D1422714

Homes & Experiences

Homes & Experiences

LIAM WILLIAMS

HODDER &
STOUGHTON

First published in Great Britain in 2020 by Hodder & Stoughton
An Hachette UK company

1

Copyright © Liam Williams 2020

The right of Liam Williams to be identified as the Author of the Work has been
asserted by him in accordance with the Copyright, Designs and
Patents Act 1988.

Quote from *A Time of Gifts* (p. 18) © The Estate of Patrick Leigh Fermor 1977,
first published by John Murray Publishers, An Hachette UK Company in 1977

Quotes from *Homage to Catalonia* (p. 82) © The Estate of the late Sonia
Brownell Orwell 1986, first published by Martin Secker & Warburg Ltd 1938
(Copyright 1938 by Eric Blair), published in Penguin Books 1962

A CIP catalogue record for this title is available from the British Library

Hardback ISBN 978 1 473 69485 9
Trade Paperback ISBN 978 1 473 69486 6
eBook ISBN 978 1 473 69488 0

Typeset in Plantin Light by Palimpsest Book Production Ltd,
Falkirk, Stirlingshire

Printed and bound in Great Britain by Clays Ltd, Elcograf S.p.A.

Hodder & Stoughton policy is to use papers that are natural, renewable and
recyclable products and made from wood grown in sustainable forests. The
logging and manufacturing processes are expected to conform to the
environmental regulations of the country of origin.

Hodder & Stoughton Ltd
Carmelite House
50 Victoria Embankment
London EC4Y 0DZ

www.hodder.co.uk

For my parents,
who encouraged me to wander (safely).

From: Paris Rosiello
To: Mark Rosiello
Jun 08; 11:42

Mark,

Got your new email address from your dad. Now locked in a thrilling email exchange with him about bike maintenance. What that man doesn't know about derailleurs isn't worth knowing, though the same holds true for a lot of what he does know . . . There's a reason he's my favourite uncle, and it isn't simply that he's my only one.

It's been a while but I think of you often – every time I encounter mention of Hull City or Graham Greene. Think I last saw you at Grandad Al's funeral. I'm still creasing at your annoyance over the fact everyone kept invoking his being Italian despite, in your words, him 'being as Italian as Dolmio sauce'. Not enough withering cynicism at funerals these days for my liking.

Forgive my piss-poor communication recently. I seem to remember you left me a voicemail about a year ago and I kept meaning to get back to it, but never did, though technically I am doing so now, so I'm not a total monster.

Anyway, how are you? Are you still writing Facebook adverts for corporations?

I've been in Greece for the last six months, working with a refugee charity there. It's a wonderful country, despite its current problems. Have you ever been?

My friend Danika, whom you might remember from your visiting me at Bristol, has diagnosed me with 'burnout' (too much sunshine and cheap beer, I think). So I'm coming back to the UK and, I'm excited to say, will be living in London for the foreseeable, which obviously represents a major breaching of a personal oath, but is pretty inevitable really.

I'm starting a proper job (once I've had a few months' 'rest' at Danika's insistence), doing various bits and pieces in the London office of the same charity, which Danika's running. So it's as a fellow Londoner that I'm getting in touch. You're probably the most 'London' person I know – certainly the only one who pays an annual subscription for their Oyster card (do you still do that?). It'd be great to get a pint and you can bring me up to speed on 9–5 living, seeing as it's a bit of an alien concept to me.

In fact, let me invite you to a fundraiser we're doing for the charity next week – invite's attached. There'll be DJs, art by migrant artists, plant-based BBQ, all of which may not sound like your scene but let me know if you do fancy it. It would be really good to see you.

P.

From: Mark Rosiello
To: Paris Rosiello
Jun 08; 13:17

Paris,

Glad as I am to hear from you, I have to start with a correction – you last saw me not at Grandad Al's funeral (the image of my dad and yours posing like minor Godfather characters under the dowly English sky is burned permanently into my visual cortex), but at your 30th, last year!

You were rightfully smashed by the time I arrived and, as I recall, in bed long before I departed. I think when I left the voicemail it would have been to say thank you for inviting me, or rather thanks to your mum for inviting me. I don't think I spoke to you much that night, though you did greet me very warmly, at least three times. I spent a lot of it chatting to your mate Danika, whom I do indeed remember from Bristol and who appeared not to have judged me too harshly for the incident when I came to stay with you in your first year.

It was my 30th this year of course. Unlike you, I did stoop to organising my own party, which was a bit of a disappointment to be frank: numbers were down on the previous year (17 vs 19), which would be stomachable in any ordinary twelvemonth, but for the 29th to yield a better turnout than the 30th is a bad sign. It was fun enough though – drinks in the Hollybush in Hampstead – until it got to closing time and I, with no irony, suggested we go to Fabric and everyone remembered they had half-marathons etc. the next day and bailed. But that's the way of it, I suppose. I grow old, I grow old.

Anyway. You were missed. I did invite you, I think, but I never seem to have your current number. I probably asked your mum to pass on the message but she's always complaining about how hard it is to pin you down too!

I'm genuinely pleased to hear that my dad has found a game recipient for his cycle chat, as I remain a committed pedestrian. Feel free to stop replying if he becomes indefatigable – that's what I usually do.

The job sounds really cool. No, I haven't been to Greece. I still haven't been anywhere really, which is pathetic. It's not that I don't want to travel, it's just that I never get round to actually doing it. Less wanderlust, more sort of . . . wander-titillation. It's funny because my job is actually now in the travel industry. So, to answer your other question, no, I'm not doing Facebook posts for Greenline Insurance any more, though just want to note that there was always more to it than Facebook posts (Twitter posts, Google Ads content, customer-facing emails, non-customer-facing emails . . . I'm boring myself). Anyway, I'm now doing a similar role for Urb, who are not a corporation. Not yet anyway.

The fundraiser sounds great. Just let me know what time to get there. Oh, and will there be a card machine, or shall I bring cash?

Best,
Mark

From: Paris Rosiello
To: Mark Rosiello
Jun 11; 21:14

Mark,

Of course you were at the birthday. Heinous failure of memory there. I definitely owe you a few beers now. And yes, I remember Danika saying she'd had a good chat to you. I seem to remember her describing you as looking like an 'anaemic Henry Fonda'. Make of that what you will. I wouldn't worry about your Bristol showing. I think she looks back on the encounter quite fondly. It was actually Danika who hooked me up with the charity as she's been heavily involved since they started up a couple of years ago and, as I say, is now running the UK operation, which I think she sees as 'settling down to a quiet life' despite it being a ridiculous workload.

Currently staying in Danika's box room in Bethnal Green. It's basically a cupboard but the flat is comfortable enough (apart from when Danika's boyfriend Tristram comes over and bangs on about his latest gritty documentary film to go viral) and, most importantly, it's cheap. Can't believe how expensive this city's become, or was it ever thus? Where are you living by the way?

Great that you can make the fundraiser. I'll be there from the afternoon to help set up so just come along whenever. Pretty sure you can use your card, mate, yeah! Hopefully Danika will be there too so you can grill her on her description of you.

Sorry I couldn't bolster the birthday numbers, I was in Greece, being terrible at communication – my mother is not wrong. I didn't even have a phone at that time!

We grow old indeed. But we'll have one last summer of fun eh, mate, before infirmity completely decays us?

I *might* even go travelling again in a very, very low-budget fashion. What are your summer plans?

P.

From: Mark Rosiello
To: Paris Rosiello
Jun 11; 22:42

Paris,

I'm living with a couple in a 'luxury' (normal but expensive) flat in Wood Green, but I think that arrangement might be suddenly up in the air as they've recently got engaged so I suspect either they or I are on the way out – and the smart money's on me, given that it's their flat. Re summer, bizarrely enough, since my last email there's been a development. It's a potential travel thing and there's half a chance it might be something you're interested in. It's better explained in person, I think.

That's funny what Danika said. Henry Fonda is a new one for me (had to google; am flattered). Anaemic isn't, though I have had it confirmed by two different doctors that I fortunately do not have the condition; I am merely pallid and wan. She clearly has a knack, doesn't she? I seem to remember at your birthday her describing you as being like 'Oscar Wilde played by Owen Wilson'. As accurate as it is complimentary, I'd say. Also, she said that you once riposted to this descriptor by saying that she looks like MIA dressing up as a geek for one of her music videos, which I agreed with her is nowhere as good.

So, I'll see you on Thursday. Looking forward to it. Will bring both card and cash for safety.

Mark

From: Mark Rosiello
To: Paris Rosiello
Jun 14; 08:19

Paris,

Just want to say sorry for last night. I shouldn't have said what I said. I could see how upset you were as you were unlocking your bike and I should have apologised there and then rather than storming off like a child. Obviously you don't want to come on the trip but I'd be up for getting a tea before I go, to talk about what happened, if that was something you wanted to do.

Mark.

From: Mark Rosiello
To: Paris Rosiello
Jun 30; 22:11

Dear Paris,

Just wanted to drop you a line before leaving for Europe tomorrow. I would have really loved to have that cup of tea with you, but this will have to suffice for now. It's one of the last items on my 'to-do list', right below 'freeze gym membership' and 'find passport case'.

I want to say sorry for my part in what happened, as much as it was my fault, though it feels futile to do so, and even though I know you won't reply, I really want to explain the reasons I decided to take the job and go on the trip, because I don't feel that I got the chance to really do that before everything happened and I just . . . well, I understand that you didn't want to come. You made it pretty clear that night. And I understand your reasons, but I suppose *I* want to be clear about my own reasons for going.

So, I'm not going to give you my life story (you know most of it anyway) but I want to emphasise that while you've been able to spend the last decade pursuing a radical, charitable, sexy mission, I, unfortunately, have not.

After uni, I moved back home and was on the dole for five months, having no idea how to move forward. My parents of course were keen for me to become a teacher but, fearful of becoming even more like them than I already was, I resisted and eventually bagged a data entry job, which entailed moving to London with only a holdall of clothes and a shitty old laptop to my name, staying on the sofa in the house essentially shared by my entire uni gang, who'd all already descended on the capital many months earlier. A bit later I moved in with strangers and have been living with a succession of strangers ever since.

The data entry job was awful: long shifts under strip lights on the other side of London and absolutely no discernible joy among the workforce. But my nights were redeemed by cheap beer, and I spent hours applying for the sort of copywriting work I thought I'd actually like and be good at. The Greenline job felt like a step in the right direction – dull but, to a basic degree, creative. After all of that, my new job at Urb felt genuinely exciting: writing copy for a start-up concerned with travel and communities. Then, when I got picked to go on the Europe trip I genuinely expected you'd be up for coming with me, particularly as you'd already mentioned that you wanted to go travelling in a 'very, very low-budget fashion' – I really thought you'd jump at the opportunity. To be honest, I'm actually quite proud that I got asked, and this is what I would have told you if you had bothered to listen.

So there I was, a few weeks ago (though it feels much longer than that), sitting at my hot desk with bad posture, on a late Friday morning that felt more like a Tuesday, proofreading a 3,000-word in-house email attachment about changes to the company's Data Protection Policy. Not abysmal, but definitely not good. That's what I remember, feeling mildly like shit, as well as worried that, even in an objectively better job, I still wasn't happy.

The woman I'd told you about – Neevie – had just left to go freelance and even though we'd kissed at her leaving drinks, I didn't know we'd end up going on several dates over the next few weeks: at that point I didn't have her number or new email or anything (the first date only happened because she waited outside work for me one evening a few days later). I was just like, 'Oh that's my favourite person at work gone.' The couple I was renting my room off had put my rent up to help pay for their wedding. *University Challenge* had finished until the autumn . . . complete existential desolation, basically.

And *then* I got an email, from a senior colleague called Bethan Decker, asking if I wanted to go for a coffee that afternoon. She said she'd read the copy I wrote for the 'Staff Easter Sours Party', which she said demonstrated an 'impressive, cogent linguistic flair' and she had an 'exciting opportunity' to discuss with me.

So at 1.55 I took my KeepCup down to Benugo and sat there waiting for Bethan Decker, trying to guess what the opportunity might be. The chance to copy-edit the company's new office refurbishment press release perhaps? The role of scriptwriter for the new employee health and safety video? As it turned out, of course, it was something even more exciting.

Bethan Decker arrived in her gym kit, but is one of those people who, even when they're wearing their gym kit in the office, make you feel like you're the one who's poorly dressed.

We engaged in a bit of small talk ('Isn't it annoying that exercise makes you feel great?', 'Aren't endorphins just incredible though?', 'Aren't people who see exercise as a kind of religion annoying?') before she came to the purpose of the meeting: Urb was going to publish its 'Authentic Europe' list, a 'hand-picked selection' of 'authentic Homes and Experiences' from across the continent.

The list, she said, was being curated as part of the company's 'Human Touch' campaign, a soon-to-launch initiative, devised in response to, as she put it, a 'growing misapprehension about the company's ethos and vibe'. As Urb had expanded, 'reaching more neighbourhoods, allowing more people to travel than ever before', there'd been 'an unfortunate but, to be honest, inevitable backlash' based on the 'false' idea that the company was somehow a 'threat' to communities, when, of course, the 'complete opposite is true!' That's what the Human Touch initiative was all about, she said.

'That's why,' she continued, 'our new slogan will be "Tourist Like a Local". It's a chance to show that just because Urb has grown very big very quickly, what we offer is not some sterile, corporate, quasi-hotel-and-guided-tour stay, and to prove that our algorithms have picked *the most authentic Homes and Experiences that this continent has to offer.'*

She stressed this last long noun phrase with such sustained vigour that I was surprised she didn't run out of breath.

After the briefest of pauses she went on: 'That's algorithms revealing Europe's most authentic Homes and Experiences, with particularly unique features.'

And they'd 'obviously,' she said, need some 'authentic, human' copy to go with it – for the website, emails, social media ads, press releases etc.

'Just a few hundred words for each Home and Experience,' she said, 'to anchor the products with a Human Touch and so we need someone to go and sample them all this summer.'

She paused.

'I reckon you might be quite good for this,' she told me, with not quite a smile, but a warmly neutral expression.

'But I'm not really a travel writer,' I told her.

'We don't want a travel writer. We don't want an "expert". You know that saying: *people have had enough of experts*? I think that's true. But I also think people have had enough of *non*-experts. Just anybody, any Joe Public, posting their opinion on the internet, it's too much! It's all too much to take in! People have had enough of it. We want somebody who's somewhere in between.'

Perhaps picking up on my slight confusion, Bethan Decker said, with the look of somebody saying something mildly mischievous: 'You know in Waterstones they have those little cards with handwritten book recommendations from the staff? Think about yourself like one of those staff – you know the trade but you're not so different from the customer.'

So at this point I'm thinking . . . I've never seen Europe. I've never seen anywhere. Never been anywhere, save for a few childhood holidays in France and a queasily-remembered trip to Amsterdam with the university football team . . . (Did I ever tell you about it: the 17-0 defeat to a team of elderly ex-pats in Den Haag, a defeat whose ignominy can be blamed entirely on performance-diminishing substances?)

That's it though, really – a stag do here and there, all experienced through a laddy, booze-fuelled and fundamentally touristic filter.

Now, rather than just looking at amazing flats and experiences via a laptop screen all day, I was going to see the real thing!

Bethan Decker filled me in on what sort of authentic 'Experiences' I might . . . experience. And though they didn't all sound *exactly* like my usual bag – graffiti tours and 'vodka workshops' – I couldn't help but feel more than willing to make the best of it. Anyway, as I began to fantasise, I'd surely have lots of time to do what I wanted, to encounter Europe the way I've always dreamed of: ambling around museums and taking long psychogeographical excursions through strange streets, until my legs, afflicted by at least three different muscle and joint disorders, began to ache and it was time to decamp to a town square Bar-Café for reflection and refreshment.

'When would I be going?' I asked, trying not to let my giddiness show.

'Beginning of July,' Bethan Decker said.

'In three weeks?' I responded quickly and with some surprise.

'That's the sort of dynamic, fast-moving company Urb of course is.'

'Of course.'

'Also the person we had lined up dropped out.'

'Right.'

And though I was slightly sceptical about aspects of her pitch – exactly how the quite exclusive-sounding Experiences she was describing could be considered 'authentic', for example, or how reliably an algorithm could detect 'authenticity' in the first place – I wasn't going to let that get in the way of what sounded like the potential trip of a lifetime.

So I said, 'Count me in!'

At that point though, Bethan Decker was like, 'That's *great*! Great to hear you're interested. *Buuut . . .*' (she really elongated the vowel in the 'but', almost turning it into a diphthong) 'we're speaking to a few people, including a few external applicants –

we need it to be someone who's a non-expert in travel, but we also need it to be someone who's *passionate* about travel; not just someone who's done a bit of tourism . . .' She adopted an ironic sort of dullard voice, '. . . *the odd minibreak, a few stag dos* – it's got to be someone who's got travel in their blood.'

Well, I was gutted of course because I don't have *travel in my blood*, as you well know. I've got *stressing and fretting fairly hard just to stay in one place, while failing, for want of cash and basic get-up-and-go, to get around to doing any travelling at all during the years in which one is supposed to . . . in my blood*. Not like you. Bethan Decker would have deemed you perfect for this role, I'd have thought.

So I just nodded with my eyes closed, to make it seem like I understood the importance of this point without giving any legally or morally compromising indication as to how much travel may or may not have been in my blood.

'So it'd be great,' she said, 'just to chat a bit more, make sure it's a good mutual fit, make sure it's something you'd be well suited for.'

'Mmhm,' I said.

'Have you done much travelling yourself?'

Reasoning that the Amsterdam football trip might not make for a particularly apposite story in what had now become an ostensible job interview, I began instead to relate a trip to Cornwall taken with my old uni gang during the summer after graduation.

'. . . we went crabbing and ate fish and chips. We even got lost on a golf course during an evening stroll!' I chuckled.

Bethan Decker looked slightly underwhelmed. Determined by now not to let this opportunity fall out of my lap, I segued quickly into an account of a two-month trip to Thailand. I'm aware how odd it was, in the self-celebratory travelogue stakes, to have prioritised a quiet week in Cornwall above a two-month foray around Thailand but I had good reason for doing so, namely that the Thailand trip was completely made up.

Bethan Decker was enjoying it though and, as I contrived tales of magic mushroom milkshakes, full moon parties, death-defying motorbike rides down winding jungle roads, and other such scraps appropriated from vernacular gap year culture, she chuckled, gasped, nodded and even at one point appeared to scribble a small tick in her notebook.

'Was the visa run stressful?' she asked after I'd just rounded off these rambunctious yarns with some sincere stuff about how the temples were, 'in the end, just incredibly spiritual places . . . *incredibly* spiritual places.'

'Oh man yeah, *incredibly* stressful,' I said.

Still don't have a clue what she was referring to.

Ten minutes later Bethan Decker bade me a smiling goodbye and promised to follow up by email. And sure enough three days later Bethan Decker's email came:

> Mark, I'm absolutely delighted to offer you the Homes and Experiences role – just lay off the magic mushroom shakes, okay!
> ;)

I genuinely shouted 'thank you', so loudly that some of my hot-desk mates almost looked up from their laptops.

Back at the flat that night, as I hid in my bedroom away from the housemates who were loudly arguing about their guest list, a feeling of doubt came upon me: what if I wasn't cut out for this? What if I'd misled Bethan Decker about my aptness for the endeavour and my sensibilities just weren't right for the kind of copy she was after? Or what if it just wasn't the right thing for me to be doing now? Things are really starting to go somewhere with Neevie. Also, maybe it was just the correct thing for me to be in London right now.

And then I thought fuck it. After all these years of static drudgery there was no question: I was going on the trip. And, having told my housemates I was moving out, which they agreed was a 'perfect idea', I emailed Bethan Decker to tell her as much, before realising that I had already emailed her to tell her as much earlier in the day.

Yes, I'll miss Neevie, but I'll see her before too long and in the meantime, she says she's going to be charting my route on a map she's bought specially!

Anyway, I have to be on the Eurostar in about ten hours and I can't find my passport cover (reluctant to let the passport go bareback given my luck with things like pens, drinks bottles, forgotten bananas etc.). So I'd better go. I just really wanted to tell you the raw facts of how I came to be in the situation I'm in, and how the job offer appeared to represent a potential escape from that situation (albeit a temporary one).

Sorry for the deluge, and for what happened the night of the fundraiser, again. I'm annoyed with myself for reacting the way I did. I think I probably will email you again, if that's okay. There's more I want to say. I wish you were coming with me, mate.

Love, genuinely.
Mark.

From: Mark Rosiello
To: Paris Rosiello
Jul 01; 09:54

Hello Paris (not quite *bonjour* yet – just left Ashford International)

So I guess I'm writing to you again. Hope this doesn't seem too weird when you do get around to reading it. Just feels helpful somehow.

I only just made my train following an argument at the self-storage where all my worldly possessions are now locked away. Won't go into it but long story short I realised only after booking the unit that I have basically no things and could likely have got away with stashing them all in a bin bag under my desk at work (if I actually had a fixed desk of my own), the cruelty of which was lost on the man on the desk who remained adamant that 'realising you don't own anything' is not a valid reason for cancellation.

So, 70 quid (and hardly more than three shoeboxes of stuff)

lighter, I'm writing to you, *au Eurostar. 'Au'? 'En'? 'Dans?' 'Sur?'*
I never properly grasped the intricacies of French prepositions
at school; perhaps this trip will occasion an improvement in my
grasp of the Romance languages, or perhaps, more likely, I'll just
slip through Paris, and the rest of Europe, like a euro coin through
the slick inner workings of a major train station toilet turnstile,
gaining no technical knowledge whatsoever, but perhaps, if I'm
lucky, accruing a little if not worldly wisdom then at least, maybe,
some . . . continental poise.

I just want to say I do appreciate my good fortune in being
able to do this. And I will make sure to enjoy myself. It is my
last intention for the ultimate import of this undertaking to be
'I went round Europe for six weeks and I didn't even like it that
much.'

Also, I read over the email I sent last night and realised that
in the chaos surrounding the missing passport sleeve (now mercifully located) I didn't actually cover what I wanted to – namely
why I invited you along, why I sort of *needed* you to come along.
So, picking up where I left off last night – Bethan Decker, after
thanking me for my second confirmation email, had sent me
some more details about the job:

- All my accommodation would be provided by Urb, in the Homes
I'll be writing about
- All my travel (primarily by air and rail) would be arranged by Urb
- I'd be paid £3,000 for the six-week job, on a 'freelancer
secondment contract' and would be able to resume my current
contract upon my return
- I'd be paid an initial fee of £1,000 just before departure, £1,000
at the halfway stage, and £1,000 upon completion in late-August
- Bethan Decker would give me a 'Trip Pack', which would detail
the full itinerary they'd booked for me. This Trip Pack was
ceremoniously handed to me as I left the office for the last time, and
is now safely packed at the top of my bag (a newly purchased 60-
litre rucksack with 'adjustable back system' and detachable smaller
rucksack; I think you'd approve). I've had a cursory look through but

should really dig into it. Broadly, as I might have mentioned to you, I'll be going to France, Spain, Italy, Greece, Hungary, Czech Republic, Germany and Holland

And then there was the bit that I was so keen to talk to you about:

We obviously don't expect you to go it alone – you can take a Travel Buddy! This could be a partner, friend or a family member. All the Homes you stay in will be able to accommodate two people. If you're going with a friend or family member, we'll do our best to arrange twin-sharing options for you in each Home, but you may have to share the odd double bed (so try to find someone who doesn't snore!).

I have to confess, my initial response to this part was to walk over to Bethan Decker's desk and, after a good two minutes of reiterating to her my excitement about the trip, ask whether the Travel Buddy was 'mandatory'.

'Well, you obviously won't want to go on your own for that long,' she said, and I found it weird just how matter-of-factly she said it.

I felt quite prepared to go on my own. As you know, this will be my first taste of solo travelling – just me and a backpack . . . (and an iPhone and a tablet and a comprehensive travel insurance policy). You meet people on the way, don't you? It's the Grand Tour tradition! *Buuuuut* . . . (as Bethan Decker would say) I've learned the hard way what scorn and ridicule we, the chronically, self-acceptingly solitary are met with upon outing ourselves, so I just stared slightly dizzy-eyed at Bethan Decker, prompting her to continue.

'Anyway, it's very much part of the Human Touch initiative. You remember the Human Touch initiative? You got the email this morning, right?'

Not only had I got the email, I'd been the one to proofread it, which was very, very easy because it was about 80 words long and genuinely as vacuous as this:

Urb has always been, and will always be, about connecting people.

We started out 11 years ago when two students in Seattle decided to open up their homes to travelling guests from all round the world. We think it was a pretty cool idea, such a cool idea that now over 80 million people use Urb every year.

It goes without saying that technology and an ever-more connected world have allowed us to do this, but as we keep growing it's important to remember that all-important element that makes Urb possible: the Human Touch.

From now we'll be making sure that the Human Touch is central to all we do – for Our Hosts, Our Guests, and Our Communities.
Urb: Welcome Home.

'Yes,' I said.

'The Travel Buddy is a key part of that – it's the Human Touch *to your Human Touch*. Does that make sense?' she asked, gently placing her fist on the desk and smiling at me.

'I'll find someone,' I said.

'Even if it's just for a few weeks,' Bethan Decker replied. 'Any other questions?'

I did have one other question, which I think you would have admired me for asking: would I be able to replace the flights with trains and ferries where possible?

'Why?' Bethan Decker asked.

'Because of, like . . . the environment.'

Bethan Decker said 'oh yeah' with the tone of someone who'd just been reminded that her holiday villa might have a mild issue with dry rot.

'Let me look into that,' she said.

'And, how sort of . . . flexible is the itinerary?' She didn't narrow her eyes as such, but did seem to sort of tense her forehead.

'It's kind of not that flexible actually to be honest. Why do you ask?'

I explained to her, as I ended up explaining to your friend Danika at the fundraiser when I told her why I wanted you to come so much, that I was wondering about the possibility of taking a few days out to visit the old ancestral village in Italy, which I've been faintly obsessed with doing, ever since your dad discovered our provenance via some genealogy website, and I looked it up on Google Images, thereafter developing a habit of, in idle moments, picturing Old Great Grandfather Domenico (basically myself but more swarthy and rustic) swaggering around this Tuscan hamlet, like a figure in a blown-up photo on a Caffè Nero wall.

'Well, that's a really cool idea,' Bethan Decker acknowledged. 'I'll see what we can do re that.'

And sure enough she emailed the next day:

> I'm delighted to say we'll be able to facilitate you going to visit your family's village in Tuscany – I can't remember the exact name of the village you mentioned. If you can find an Urb Home nearby you will obviously be reimbursed. Otherwise you might need to find another option.
> How are you getting on with choosing your Travel Buddy?

Not well, Bethan Decker, not well. I hadn't asked anybody. I hadn't even thought about asking anybody, except Neevie, and even though we'd been on three good dates, it occurred to me that it might be considered mad to ask someone, after only three good dates, to spend the whole summer travelling around Europe with you.

I took myself to the breakout area, where the ceiling and general calmness levels were higher. There I sat, fingering the already ragged cork band of my KeepCup, trainers tapping on the cross beam of the high stool. And then, as the dishwasher droned meditatively, it dawned on me . . . the answer had been sitting there all along in a Gmail Data Centre I know not where, a single sentence of text in your email: *But we'll have one last summer of fun eh, mate, before infirmity completely decays us?*

It just felt so serendipitous! It would be you! You were, Paris, the first person I asked to be my Travel Buddy. Does that seem sad? To quote your mock-hero, Patrick Leigh Fermor in *A Time of Gifts*, at the outset of his own admittedly more intrepid European Odyssey, *'To change scenery; to abandon London and England and set out across Europe, like a pilgrim or palmer, an errant scholar, a broken knight! All of a sudden this was not merely the obvious, but the only thing to do.'*

We would reverse a lifetime's steady estrangement in a glorious, Byronic *dérive* across the continental sharing-economy, which to you might seem about as adventurous as a trip to Whole Foods. But to me it seemed wonderful and exciting, the prospect of six weeks of Urb apartments and TripAdvisor recommended restaurants and the chance to see a few paintings and towers and things, and drink a few half lagers in the town squares, as I found out how all my old anxieties and preoccupations would stand up across a fairly narrow span of time zones and climates. Who knows, perhaps there'd even be time for an epiphany or two along the way?

And yet more excitingly you would take me to renowned left-wing neighbourhoods, refugee camps, community centres, bars where artists, and rebels, and dissidents drank – damnit, where they still drink! And I would have to work of course, drag the two of us around boujie tourist activities – Zorbing and Segway-touring – but you wouldn't resent it too badly. You'd enjoy it in fact, and laugh, laugh at the frivolity of it all!

Except, it turned out, you wouldn't. You laughed at the very suggestion, in fact.

'Travel Buddy?' you sneered after I'd made my proposal at the fundraiser, not even meeting my eye, too bothered by what else was going on in the room.

I understand you were busy – you were effectively at work, you had people to talk to. But why invite me simply in order to snigger and fob me off by telling me 'we should have a drink soon to discuss it'? We could have had a drink and discussed it there and then! We could have at least had a ten-minute chat. Or perhaps we didn't need to because you managed to convey exactly how you felt about the proposal by saying basically nothing. Anyway, I regret the way I spoke to you and in the cold light of day I can't resent you for it. It just came as a major disappointment, that's all. And that's why I said what I said, and I've told you already how much I regret it and obviously I regret it all the more now.

So anyway, the morning after the fundraiser, I sat again in the breakout area, nursing a soy decaf latte (not from my KeepCup, though, as I'd left it on the kitchen table that morning – you can see I was falling to pieces) and thought through my abiding options.

I thought about asking one of my old uni pals – some of whom you must have met back in the day – but a quick email to the group put paid to that idea (holidays with partners; 'training' for an ambiguous fitness event; lecturing at a summer school; and most gallingly of all, *no response* from film-directing 'global *flâneur*' Dyson). I thought about my school friends (now strictly Christmas-time-only drinking partners), workmates (all, by definition, working) and occasional five-a-side teammates whom I met through an app (realising instantly that it would be irredeemably terrible if one of them came).

So you can see why, in the end, I *did* in fact ask Neevie to come. I thought about those three dates: a nice coffee in the new development by King's Cross (you know there's potential there when you can genuinely enjoy a hot drink date with someone); a wonderful boat trip on the Lea River; and a terrible one-man play about OCD by someone who didn't have OCD. The writer/actor, an inconceivably arrogant man called Gart, was the boyfriend of Neevie's mate and, in the pub after, she (Neevie) was extremely apologetic about making us go. I was effortfully gracious and relaxed about the whole thing and even feigned appreciation of the piece in a way which I think amused Neevie.

And it was this amusement that gave me the conviction to ask her the big question, on our fourth date, as we sat in a Thameside beer garden, the sunset picking out the gold tones in her wavy hair, the freckles on her shoulder as pleasant to look at as the sunlit features on the water's surface, in a conversation that went along these lines:

Me: Have you got summer plans?

(My intention was to ask in a low-key seductive way, as if I was an impressive chocolatier asking a customer whether she'd like to try a new, exquisitely dark chocolate, but instead I probably sounded more like a local radio DJ asking an unsuccessful competition entrant whether they had plans for the bank holiday.)

Neevie: Hmm, not sure yet really. My family always go down to Cornwall for two weeks in August but I don't know if I can this year because I just don't know what work I'm gonna get. Meg [the friend whose boyf did the bad play] and I were talking about going somewhere in July but that is really soon suddenly and I'm thinking I should probably be sensible with money. So I dunno really. How about you?

(Perfect. Ideal. Perfect.)

Me: Well . . . how do you fancy going to Europe?

Neevie: Europe?

Me: So basically . . .

(and with my best chocolatier/drivetime veteran's tone I explained everything. Neevie's response was one of great excitement . . .)

Neevie: Wow, that's so cool. You'll have an amazing time!

Me: Yeah, yeah, I'm very excited. And do you fancy coming along for a b—

Neevie: *(the fastest I've ever heard her speak)* I mean, I can't do six weeks away.

Me: Haha! No, no obviously not for that long! We'd be *sick* of each other [a massive lie]. I just meant for a shorter time. Like just a few . . .

Slight pause.

Neevie: A few days? I mean . . .

(I'd been about to say 'weeks'. I'm supremely glad I didn't.)

Neevie: I mean yeah! I mean yeah! Why not?? That could be okay, couldn't it!

Neevie's quite mild enthusiasm emphatically expressed, it was just a matter of talking through the itinerary in order to pencil

in a plan. We omitted cities that Neevie had already been to –
ostensibly most cities – until deciding on Athens as somewhere
she'd like to go if she could make the dates work.

And with that, I went to the bar. Smiling my head off.

I slightly lied to Bethan Decker the next day, telling her that
Neevie would 'definitely be joining me in Athens' and might even
stick around for more of the trip once she'd got her summer
plans sorted, but she didn't seem that fussed about the intricacies.

I don't frankly know much about Athens, other than that it
has the Acropolis and everything and – via some trendy New
Media people I follow on Twitter – that it's 'affordable'. So cheap
cocktails and chapiters? Ideal for a fifth date, I reckon!

You must have been to Athens loads of times during your time
in Greece? Oh and by the way, I've been speaking to Danika
and it looks like I'm going to be doing a week of volunteering
myself at the charity's base in Thessaloniki! Hope you're
impressed.

Anyway . . . may I find life-changing days on a budget in
France, Spain, Italy, Greece and beyond; and may I not suffer
some creeping six-week panic attack across a series of indistinguishable town squares under sterile tourist skies. Speaking of
which, we're now approaching the outskirts of Paris, so I'd better
wrap up. Goodbye (though I'm not really sure if this is actually
goodbye, as I suspect I'll probably email you again). So for now
let's just go with . . .

Au revoir.

Mark.

From: Paris Rosiello
To: Mark Rosiello
Jul 02; 01:37

[blank email]

From: Mark Rosiello
To: Paris Rosiello
Jul 02; 10:17

Dear Paris,

I got a blank reply from you in the middle of the night. Weird. Some sort of glitch?

Anyway, hello from Paris.

I haven't thought of the old Paris homonymy in years – not since I came with Grandad to watch you play football at, like, U13's in, I *think,* Wetwang and you had just scored a header from a corner without even jumping, as I remember, and once the celebrations had died down someone asked why you were called Paris and Grandad said, 'He's named after the lad from Greek mythology, because his mam and dad met studying classics,' to which one of the dads replied, 'Oh so it wasn't because he was conceived in Paris then?' and everyone laughed, even Grandad. *Especially* Grandad!

This was roughly in the era of Brooklyn Beckham's babyhood, and everybody was pruriently obsessed with the conception places of other people's babies. Where *were* you conceived, I wonder? I was conceived, as far as I know, in Hull. I'm guessing, by the same calculation, you were York. Or maybe New York, or Athens, or Cairo, or wherever academic conferences might be held, including there's every chance, I suppose, Paris! Maybe the whole supposed Trojan allusion is just a saucy ruse after all . . .

Did I tell you that I've never been to Paris until now? You must have been, I'd estimate, upwards of seven times, the most famous occasion being the 2015 climate conference protest-cum-romantic weekend with that English film distributor.

Anyway. I'm emailing you because I've just had a coffee, so am artificially stimulated to the point of over-sociability. Can you tell? I'm also trying to make an 'event' of it, because the coffee itself was literally egg-cup-sized so was over in about three minutes.

Feels kinda weird making an effort to sit down and savour an espresso for pleasure. It's just not British. It'd be like going out to a bar to order a shot and sitting down and taking half an hour to drink it, which, it occurs to me immediately, a French person might very well do, with a brandy or a pastis, or a very small wine or something. Perhaps the French do it better, is the grander point I think I'm angling towards. They're able, it seems, to extract greater pleasure from smaller measures, to derive from 30ml of liquid consumed at least as many minutes of mental occupation.

Despite the urbane sultriness of this moment – the coffee and the pastry; the impassive waiter, deft and dexterous as a snooker referee; the bicycles and the scooters passing by; and the mechanised recycling station a few metres to my right – I am writing to acknowledge that you might not have been totally wrong in your assessment of the city as a 'playground for vain, white, middle-class yuppies intent on remoulding the city into a near-empty studio space containing only iMacs and fronted by one, unending terrace of people in New Balance trainers drinking half pints and small coffees'. Or words to that effect. It's an alarmist vision, I feel, but not a wholly unfounded one, at least as far as the impression gained from the eight or nine streets I've so far encountered between my Urb Home and this café terrace would suggest.

Speaking of my Urb, my first Home of the trip, 'La Maison Authentique' is located in the quiet neighbourhood of Olympiades in the 13th Arrondissement and gained its place on the *Authentic Europe* list as it was apparently identified as the 'most Authentic Home in a low-density Authenticity area within the typical first-time customer price bracket'. In other words, it's homely and, by Urb standards, cheap. My first introduction to the house was from Bethan Decker's Trip Pack – which, now I'd had the chance to look at it properly, I found to be an informative compendium of 'Host and Home profiles' and photos of all the Homes and Experiences I would be sampling, in both PDF and glossy-brochure formats. The photos it contained of the Paris Urb seemed to bear out the homely descriptor – a large, rustic kitchen, with antique aga; a living room, or, should I say, a _salon_, containing what looked like early 20th-century furniture along with some subtle modern accessories, and a large neon installation on the wall reading 'HOME'.

Along with each Home and Experience in the Trip Pack, a short, usually first-person profile of the Host was included, as well as a photograph. My Parisian Host would be 'Elisabeth', who stated in her profile: 'I am a normal Parisienne woman, and mostly a stay-at-home mother. My interests are cooking, theatre and raising my children.' She sounded, and looked, a very pleasant person.

As I neared the Home yesterday, after a thrilling Metro ride and a short walk taking in a baroque church; terrace cafés; artisanal and ethnic bakeries; a middle-class friendly mural naturistically depicting a quizzical child in bold primary colours (I could have been in Bristol!), I messaged Elisabeth to say I'd arrived early – having left myself over an hour to complete the journey from Gare du Nord but actually completing it in less than 20 minutes – and was it okay to check in now? Elisabeth replied to say that she was 'stuck' at the supermarché – presumably being held up by her native appreciation of good produce – but that she would return home as fast as possible and that the door would be left open for me.

I questioned how she might organise the leaving open of the door while she was in the supermarché, but, realising that this conditional passive-voice construction was probably just a translingual mistake and that she in fact meant that she'd _already_ left the door open, I continued to make my breezy, whistling way along _la ruelle_ towards the house.

I inspected the building the Home was situated in – charmingly spindly and leaf-hidden amongst a terrace of beguiling 1920s villas – and sure enough discovered its door to be open. I gave a knock which I intended to be stylistically quite French – a little quieter and rhythmically more elaborate than the stolid knock-knock-knock I tend to dole out on home soil. No answer came.

I peered in and discovered that familiar, inviting, almost rustic kitchen, with more high-tech touches than the photo betrayed, but no human presence. Only *deux chats* lolling about on the worktops, one quite boring with short black fur and one absolutely *merveilleux* with long grey coat and a clear addiction to rolling about.

I called out 'hello?' and then '*bonjour?*' as if anyone who was in the house might not have replied the first time because they simply hadn't understood me. No reply came in any case and I continued to stand in the kitchen a few moments, watching the cats, not really knowing what else to do. Hearing footsteps in the courtyard outside, I wheeled round and instantly heard a smash on the floor behind me, which I knew even before looking down, had come from a vase of flowers sent to its obliteration by my big bag. One of the cats basically screamed and the other dealt with the trauma by beginning to scratch at the wall. A moment later Elisabeth walked in.

We made acquaintance in a flurry of slightly garbled French, English and non-verbal communication, before I offered apologetic explanation for the vase.

'My bag is too big!' I said. '*Mon sac est trop grand!*'

'Oh please . . . do not worry, please!' Elisabeth cried. 'It is my fault for leaving this vase here, I should have realised you would have a big bag!'

The logic of this claim I wasn't totally convinced by as I watched her quickly sweep up the shards and dump the wet flowers in the bin, but I appreciated her emphatic, friendly efforts to ease my guilt and bid me welcome. Was it prejudiced of me to have expected from a middle-aged, middle-class Parisian home-owner, if not outright unfriendliness, at least a degree of . . . froideur? Well almost certainly yes, but all the same I couldn't help be taken by surprise by her genial enthusiasm as she showed me around the place, speaking in decent if pausey English and blinking chicly behind her glasses.

As we climbed three steep flights of stairs, I asked how long she'd owned the house.

'Twenty-two years, wonderful years in this wonderful Home,' she replied.

And how long had she listed it on Urb for?

'Just one year, a wonderful year.'

Why she kept saying wonderful so much I don't know, but I know I liked it.

The wood-panelled walls of the stairway were brightened by paintings and photographs, and I stopped a second to enjoy a print of Daumier's painting of Don Quixote. Not sure if you know but I'm something of a fanboy for Miguel de Cervantes' (possibly by today's reckoning quite seriously mentally ill) knight-errant and will be visiting La Mancha, his hailing place, as an excursion from Toledo. Looking at pictures and going on day trips is obviously a much lazier way to appreciate the tilting Don than actually finishing the book, which I intend to do on this trip. Then again, finishing things isn't really in the quixotic spirit.

We reached my *chambre*, an elegantly empty room with a neon sign reading BED above the bed, wooden window shutters and a floor-to-ceiling black velvet curtain running along the opposing wall.

'It is nice,' I said.

'Mmm, wonderful to sleep in, wonderful to be in, my guests always find,' Elisabeth replied.

She told me she would be back later to feed the two cats, now skulking schemingly in the doorway, and, without explaining whether she actually lived in the house or not, she bade me '*bonne journée*'. At this stage I was pleased to be left alone with just enough time for a nap (once I'd texted Neevie to tell her I'd arrived) before taking 'Cocktails on the Seine' that evening.

This 'Chance to Explore Paris from on board a Luxury Boat' would be the first Experience of the trip proper but, in a feat of beneficence from Urb, not one I was required to write about. It would be a soft landing, the opposite of a baptism of fire . . . or, judging from the Trip Pack, more like a baptism of Sour Cherry Gin Smash. Bethan Decker had emailed me the morning of departure to say that this would be a chance to 'relax and have fun', which felt more like a plea than a suggestion (perhaps a response to the string of anxious emails about various, I now see, trivial logistical concerns I'd dispatched in the hours preceding my departure). Embarking upon the fairy-lit gangway at Port de l'Arsenal, I felt about as capable of relaxation and enjoyment as an ostrich must of flight.

Certain advertised elements of the event were already inducing a state of mild anxiety: that this would be an event attended by around 20 people – too many to make polite, inclusive conversation a necessity for all involved but not enough to make hiding in the crowd a real possibility – and, worse, that these people would be 'an exciting and unique assembly, made up of Urb Superhosts, Gold Level guests, and valued Urb Associates, making for an elite Parisian welcome experience.'

Almost every word in that sentence had contributed to a certain fraughtness of mind and my taking an inordinate amount of time choosing a shirt (in the end, light blue flannel rather than dark blue flannel), 'doing' my hair (arranging it into a rough side parting and then spraying 'sea salt spray' all over it, at my barber's ongoing, expensive behest), and, finally, stopping at a bar between the Metro and the boat to drink three half pints (*demis*) and listen to the first 40 minutes of that morning's *Today* programme on my phone.

At about 8.40pm, I approached the 'Refurbished Replica Traditional Chinese Junk Ship, Embodying Worlds Old and New', corralling my psychic energies towards the purpose of seeming confident and relaxed, made slightly easier by my being already a bit tipsy. In fact as I wandered through the evening streets near Port de l'Arsenal I began to feel a great deal lighter, suddenly quite free from the tedium of my life in London. Here in Paris, on the first night of a famous summer, was a chance to start again and to reinvent myself . . .

It was a shame then that, as I plunged into these reflections, my walking slowed considerably, and I almost ended up missing the boat, having to literally jump from the bank onto the departing vessel, naturally becoming quite stressed again in the process. As it turned out, 40 minutes late was not 'fashionably late' but just late, late enough for the rest of the exciting and unique people to have already arrived and disappeared beneath deck to escape the rain.

The man who'd been responsible for unmooring the boat, and who'd positively scowled at me as leaping momentum carried me stumblingly across the deck, now became a sort of Greeter – almost literally spinning on the spot and adopting his new guise like a Brechtian actor – and smiled at me as he said *bonjour* and gestured me welcome into the vessel's converted saloon. Inside, I found a humid and confined space, a bit claustrophobic even – a dark, and slightly lurid haze of exaggeratedly old wood and LCD screens advertising Drinks and Events. The ceiling was low, which made the already probably quite tall throng gathered here look all the loftier.

They'd arranged themselves, possibly not consciously, into a formation that seemed designed for maximal inaccessibility for a below-average-height, late man arriving alone. At least eight were sitting around a very large, round table – one of only two or three tables in the space – and some on a kind of couchette fixed to the wall. The other 10 or so people were standing in a loose phalanx, closed off to the foyer area of the room, centred roughly around the small bar, attended by two staff members, including the one who'd just greeted me on deck.

I resisted the urge to get my phone out and look busy (i.e., stand refreshing Twitter over and over), and instead decided to make a fist of trying to socialise. All I needed to do was get to the bar and find a place to lean.

I was instantly thwarted in this endeavour, my path blocked by a fella, perhaps the loftiest of them all, whose entire demeanour and physical vibe in that moment seemed designed to obstruct the path of anybody who needed to pass by him. He was talking to two people and gesticulating so widely and muscularly that he might have been a supporting artist in the background of a movie battle scene. I offered a quiet and useless, '*Excusez-moi!*', which I suspected this guy, deep in the bowels of a big conversational set piece, had little chance of hearing. I had another go, this time in English, and still wasn't heard. It only now occurred to me how loud the music in this boat was, yet this guy was not struggling at all to make himself audible. There was no aural solution; passage could only be negotiated physically. I did a bit of shimmying to my left side to try and get into his field of vision, but if he saw me, he didn't look at me.

I was beginning to panic a bit now. The first night of the tour. The beginning of what was supposed to be the most freeing, exciting phase of my life, was about to be cancelled because I couldn't get past a man in a bar. Just as I felt my breathing start to go a bit weird, one of the other interlocutors, the woman – flaxen-haired and well presented, who'd just been nodding intently – spotted me looking, presumably, quite agitated and alerted the expressive man to my presence. He spun round and, in perfect middle-class Estuary, bade me 'Sorry bro!', while looking not the least bit sorry bro, his features pronounced as knuckles, his stubble dense as Brillo wool.

'*Pas de problème,*' I replied nonsensically, and moved into the narrow space he had vacated, feeling as I did so his large hand on my back in a sort of faux-helpful shove. Again, I bet in your entire adult life you never experienced such a thing, being too big and self-possessed to seem shove-able.

Anyway, only slightly psychologically unravelled, I was through to the bar area and I only had to wait about nine minutes to get served, after two separate parties had ordered multiple complex cocktails. I asked for a Heineken and, thus armed, standing on my own felt a less awkward undertaking. A moment later, I felt a ripple of excitement as the flaxen-haired woman from before tapped me on the shoulder and politely asked if she could get to the bar.

'No problem,' I replied in perfect English, and she asked me where I was from. Here it was: a chance to interact, perhaps even get in with a group. The adventure's real beginning.

'London. Hull originally. You?'

I was fucking nailing this.

'I've never been to Hull,' she said, with an implied *and I never will*. 'I live in Paris but I'm from London.'

'Nice one, what do you do in Paris?'

I was just getting better and better.

'Oh god, quite a lot of stuff. I do some influencer bits and pieces, including in the travel industry, which is why I was invited to this thing. But . . .' She leaned close to theatrically whisper, 'I'm really just here for the free cocktails.'

I felt a momentary ASMR shiver and smiled clumsily. I waited while she ordered drinks, not really knowing where to look.

'What brings you here?' she asked.

'I'm a copywriter for Urb,' I said, and it occurred to me that this stock explanation of my purpose in the labour market had a new significance here. It felt elevated somehow, almost exotic. Where in London I was just another smart-casual hot-desker, dispassionately serving the digital economy in a distinctly unre-warding way, here I was . . . special, select, transcendent almost of the trappings of ordinary wage labour and its routine effects.

'Ah, you're part of the Mafia.'

I laughed but didn't really know why.

'So who are you here with?' she asked.

'Just on my own,' I told her.

'Ah that's great. That's cool actually.'

I smiled again, having nothing good to say.

'There's actually one or two other people here by themselves too. Let me introduce you.'

'Cool,' I said, fighting down an internal wave of panic at the prospect of getting the very thing I wanted.

'I'm Ellie by the way,' she said.

'Mark,' I replied, a bit too loudly.

'I've just got to deliver this to my boyfriend,' she said, taking up a dark pint from the drip tray in front of her. 'What sort of a guy goes to a FREE cocktail party and orders Guinness? Err, ma boyfriend, that's who!'

She delivered this last statement in a skilfully goofy way, with a slight put-on American accent.

As I followed her over to the table area, I wondered whether in the past I might have been thrown by such a revelation, or 'the boyfriend bomb' as it was once inanely known. Had age and a more feminist culture improved me? Possibly. Just as likely though, it might have something to do with Neevie. We never had any sort of conversation about whether we were 'exclusive' or 'allowed' to get with anyone else or whatever but, I was actually finding that I didn't really want to anyway. To be released from that inchoate, stupid compulsion to regard every to-even-the-mildest-degree-gregarious interaction with a remotely attractive person as a potential romantic opportunity and suffer consequent disappointment when it didn't transpire to be one, felt . . . good.

So, I was still buoyed as I arrived at the tables. I met Ellie's boyfriend who was an extremely genial Frenchman, called Philippe and who, I now recognised, had been talking to the man who'd shoved me in the back minutes earlier. Philippe was sitting at the table of about ten people, about half of whom – the half furthest from me – were engaged in loud and animated conversation and seemed a world away. On the other side of Philippe, closer to me, were the back-shover himself and the woman he'd been talking to/at. Ellie crawled nimbly under the table to sit on the couchette opposite Philippe and next to the back-shover. Sensing me hanging awkwardly behind him, Philippe stood up and collected a chair from the next table, which left me looking rather foolish and, as I sat down gratefully, Ellie said, 'God sorry, Mark. This is Mark, guys.' The back-shover looked at me like he was going to strangle me for a second and then smiled and offered his hand.

'How are you doing, dude? I'm And.'

'And?' I said.

'Yes,' he said, a hint of annoyance shaking his smile.

'Short for Andy,' Ellie explained.

I shook his hand and, naturally, he placed his other hand on top of mine. I find it wonderful and astonishing that people (men) still do this, about 20 years after everybody in the Western World learned it to be a supposed body language power-move favoured by now fallen turn-of-the-century Anglophone statesmen.

Philippe asked me a few questions about what I was doing in Paris and I reciprocated. He laughed and told me he'd grown up in Paris and reached for the phrase 'born and bred', which I confirmed was correct. One of those shaming moments where you, as a near-monoglot, remember that you're a trillion miles away from being able to speak any other language with any sort of idiomatic flourish and you never will. Of course, you'll have no idea what that feels like, Mr I Taught Myself Arabic Before the Age of 20 (imagine if you actually changed your name to that!).

I was soon in the midst of a conversation with the woman next to me who was called Greta. She was from Italy but had an American accent from going to international school in Milan. She was living in Paris, studying interior design, had been to London quite a few times, preferring to go out in the east of the city. This was easy, I thought. Talking to strangers, it turns out, could be fun, if you just went with the flow a bit.

I smiled at the general scene. Ellie noticed and turned towards Greta and me.

'We're just talking about apartments, guys,' she said. Where are you living again, Greta?'

Greta said she was living in Montmartre and I, having superficially gleaned the neighbourhood's charms from work, commented that Montmartre was supposed to be lovely.

From the other side of the table, And then said 'Montmaaaaaatre's suppooooooosed to be loooooooovelaaaaaay,' in a caricature Yorkshire accent, and not even a Humberside accent – let alone one slightly softened by a near-decade's southern exile – more just a generic Yorkshire accent, like the Harry Enfield Yorkshireman character, but sadder-sounding.

Ellie and Greta laughed and I tried to laugh too, but not quickly enough to avoid betraying my self-consciousness.

'It's all right mate, I'm just fucking with ya, I'm just fucking with ya. No worries,' And told me, reaching over to squeeze my forearm meaninglessly.

This was by no means a novel experience. Since uni, I've been used to people parroting my accent back to me. I remember at the very outset of my time at Sussex, during some kind of Freshers' meet and greet, a guy talked to me in a Yorkshire accent for the entirety of our 10-minute conversation and I only found out a week later that he was from St Albans. He even continued to talk to me in a Yorkshire accent for the remaining three years!

Sometimes, I know, it's intended affectionately – my friends Dyson and co. would mimic not only the Yorkshire accent but the dialect as well, employing phrases and idioms that I wouldn't in a lifetime ever use – *'Put t'kettle on then, lad'* and so on (note how much non-native Yorkshire speakers struggle with the glottal stop in definite article reduction).

Did you ever get this, I wonder? Possibly not, your Yorkshire traces having become so mild as to be almost undetectable. I remember when you came home at Christmas during your first year, I was appalled by your newfound Bristolian inflections. Over time I've noticed it less, a product of your evening out into an inevitable Estuary/RP default, perhaps, or maybe my own acclimatisation to more southern strains. Or both. When I go home now, people even tell me I sound like I'm putting on a 'London voice', which I can do little to counteract. And, yet, in London, still, I am mimicked as the Stock Yorkshireman. Even Neevie's taken to it, saying 'nowt' to mean nothing, and calling me 'our Mark' in a dodgy northern approximation. And it goes without saying that I like this a great deal because I'm already fond of her and I trust she's fond of me.

But this guy, And, I didn't know from Adam. And whether he'd meant it as a good-natured joke or not, I was now completely out of commission for the rest of the conversation. The others spoke knowledgeably about Montmartre and various other favoured Parisian neighbourhoods and I listened dumbly, the conversation having become far too intricate for me to have any chance of getting involved. I got my phone out to check the time and saw that it was 9.20pm, 40 minutes before the boat was supposed to dock. I excused myself to go and get another beer, but instead of returning to the table I took it out onto the deck, where the rain was lighter now. I tried to look at Twitter but the 3G was bad and the screen quickly wettened so I just gazed out over the river.

The air was fresher now and the breeze felt good. Across the river the lights of the buildings looked beguiling through the gathering dusk. I was only now taking proper regard of my surroundings. Set back slightly in the mid-distance was . . . the Eiffel Tower. The fucking Eiffel Tower! Right there. It was almost like a joke. I'd hardly been able to see the wood from the trees thus far, in terms of what was Paris and what was just a city. But suddenly there was the Eiffel Tower, glowing like metallurgy against the gloaming sky. And there was the Left Bank and the water of the Seine – city of De Beauvoir and Sartre and Camus and Rimbaud – and what was I doing sulking already?

There was nobody else on the deck, just the rushing air and the sound of the hull breaking the water. On the riverbank, cars looked graceful and quiet. People were walking – *en marche*, if you will. I stood there for a while, making the most of the moment.

We were nearing Port de l'Arsenal again. I went back down-stairs where the guests were making to leave. The music seemed better than before, more melodic or something. As I walked towards the bar Ellie grabbed my shoulder. She looked drunk, but in a nice way.

'Hey, where have you been?' she shouted.

'I was just on the phone,' I replied. Not technically a lie.

'A few of us are gonna go back to ours for a little sesh if you fancy joining.'

'Yeah, great!' I had literally nothing else to do. I was truly free.

We chatted a bit more about our respective Parisian callings and then Philippe came over and slapped me on the back, but not in a dickish way.

'Mark's gonna come with us,' Ellie told him.

'Cool,' said Philippe.

He went off to find his jacket and I followed Ellie upstairs again. She went to the toilet and I told her I'd wait on deck, where the deckhand-cum-bartender was gathering ropes, ready for docking. Most of the guests were up here too now.

I watched the docking of the boat, the swift alignment with the fluorescent-lipped bank; the slight ricochet as the vessel made contact; the barman-cum-deckhand's leap onto land and expert ropework in bringing the junk to harbour.

The barman restored the metal gangway with a kind of winching device and the people began to filter off the boat and onto the bank. They were laughing and shouting, and their movement was variously giddy and tired. Some stood together on the quay and some passed through the small port to the road beyond, where cars were waiting. After a moment, I saw And emerge onto the deck, throwing his shoulders about, singing like an opera singer, though I couldn't tell why. Greta was following him and laughing. After them came Ellie and Philippe, arm in arm.

I quickened my step as I followed through the port and caught up with them just as they were all piling into an Uber.

'Oh shit, we need a six!' Ellie said.

'Well, I can't cancel this one,' And cut in from the front seat.

'I'll send you the address,' Ellie told me through the back passenger window.

'Okay,' I said.

And said something to the driver in French and the car pulled away from the kerb and away into the night. I took my phone out and realised immediately that Ellie did not have my number.

I felt fine. I still felt fine. I walked towards Oberkampf Metro and sat down at a terrace. I ordered a *demi* and sipped it as I chewed over the evening and decided it hadn't been so bad. I'd done all right chatting to Ellie and Philippe. A late evening spent alone was, no question, better than any more time spent near And. As you well know, I have long been absolutely fine on my own. In the right solitary conditions, I thrive. I am a near-introvert and proud of it. I wasn't going to let histrionic self-pity get the better of me after one weird night in Paris.

What did it matter, I thought, as I sat tipsy on the Metro, if a doltish man had been a bit rude to me and I hadn't gone to an afterparty? How dare I pity myself in such a position? I'd just been on a boat in the most beautiful city in the world, drinking free cocktails. Well, actually drinking free Heinekens but having the license to drink free cocktails, if I'd so wanted. I was here now, and I was going to enjoy it!

So last night was not my scene, and there'll be a lot of teeth-gritting to come as I endure some fairly annoying situations doing this job, I'm sure. But, as I told myself while lying in bed last night and listening to the cats scratching at the bedroom door, in Paris, and in other cities too, I *will* find the places and people to make real my long-overdue European Odyssey of discovery. Perhaps I'll just have to work a bit harder to find them than I'd anticipated.

Well, that's been quite an email. Amazing what one coffee can do. I will now leave you be. Should probably get moving myself – don't think this café is particularly unhurried-millennial-with-tablet-friendly, judging from the looks I'm starting to get from the waiter.

I only wanted to give you my first impression of Paris. It is, overall, a good one. Though I appreciate I've only actually seen about three neighbourhoods in the centre, which can't be said to represent much of an insight into the 'real city', I admit.

Et demain, je vais visiter le Louvre! Haha. Quite excited actually. I'll be going round as part of a 'non-boring' guided tour, my first 'Experience', to be copywritten about. Today, I'm just gonna wander around, get a sense of the city.

Oh and Neevie eventually replied, saying sorry for taking so long to get back. I hadn't really thought about it being a long time until she apologised for it being a long time. I've become accustomed to the particular rhythms of her creative brain. Anyway, she's been busy designing the marketing for an affordable art fair, which sounds very cool. Also I'm not on Whatsapp at the moment, which probably doesn't help things, reply-speed wise. It's the cross I bear.

Okay. *C'est assez.*

Salut,

Mark.

From: Mark Rosiello
To: Paris Rosiello
Jul 04; 09:52

Bonjour!

C'est encore moi! I'm having my morning coffee and couldn't resist writing again. This morning I've shunned the genteel but all-too-swiftly devoured offerings of the traditional café in favour of a place that not only will serve americano, but also give it top menu billing. It's called like 'Bon Fresh' or 'Oui Food'. It's Pret, basically. I've got my big coffee, it's in a disposable cup and, having paid for it contactlessly, here I am, sitting at a long counter, on a high stool, like a schoolchild in a CDT lesson.

So, an odd thing happened last night. Back Home after the Louvre tour and a bistro dinner – an asparagus salad which I'd expected to be an asparagus pizza and was too nervous to try to change – I made my way through the dark *maison*, past the cats purring at their ease on the kitchen table, and found, upon reaching my bedroom, spread across the carpet like an oil spill, the black curtain, visibly torn down from its rails. Where the curtain had hung I now saw . . . an alcove, spanning almost the width of the room and a couple of metres deep.

In this space were deposited, quite haphazardly it seemed, a great number of storage boxes, some piled almost to the ceiling, some at floor level, open and overbrimming.

I stepped into the recess to examine the contents more closely and saw the apparent trappings of a teenage bedroom: trainers, deodorant cans, framed posters of bands and footballers. It all felt uncannily like the stuff you and I would have had in our bedrooms in our mid-teens, with the exception of a few decidedly modern items: a whole crate of PS4 games, a Bluetooth speaker, an electric scooter leaned against the back wall. It was as if an entire adolescent life had been hurriedly moved into a shipping container.

Who on earth had torn the curtain down, I wondered for all of three seconds until I realised that I'd left the bedroom door open when I'd gone out. I knew there'd been something especially insouciant about those cats as I passed them on the way in . . .

This morning, just after waking, I heard Elisabeth let herself in. After dressing, I went directly downstairs to hear her moving around in the kitchen and talking in hushed and apparently earnest tones to the cats.

'*Bonjour!*' she called before I'd even entered the room. 'And good morning. Was your sleep very good?'

It was, I assured her, as I shambled into the kitchen.

'But,' I continued tentatively, suddenly aware it sounded like a quintessential fib, 'I think the cats pulled down the curtain in the bedroom . . .'

'Oh not again . . . I am so sorry!' she said.

'It's okay,' I told her, taken aback at just how easily she had received the information, 'I didn't know how to put it back so I just left it, I'm afraid.'

'Please. Don't worry. I will do it when you go out. I am well practised.'

She smiled and I nodded and smiled back and then we just continued to stand and smile at each other and the cats both lay sphinx-like on the table and seemed to smile too.

'Erm, that stuff behind the curtain . . .' I said after a moment.

'Yes . . .' she said.

'. . . what is it?'

'Oh nothing, I am sorry you had to see it, hope it doesn't affect your opinion of the room.'

'No, not at all. I was just curious about it.'

'Well, it is not important but if you want to know, it is my son's.'

'Oh,' I said. 'Is it his room?'

'No,' she said, almost sternly, 'it is *your* room!'

'I mean usually.'

'Well, when there are not guests here . . . yes.'

'Where is your son now then?' I asked.

'He and his sister are sent to their father's.'

Elisabeth now moved from the middle of the kitchen and began doing something with the coffee machine on the other side of the room.

'Oh, not on my account, I hope,' I said, to her sleek hair.

'Mark, please, do not worry.' She turned and smiled again. 'Would you like a *café*?' she asked.

'Yes please,' I said, and sat down at the kitchen table to stroke the cats.

As if all of that wasn't stimulation enough, I also went to the Louvre yesterday.

Arriving after lunch, early for my tour, I negotiated the crowds, which frothed like currents of water through a rock pool system, and then had a good, long stand and look at that famous glass pyramid and found the tour group nearby.

The Experience was fairly enjoyable really, once I made my peace with the hurried, unsatisfying pace of progress, affording only fleeting glances at amazing Durers and Bosches and Bonheurs, and with the guide, whose name was Alex. Slightly bearded, open-collared, intimidatingly good-looking and just a little too cocksure and performatively extroverted to be genuinely likeable, he delivered a tour that was two parts salacious and inconsequential apocrypha about the paintings to one part useful analysis/exposition. But what else is to be expected from a tour that's called 'A Cheeky Time In The Louvre (And You Might Learn Something!)'?

The cheekiest moment of all came as we looked at La Joconde herself, or rather looked at the six-body-deep crowd looking at her (past two stewards and a bullet-proof screen), and Alex insinuated that the eponymous Lisa might have been receiving cunnilingus beneath the frame of the painting. I looked around at my seven or eight tour-mates, for some unspoken, collaborative disapproval but found the majority of them to be laughing appreciatively, and the couple who weren't hadn't seemed to understand very much of the tour prior to that point. The worst thing was that Alex appeared to be directing a great number of his jokes at me, saying things like 'This cherub looks like he has enjoyed too much wine!' or 'This tree looks like something you might see in a porno!' and then just staring at me with desperate anticipation. Eventually I realised it was easier just to laugh without reservation, sometimes before he had even finished the joke, so as to permit him to move on as fast as possible.

I got the sense that this performance was being delivered with the aim of impressing me, as the person who would be capturing his Experience in the form of copy. It seemed quite unnatural and unnecessary though, just as it had been weird that Elisabeth would completely vacate her home and evict her own children for me.

After the tour had finished, Alex asked me whether I would like a 'personal tour' so he could tell me some 'even more cheeky secrets of the Louvre'. I politely declined and he nodded, gripping my hand as he wished me 'the very best luck with the writing' before staring deep into my eyes with an almost pleading expression. Blinkingly, I thanked him and exchanged with him a slightly clumsy broshake, before hurrying to the nearest bar, or the nearest one not brimming with tourists, a good 10 minutes' walk away.

While I waited for my *demi* on a quiet side-street terrace I reflected that the Cheeky Tour wasn't exactly my bag but it was a distracting and occasionally informative couple of hours. I can now sort of see the appeal of doing a guided tour, having spent my entire life doggedly shunning such curated experiences. I'm prepared to accept that a certain amount of structure and purpose and narrative, in such a sprawling overgrown cultural sandbox of a place as the Louvre, can be helpful.

I drank four *demi*s while writing up the copy of my first Experience while it was still fresh in the memory. In the end, I was pretty pleased with it. Bethan Decker, however, when her swift reply came, was not:

Hey Mark,

Glad to hear you're enjoying Paris and that the Seine Cocktails were fun. I've done that Experience a couple of times myself – I trust you sampled the Artisanal Grog, 'tis truly the stuff of dreams!

And thanks for sending the Louvre copy so promptly. I have just a few thoughts that I think will help to improve it and the first is to completely rewrite it.

My main issue with what you've written is that it reads more like an art essay than Urb copy. For people looking through the Featured List, it won't be important to know that:

'While many of the figures in Veronese's famous Wedding at Cana interact with one another, not one of them is seen to be speaking. This is because the painting would hang in the refectory of the Benedictine monastery at San Giorgio Maggiore, where monks must observe a vow of silence.'

Similarly reading that **'the gradated legal punishments enshrined on the Code of Hammurabi, which privilege property owners above the rest of society, seem an eerie antecedent of our current crisis, rendering the Babylonian stone a strange harbinger, uncannily reminiscent of Kubrick's monolith in its (accidental) power to herald the repetition of history's mistakes'** is not something likely to make guests more interested in the tour. The important thing is just to make it sound, yes, interesting, but more importantly, fun, given that galleries can often feel a chore! Remember this is about the Human Touch, not the Intellectual Touch.

What was Alex like as a Host? How did he bring the paintings to life? Did he tell any funny stories or jokes? It's also not relevant that you found his style **'affectedly demotic at times'** and his anecdotes **'tending towards the frivolous'**.

If that's how you felt, then fine, but don't mention so in the copy.

And, furthermore, I would urge you to stay mindful in making sure your personal feelings are as close as possible to what we want to inspire in Urb Family Members checking out the Featured List! We're looking for authenticity, but it has to be the right kind of authenticity.

It will be much more enjoyable for you to feel like you're in tune with the Homes and Experiences in terms of feelings. If a tour is offering 'laughs' let yourself laugh; if a particular Home is known to be 'cosy' let yourself *be* cosy.

I appreciate this is your first submission of the trip and it's naturally going to take a little while to 'get your eye in' as it were. I also think it's great that you're brimming with ideas and impressions and there's definitely scope to let your exciting, subjective, personal take on things shine through. The important thing is to make sure that that personal, subjective take is a little more in line with what we're looking for in terms of making the Featured selections sound as appealing as possible. Hitting that key information in a fun, engaging way is something you're usually very good at in your copywriting and I'm sure you can get there with this.

Have another go at the copy and get it back to me by tomorrow afternoon if you can. Want your mind nice and fresh for your mountain retreat in the Pyrenees!

Bethan.

Bit annoying, but I take her point. Clearly I got carried away, probably a result of the infectious pomp of the Louvre, and of Alex's frustratingly non-intellectual approach, and of the four *demi*s and of the whole Parisian *mise-en-scène*.

It's fine, I can deal with it. It's just annoying that I've got to sit here and write it again. It's not coming easily this morning either. That's why I've broken off to email you again. For displacement, I guess.

Rather than try to rewrite my Louvre copy now, let me tell you of what I *have enjoyed*:

The Eiffel Tower

•   The day before yesterday I walked from the Pantheon to the Eiffel Tower, and it began to rain just as I came close enough to the structure to be able see its red lift ascend. I wanted to get a good selfo with the comically famous tower, so I sat and waited for the downpour to stop under a parasol, drinking an ice tea – strong Proustian flashbacks to our childhood La Rochelle holidays here where I drank gallons of the stuff! At the next table, three well-dressed women who might have been younger than me sat and talked good-humouredly, each holding a very young baby. A couple of dogs sniffed around the tables. A loud man in shorts drank a Coke while his family looked at their phones.

The View From the top of the Institut du Monde Arabe

•   From here you can see right out to Paris's dimly visible suburbs. The museum collection is fascinating too, most of its content – taking in early Bedouin tribes up to artistic responses to militaristic destruction of contemporary Arab lands – so far beyond my ordinary ken, that, combined with the more literally far-reaching view from the roof, it left me feeling like I'd really broadened my mind.

Art

•   To compensate for my slightly underwhelming experience of the Louvre, I did manage to get to l'Orangerie to see the Water Lilies followed by Musée d'Orsay, which I found truly wonderful until, looking at a Goya, I started to feel weird. I had contracted, I suspect, Stendhal syndrome – the condition induced by the viewing of an abundance of sublime art, whose symptoms include faintness, dizziness, nausea. You've probably heard of it. It's like whiteying on paintings basically. I've experienced the syndrome once before from looking at a Turner at Tate Britain, though tbh on that occasion the symptoms could equally have been attributable to a hangover. This time, I didn't discount it being from too much walking. Whatever the cause of my malaise, I decided to back away from the Modiglianis and the Sisleys and went to sit in the café to have a cup of tea and play a pipe-puzzle game on my tablet.

Not a bad few days all in all and not totally taken up with work. But still . . . I can't help thinking, as I sit here nursing my non-recyclable ripple-wave paper coffee cup, that I might have done more during my stay, and, as time passes and all that is left are memories of Paris, those same memories might be coloured just as much by all that I didn't do as that I did.

I didn't go up the Eiffel Tower, see the Arc de Triomphe, or the Bastille. Didn't visit the catacombs or the medieval museum as I'd hoped to. I didn't go back to Ellie and Philippe's flat; I didn't make any new friends; I didn't observe the realities of working-class life in and around the city; I didn't drink a Pastis; I didn't read any Sartre or De Beauvoir or Camus or Baudelaire; I didn't, if I'm honest, manage to have a single conversation with a person with whom I wasn't effectively involved in a commercial or contractual transaction.

I feel a bit shit about that. Like, that's it: that's Paris. Just a handful of fairly touristic experiences and an overwhelming sense of a city unseen. I will come back, I hope, but I suspect now that the more I return, the more I'll realise how vast and unknowable the city is and how impossible it will be to ever gain anything like an 'authentic' experience. It's like a classic case of 'the more you learn the less you know' or something; the more I understand Paris the more I'll see just how little real affinity with the place I have.

Now, having been here for the first time, it's like some fantasy version of Paris has died. I've seen the reality of it and realised that the mad, strangely lit cinema montage version of my potential Parisian experience, like a Truffaut film or a Eurostar advert, a seemly debauch of wine and sex and endless prestige leisure, is impossible, and in reality, the default Parisian tourist experience is at least 60% boredom and frustration and negotiation of personal psychological shortcomings and generic civic infrastructure, just as in London or any other big European city.

Prior to this week I'd always had a stirring sense deep within me that I was *meant* for Paris. That I, in some incommunicable way, shared its spirit. That arriving here would feel like coming home. Now, after three days in the city, I know only that it's big and I literally can't travel more than about 300 metres within it without first having to squint at Google Maps for about two minutes. To really *know* the city you would have to live here. For years. And am I ever going to? Probably not.

I'm being morose. Just the coffee wearing off, I guess. Something to do with 'adenosine' and dopamine or something. I must go. I'm going to Foix tomorrow. No, I don't know either. It's in the 'Midi-Pyrénées' apparently and I'm going to be staying on a 'retreat'. Must admit I'm quite intrigued.

Right, I better get this fucken Louvre copy done. If I get a move on, I'll still have a few hours for some *flânerie ce soir*.

Jusqu'à la prochaine fois,

Mark.

From: Mark Rosiello
To: Paris Rosiello
Jul 07; 10:58

Hi Paris,

It's me, writing to you again, this missive arriving in your inbox from the train to Barcelona. We're just leaving Toulouse, and this is the freest, most fortified with excited sureness, most untroubled by my familiar cares that I've been, *basically ever*. Hence writing again, I suppose. Also because Foix – pronounced like 'foie' (liver) as in 'foie gras', which homophony is actually the source of an 'amusing' rhyme told to me by my Paris Host, about an old woman who goes to Foix to sell some liver – and its environs were as funny and whimsical as the name suggested it might be.

I was in decent enough spirits after that last email I sent you. I got my Louvre copy done and even had time for a parmigiana before bed. Next morning, filled with a sense of quixotic purpose, I departed Gare d'Austerlitz in the direction of Spain. Was a bit sad to say *au revoir* to Elisabeth's cats, to be honest, but was looking forward to the train nevertheless.

As I've probably told you umpteen times, the taking of a long train journey surely ranks amongst my three greatest pleasures, unless I'm facing backwards, in which case it probably ranks amongst my three worst pleasures. Sadly it was in that vestibular-system-confounding orientation that I travelled from Paris to Foix, known colloquially as 'the gateway to the Pyrenees'. All hope of reading or writing abandoned, I adopted a 700-mile grimace, stared out at the beige and graffitied engine sheds and listened to Kendrick Lamar's *DAMN* and then Laura Marling's *Semper Femina*, and then Laura Marling's *Semper Femina* again, because I am, at heart, a drip. Within a few hours, all sense of purpose, quixotic or otherwise, had dissipated and I just wanted to go to bed.

Despite knowing that my next Home (the Wellness retreat high up in the Pyrenees; the common-noun-made-proper feeling more of a stretch than ever here) offered '*intelligent movement*', '*intuitive nourishment*', '*three-dimensional detox*' and '*free parking*', I didn't really know what to expect.

About three listens and a change of train later, I disembarked at the Gare de Foix in the mid-evening to find one minicab in the car park, a grey Renault Mégane, with 'FOIX TAXI' emblazoned on its side, crouching solitary and rain-beset by the station entrance. Around it were only trees and charming street lamps, each with three upright glass bulbs, like berries on a branch or three bowling balls on a rack or three old friends talking closely. From the surrounding mountains, just visible through the rain, came a feeling of being half watched from above.

On seeing me approach, the taxi driver – a short, wiry-haired man in an old-school rugby shirt – got out and bade me a low-energy *Bonjour*. I responded in kind, and began lining up my next sentence, which I reckon would have been at least a B-standard on a GCSE French oral exam, but he was already hurrying around to the boot, the size of my bag being the plainest fact about me I suppose.

The by-now, quite damp, 60-litre rucksack deposited in the boot on top of some old newspapers and what looked like a broken piece of garden fence, the driver asked me where I would like to go.

I was, perhaps, over-prepared for this moment, given that I'd delayed watching *Ray Mears' Adventure Special* on my tablet the previous night in order to practise learning and saying the name of the Urb – La Forteresse de l'Esprit – and to do a little bedtime reading of my Trip Pack, which had furnished me with 'everything' I needed to know for my arrival: that Foix is a medieval city on the edge of the Pyrénées Ariégeoises in south-west France, playing host to a well-preserved Cathar castle, surrounding medieval streets and, most saliently in the Featured Destination stakes, the aforementioned *'Forteresse de l'Esprit' Wellness Retreat'*, *'nestled mindfully in the hills above the town'*. How a Wellness retreat might nestle mindfully I could not guess, but I was already looking forward to mindfully working this boast into my copy.

So anyway, I carefully enunciated La Forteresse de l'Esprit to the driver, to which he frowned and said *'Où ça?'* This response, given as it was in French, encouraged me to think for a moment that my accent might have seemed decent enough not to betray my provenance, before I realised it was more likely because he didn't speak English. I was not in Paris any more.

I re-pronounced the name, even more laboriously than before, but he just frowned and began to shake his head with the steady rhythm of a hypnotist's watch. I took my phone out to show him on the map, but the screen was so immediately wet that I couldn't unlock it, prompting the driver to usher me into the back of the car, which was overwarm inside and smelled of cigarettes.

With the screen dry, I found the Urb, which looked to be a couple of miles from the station. I showed the driver who squinted at the phone and took it from me, zooming in and out a couple of times before shaking his head again and copying the address into his own satnav (this took about 90 seconds, during which I genuinely could not imagine the task ever being completed – it reminded me a great of deal of Grandad and his last Christmas present of an iPad, which he, if memory serves, genuinely threw in the bin and let be taken to landfill).

Seeing the destination, the driver jutted a lip and said something in French, with a note of gruff surprise. It wasn't immediately obvious whether he expected me to answer, so I did what I do in any conversation with a French speaker whom I do not wish to sense just how incapable of French-speaking I am, i.e. not ask them to repeat what they've said until it becomes completely necessary. Accordingly, I just nodded, prompting him, after a dead pause, to look and me and ask '*Alors?*'

'*Pardon?*' I said.

'*C'est une ferme?*'

Was it a farm?

'*Ah non, c'est une . . .*' It occurred to me that I had zero idea of how to say *Wellness retreat* in French. I could, now I think about it, probably have ventured 'Spa' and been understood but in the dampness of the moment I went for *Château de Bien-Etre*. At this, the driver asked if I meant I wanted to go to *the* château, but appealing though that was I told him *non merci* and just said the place was *un hôtel*.

Driving away from the station and along the river which edged the medieval commune, the driver told me, I *think*, that the place used to be a farm owned by a man, *possibly*, called Monsieur Durand, who died a few years ago of, I *believe*, untreated gout.

We passed all the classics from the vocab sheets – *la banque*, *l'hôtel de ville, le Crystal and Healing Emporium* etc., all of them looking, in the summer rain, somehow uncanny in their Frenchness – and left the town by a small road that climbed upwards away from Foix into the mountains. From the stuffy backseat, I watched the satnav as we left the familiar suburban world, denoted with a grey shade, and entered a wilder land, a strange green expanse that stretched beyond the edge of the screen. Soon, reaching a dirt track, we left the mapped road entirely and were just an unbound blue dot bearing down on our target, a blue teardrop icon.

And, sure enough, soon it was visible through the windscreen

– that great screen which mediates the hard content of the putative real world – a vinyl 'Welcome' sign in pastels and plain helvetica, then suddenly a paved road leading towards a crop of farm buildings dolled up like the imaginary fundaments of a Kevin McCloud wank, along with a couple of very modern glass-and-oak buildings with high slanted roofs. There were neat herbaceous foliage and water features which were serious, and laterally insistent. This was not the residence of a farmer with gout.

The driver brought the Mégane to a rumbling halt by the awning-covered entrance, alongside the eight or so other cars, many of them *Top Gear*-worthy. Having paid the driver and watched him disentangle my bag from the garden fence pieces, I hunched my way through the rain towards the glass porch cover and a hefty door, which had a Samsung keypad where a keyhole might be, and two thin panes of frosted glass, corrupting the general veneer of welcomeness.

Just to the left of the door was a buzzer and above it a smaller sign, which read, in English, 'If door is locked, please press bell', which seemed self-obvious and faintly extravagant, especially given that the sign appeared to have been made bespokely, ostensibly by one of those laser cutter machines they had in CDT at school. Did you even do CDT at your posh school or would that have been considered dangerous (in an ideological as much as a literal-physical sense)?

I pressed the bevel-edged bell, which felt like porcelain, and waited a minute, maybe more, before pressing it again to hear a skeuomorphic bell SFX resound for a second time.

A moment later, the door was answered by an angular-featured man of about 27 wearing a crumpled white vest and smart trousers. He had fair, chin-length hair, slightly curly – a bit like yours, but darker – which he ruffled as soon as he opened the door.

'*Bonjour!*' I said loudly, a key interpersonal policy of this trip being to use volume as a sign of amity.

'*Chut!*' he rasped and raised a willowy finger to his curling lips.

'*Ah pardon*,' I said, loudly again, which made him say '*chut!*' once more.

'*Je suis désolé*,' I whispered and raised my own palm towards my lips, in the flinchingly contrite manner of a sitcom buffoon with delusions of sophistication.

My piss-poor accent must have alerted him to my Englishness, or at least my non-Frenchness, because he now began speaking to me in English, asking next, in a stern whisper:

'How can I help you?'

'*Je suis l'invité d'Urb*,' I said, not yet ready to admit lingual defeat.

'You are with Urb?' he asked.

'Yes,' I confirmed.

He regarded me searchingly for a few seconds and then, perhaps finally taking account of the persisting rain, told me to follow him inside. Pausing a second to watch me shut the door, he padded in his bare feet across the dark wood floor to a very high desk with one succulent and a single pen on it. A couple of warm, orangey lamps shone against the room's deep blue walls, and there was a sense of benign, low-level activity, deriving primarily from two beige curviform machines on small, low tables, which were near constantly squirting out vapours like cetacean blowholes.

I reached the desk where the man was now staring at a printout of a spreadsheet covered in grey crossings and annotations, floating his pencil over its surface.

'You have a reservation?' he asked.

'*Oui*, yes, *oui*,' I said. 'Mark Rosiello. Or maybe under Bethan Decker.'

'For today?' he clarified, clearly not perceiving in me enough basic intelligence to check what day it was before setting off to stay at a Wellness retreat.

'Yes, *oui*.'

'I cannot see here,' he said, an accusatory note growing in his voice.

'Can you check on the computer system maybe?'

'We have no computers in public areas.'

'Right. So . . . so how do you know who's staying?'

'We have the information here,' he said, gesturing down at the paper. 'It is printed for us in the town and delivered here for us by the baker.'

'By the baker?'

'Yes, he does a mindful patisserie class, he delivers the fresh bread and he brings the emails and the booking sheet each day.'

'Right.'

'And today I cannot, I'm afraid, see anyone from Urb.'

I closed my eyes and let a wave of useless anger roll over me. I could prove to him who I was. I took my phone from my wet jeans whereupon the man flinched like Superman seeing a photo of some kryptonite.

'You cannot have this out in this room!' he hissed.

'What?'

'It is no devices in this space. Only in the Devices Room.'

'Where's that?'

'It is within the retreat.' He gestured to the door behind him.

'Well, can I go there now because I can show you the email—'

'No, you cannot go now.'

'Why?'

'It is only for guests.'

By this point, Paris, I was well on my way to losing my *merde*.

'There must be a mistake, the list could be wrong or—'

'There is no mistake, the baker who brings the list will not come back until tomorrow.'

'Can't you phone him?'

'I do not make phone calls after 3pm.'

I huffed like a child. 'Well, if I can show you this email you'll see . . .'

He looked sceptical, taking in my appearance once more – my wet jeans, my nondescript baseball cap, my sweaty T-shirt, my hulking backpack. I'd given little thought to my appearance since the cocktail Experience in Paris, but assessing it now I probably looked something like a pale teenager who'd gone to a fancy-dress party as a middle-aged American tourist. He told me I could look at my phone outside under the cover. Released once more into the device-permitting kingdom of rain, I began searching my inbox for an email that would confirm my reservation, the whispering man waiting barefoot on the step, arms folded, as dull water chugged in the gutter.

It was only then that it began to dawn on me: I didn't *actually* have any definitive email about my reservation. Neither was I using the Urb app. Bethan Decker had organised all the reservations directly with the Hosts, possibly even outside of the app. All I had was the Trip Pack and a travel itinerary with the dates and details of the Urbs and their Hosts. The vest lad exhaled a loud breath, one that seemed to say, 'I'm increasingly beginning to think you're a con artist.'

Hand shaking a bit, I found the entry for Foix on Bethan Decker's admin PDF and zoomed in on the name of the Urb and the dates of the stay. The man leaned towards the phone to read the screen and simply said: 'This is not a reservation.'

'No, but as I said, I am here working *for* Urb and my boss made—'

'You are working *for* Urb?' he clarified.

'Yes.'

'I don't know of this,' he said after a few seconds.

'Bethan Decker?'

'Excuse me?'

I grew louder and less self-possessed with every word: 'Bethan Decker is the name of my boss at Urb,' I held out the phone once more, 'she's the Director of Content at the Urb headquarters in London, and I'm here to write copy about this place for the website to increase the likelihood of people actually bothering to come all the way to Foix to stay here.'

The man looked at it and, still not taking it in his hands, replied again: 'This is not a reservation.'

I snapped at him. 'I know it's not a reservation! She boss of me. She work for Urb. Maybe you remember emailing her?' I said to him in pedagogical staccato. Why I was now adopting this bizarre rhythm and grammar to a man who spoke pretty decent English, I have no idea.

'Hmm, maybe my manager, I don't know.'

'Could I speak perhaps to your manager then?'

'No, she is in India.'

I turned away from the man and the Urb as if a solution to this conundrum was about to come crawling over the wet fields from the dim town beneath.

'I will ring *my* manager,' I said.

I was panicking, catastrophising. This felt like a crisis, but it wasn't really. I would call Bethan Decker and she would send over the necessary document to prove my reservation, I would show it to the man, he would apologise for being so obstinate and within five minutes I would be inside drinking an Ayurvedic tea and smiling..

The man shrugged again. I would show him. He would soon be shown by me!

I turned away and called Bethan Decker, but it went straight to voicemail. Staving off another wave of internal panic, I called her again. Straight to voicemail. I called her again. Straight to voicemail. It was 7.22pm, so 6.22pm in London. Bethan Decker would be on the tube most likely, but others would still be in the office. Surely someone would be able to dig out the reservation.

I phoned the Urb office and got through to Florence on reception who said that according to her synced calendar, Bethan was in both New York and Bogotá. I asked if Bethan Decker's assistant was in and was told that he was also in New York and Bogotá.

I explained my predicament and asked if anybody in the office might have access to the Urb reservation. She said she was really sorry to hear about it and that she'd be willing to give me Bethan Decker's personal mobile number as it was such an urgent issue. I told her, getting increasingly high-pitched, that I already had Bethan Decker's personal number and that she wasn't picking up. Florence told me that she was really sorry that there was nothing more she could do to help me and I hung up the phone without saying goodbye, which was unfair really, as it wasn't Florence's fault.

I took a deep breath, looking out at the rain-drenched gateway to the Pyrenees, before turning to tell the man I had no access to my reservation. He looked unsurprised but not completely without sympathy.

'How much will a new reservation be please?' I asked. This was going to hurt, but I forced myself to remember that Bethan Decker would soon reimburse me. The inconvenience of having to shell out like this might even buy some pity after grudgingly, I sensed, accepting my copy for Paris after the rewrites.

'I cannot offer a new reservation for today,' the vest man replied. 'Check-in time for guests without the reservation has now closed.'

Enough, I thought.

Bethan Decker would soon call back and then she could call him up and sort it out herself. For now, I had to get away from this barefooted neo-luddite. With as scathing a look as I could muster, I walked away from the awning to the edge of the car park and then down the damp, gritty road. I might have been crying, or – as I often do these days when I feel I want to cry but physically can't – contorting my face into a lachrymal expression and growling. The rain, at least, was now easing.

The road progressed in a mocking zigzag that made it feel like I was having to walk about twice as far as was logical. 12 minutes into the walk, Bethan Decker's phone still going straight to voicemail, I'd checked my phone and seen that Neevie had been on Twitter but still hadn't replied to my text, and I was still nowhere within spitting distance of the bottom of the mountain. It was then that I heard a vehicle rumbling increasingly louder above me. I turned and saw a small, pristine Citroën round the bend, pass me and come to a stop a few metres away.

'Monsieur Rosiello, please accept my apologies!' the retreat man beseeched me as he climbed out of the car and attempted to wrench my bag from my back. 'There was a terrible problem, but my manager has just called to check that you are here safely and I realised there has been an error with the system, so I have come to take you back so you can begin your stay with us!'

'Oh . . . *de rien!*' I replied, having only since realised that this in fact means *You're welcome* rather than *It's nothing / Don't worry* as I'd supposed. I climbed into the front of the car, steaming slightly.

'Thank you deeply, Monsieur Rosiello,' he said while performing a tricky three-point turn in the road bend.

I told him to call me Mark and he told me his name was Sylvain before proceeding to explain, as we drove back up the hill, that the 'terrible problem' came about because the baker had simply printed off the bookings sheet and not gone into the special folder in the webmail account, which anyway is a new webmail account with a new service, which to be honest, has some problems! And so he had not brought the special information about my visit, which his boss (i.e. Sylvain's boss) wanted him (i.e. Sylvain) to admit was not her (i.e. the boss's) fault and that she definitely had told him that Monsieur Rosiello (i.e. I) would be coming today and that he had forgotten, and indeed he himself wanted to admit that too and to apologise as well – he had been very busy with an extra high number of guests this week, a sign of the increasing popularity of the Forteresse de l'Esprit, which remains very devoted to its exclusive and refined guests, plus his boss is in India at the moment and with the time difference a lot of things were getting lost this week. Not that that was an excuse. And – by this point we had arrived back at the premises – perhaps I would like to come inside, where all would be made up to me.

As we approached the entranceway, Sylvain offered to carry my bag, which I declined as it would have been pointless and we both knew it, but I appreciated the gesture and I was beginning to warm to him, seeing him now as a sort of high-functioning buffoon, where just half an hour ago and without the suggested hinterland of a difficult boss and her ridiculous communication system, he'd just seemed a bit of a tosser.

He led me through the previously restricted door to a large,

open-plan room with a glass ceiling, slanted along the obvious
former contours of a high gable. The room was excitingly ambiguous in its function: to the left was a showroom-style kitchen
which a woman in a grey polo shirt was mopping; in front and
to the right a kind of sprawling lounge area whose various furnishings – bookcases, low tables, sofas, potted plants – cohered with
the perverse harmony of elements of an ancient woodland. There
were a few people in the space, presumably guests, some in pairs
chatting and others alone reading or sipping teas and juices.
There was a span of ages but they were mostly white and seemingly well-to-do. Lots of linen garments and expensive sunglasses
crowning foreheads. Many had kicked off their flip-flops. I felt
an inexplicable ripple of intimidation.

I followed Sylvain past a bookcase and an industrial-size lamp,
which looked as though it had been plundered from an old movie
set, to an extension at the far side of the space, signed as the
'Devices Room'. I now deduced the building to be the converted
farmhouse of the man with gout, with its inner walls and upper
floors deleted. Separated from the main space by a thick,
many-panelled room divider, the extension looked newer, being
of a slightly different style brickwork, though still more or less
in the same partly exposed/partly pastel-washed scheme and with
yet more expensively mismatched furniture.

'I have for you a plate of fresh apology fruit,' Sylvain said and
gestured to a glass table with burnished, cast-iron frame, on which
sat, sure enough, a dinner plate of sliced fruit. Melon, pineapple,
kiwi, strawberries. All the good ones. Without anywhere near
enough faux protestation modulating into politely giddy accept-
ance, I dropped my bag and sat down to eat. The fruit was
delicious, sweet and cold, and I worked through it quickly and
quite messily, like the ingenuous protagonist of a fairytale, being
baited for a villainous trap.

'You are enjoying the fruit,' Sylvain said and I replied '*Oui*,'
as if it was a question, though it might not have been. He asked
to see my passport so that he could copy down the details, and
after handing it over I sat and ate all the fruit on the plate, looking

up occasionally through the skylight above. After a few minutes Sylvain returned and handed me back the passport.

'You look very young in your photo,' he said and I laughingly agreed, even though the photo was about six months old.

Sylvain then removed the wet fruit plate and in one motion placed a tablet in a wooden or wood-effect case on the glass surface in front of me.

'I would like now, if you don't mind, for you to speak to Cindy.'

'Who's Cindy?' I asked.

'She is my manager. She is the owner of the retreat. She would like to apologise to you about all the problems.'

'That's really not necessary,' I said.

'It would be very important to us,' Sylvain said, as he opened the tablet cover and made it tilt upwards to look at me.

'Okay then,' I said.

'Excellent, thank you.' Sylvain smiled, now leaning in front of me to start pawing at the screen. It felt wrong to watch him as he unlocked the thing and started moving between apps so I looked out of the skylight again until I heard the strange ripple of the Skype call outgoing.

'Okay,' Sylvain said. 'She will now hopefully answer.'

As soon as he'd said this the call window showed a woman sitting before some palms. She had a large, attractive face, with a slight suntan, framed by silvery blonde hair, and wore a sort of white shirt.

I smiled and felt my eyes dart around the screen a bit. I could see the video image of myself in the bottom right of the app window. I was well lit, almost holy in the funnelled sunlight from above, but also looked pink and oily. I took my cap off and saw that my hair was wet and matted with sweat.

'Hello Mark,' said the woman.

'Hello,' I said.

'I'm Cindy,' she said, 'how are you today?' Her accent was RP English, with an airy, possibly slightly Americanised lilt.

'Er, good thanks.'

'Yah?'

'Yah. How are you?'

'Well, I'm good but I'm really, really sorry for what happened today, Mark!'

'Oh it's totally fine. Totally fine.'

'It's just so not exemplary of how things are at La Forteresse De L'Esprit,' she said, delivering the name with a confident French accent. 'I'm sure Sylvain explained the anomaly of what happened.'

'Yes, with the baker and the emails and everything.'

'We've been incredibly let down by a new webmail service we're using.'

'Right,' I said, with a, I think, quite convincing air of interestedness.

'You know I'm always really keen to support new businesses, new start-ups.' She said 'start-ups' in a slightly Californian way, like with a 'd' instead of a 't' and an 'a' instead of a 'u'. 'So these guys contacted me, said would we be interested in trialling their new system, I said sure. Well, ya know, be careful how much trust you give someone because this incident has proven that things can go wrong.'

'Right,' I said again.

'Basically they offer a feature where important long-term emails or documents or whatever are stored in a separate inbox and sent *into the main inbox on a marked date*. How many emails and messages and things do we receive and think "hmm I know I can't really deal with that right now but I know that's going to be important soon so I'll just hope I remember to come back to it"?'

'A lot,' I said.

'A real lot,' she said. 'So that's what this service is supposed to make simple: you get an important email – in this case, letting me know that you would be coming to La Forteresse to write fabulous copy for us – you mark that as important and request it to be resent to the main inbox on a given date. That didn't happen.'

'It didn't send?'

'It didn't send it through, Mark.'

'Oh no.'

'So you've had some fruit, Mark?'

'Yes.'

'That's great. And you know, I'm so sorry again. I've spoken to Bethan. She's just gorgeous. She's amazing. You're obviously a cool guy. You know, Sylvain says you've been so understanding. Because you know that's so rare these days. And that's what we do, what we celebrate and what we *cultivate* at La Forteresse.'

She then gave a, I would estimate, upwards of seven-minute-long account of how she came to be the absentee owner of a Wellness retreat in the Pyrenees, taking in: years spent at art school and in squats; allusions to ambivalently enjoyable drug use in the '80s; a lucrative but exhausting career as a commercial radio executive in the '90s; flights to India and elsewhere in the '00s where many self-questions were posed, the cumulative answer to which seemed to be 'now it's time to buy a very cheap farm in the Pyrenees and turn it into a Wellness retreat and get a skittish man to run it'.

'And what we do now,' she said, 'is offer a new space, a space that isn't available much in modern western life. A space where the conditions are right for healing, and for understanding who we ourselves are. And through that there comes a calmness and a peace and a decency that is getting harder and harder to achieve for most modern people in the West. And I can tell you do have that. So I think you're going to have an amazing time. Have you been to a Wellness retreat before?'

'No, I haven't actually,' I said, with a note of bright surprise, as if I'd only just realised that I'd never been to a Wellness retreat before.

'Oh!' She brought her hands up to her chin in a poise of abrupt, almost pained gratitude. 'Well, I think you'll love it. I hear you're a really *strong* copywriter. And I've told Sylvain just to let you *experience* what we do. And create your own take on it. Because you know – I wrote copy for our website and things, and we've had copywriters in the past. But this is what's so exciting about being chosen by Urb for this list, because Urb cuts through that – pardon my French – but that bullshit! It's so direct, it's so real, it's so human. And that's what Bethan tells me your writing does – shows things through that modern, no-bullshit lens, which is so refreshing. And that's what we need for our retreat.'

I nodded and then noticed myself nodding and then tried nodding again just to see what it looked like. I felt somehow that my nod lacked conviction so I tried nodding again more confidently. This might have gone on for 20 seconds before I tuned back to what she was saying.

'I can see you're nodding Mark, and, *ya know*, we do well, we're always full. We could be *fuller*. But we keep going and I don't do it for the *money*. I do it because I want people to find this space. This space that is so hard to find now. And that's the literal space of the retreat, in this beautiful part of the Pyrenees. But it's a more metaphorical space. I'm not gonna say a spiritual space, because it doesn't need to be that. But it's a mental space, it's a mental space, it's a place of selfhood, of difference from the way—' She raised her hand and aimed her open palm towards her own head in an emphatic gesture '—things generally are, out *there.*' She tilted her hand so that her palm faced away from her and now gestured outwards, beyond the edge of the Skype window. 'We need to detach from that.' She nodded at her own words. 'Look, I've rambled on long enough. I probably sound like some mad old hippie.'

'No,' I said.

'I'll let Sylvain look after you. And I hope you find the retreat very calming and very restful.'

'Thanks!' I said.

'Okay,' she said.

'Okay,' I said.

'Goodbye,' she said, smiling.

'Goodbye,' I said, smiling.

Then we both just sat there slightly frozen for a couple of seconds before she seemed to wake up and call for Sylvain once more. He slid back into view and they spoke French again but not long enough for me to feel compelled to look out of the skylight. When they'd finished talking and he'd ended the call and picked up the tablet, Sylvain said he would show me to my room.

I picked up my bag and followed as he walked, barefooted naturally, across the room to the doorway, which led into a glass-covered walkway that might have felt like some feature of museum infrastructure, were it surrounded by some thrilling display of e.g. model dinosaurs, or a gigantic model replica of the human digestive system, and not a hectare of lavishly refurbished French farm buildings.

After a dozen or so yards the walkway forked, thricely, each prong leading to another building. Sylvain turned left, telling me 'We go this way!' and I followed him down a longer walkway, leading to a door in a structure that was once perhaps a barn but now more like the kind of very large functional space you might find behind a Home Counties gastropub.

The building's rural-rustic ostensibilities were betrayed as Sylvain led me over its threshold into an entrance area of deep, deep reds and golds, Buddha statues, candles and incense.

'This is the Eastern House,' Sylvain said, 'where you will stay. Let me show you the place.'

He took me around a series of rooms slightly less orientalist than the first, or perhaps it was just that the shock of it had desensitised me to the rest. There was a small kitchen, which he said was mainly for corporate bookings.

The meditation room was actually very nice: mid-brown parquet flooring; subtly off-white walls; plush low cushions; only two or three Buddha statues by my count. Sylvain said this space was mainly for use if it was raining. On a brighter day he'd encourage me to use the Meditation Barn, just to the east of the Eastern House.

The lounge was a lot like the meditation room except with armchairs as well as cushions and, I think, one fewer Buddha.

My own room was, needless to say, pretty luxurious. You'd

have hated it. The less said about the Super King-size bed and
the artisanal toiletries and the yoga balcony the better, I
suppose. More judicious probably to tell you about the wifi
situation.

Sylvain told me he would show me the rest of the retreat in
the morning, and until then I was welcome to enjoy my room
and the rest of the Eastern House. I thanked him and asked for
the wifi details, as if the thought had just occurred to me and that
this wasn't something that had been plaguing my mind since the
moment I walked onto the premises.

'Ah yes,' Sylvain said, 'wifi is from 7 until 8 o'clock.'

'That's the name of the network?' I said, half listening as I
took my tablet from the top of my bag.

'No, it is that wifi is only available until 8 o'clock, so won't be
back on until tomorrow,' Sylvain explained.

'What?'

'In the Devices Room.'

'Where's that?' I asked, losing all effect of equanimity now.

'It is where you spoke to Cindy.'

'Right,' I said.

'Usually there would be no devices in the area after 8 o'clock
but Cindy decided it was exceptional circumstances.'

What he said next sounded like spiel. 'What we provide at La
Forteresse de l'Esprit is a "3D Detox". This concept represents
a detox of the body, mind and spirit. It means we have no poisons
of the body, such as alcohol and caffeine. We limit the poisons
of the mind such as wifi. And we prevent poisons of the spirit
such as negative energy.'

'So there's no wifi *here*?' I asked, gesturing quite urgently to
the space immediately around me.

'No, there is not. This is because we feel it is very important
to have liberty from the intrusions of the modern word into the
psych—'

'Sure, yep,' I said. 'So where do I go for dinner?'

'Dinner is between 6 and 7 o'clock.'

'So I can't get any dinner tonight?'

'You have had some fruit.'

'Yes, I have,' I said, already feeling the pangs of hunger coming on.

'So what should I do now?' I asked, afraid to take my phone out to check the time for fear of another passive-aggressive reproach but sensing there were still a few growingly hungry hours left in the evening.

'You could go into the Together House and meet your fellow guests perhaps? Or onto the patio for sunset yoga? Or you may just wish to meditate and sleep. And in the morning I will give you the full tour.' As he said this, Sylvain reversed out of the room smiling and bowing, quite unaware, I think, of just how thrown I'd been by the wifi reveal.

I now checked my phone and saw that it was only just gone 9, hours still until bedtime. I would struggle, I knew, to watch content using 3G but I might at least be able to get a podcast or something to play. Leaving my unpacked bag on the floor, I lay on the bed and took out my phone and saw that I had no 3G. I went onto the balcony and found none there, then tried the bathroom, kitchen, meditation room, and halfway down the glass walkway. No 3G.

I had no choice but to accept my supposed freedom and pursue a non-digitally-mediated passage to sleep. I lay on my bed and thought about writing a modern, perhaps parodic children's book in the vein of *The Bear Who Couldn't Sleep* called, like, *The Meerkat Who Couldn't Get 3G*, or *The Unicorn Who Couldn't Connect to the Wifi*. No wifi. No dinner and no booze either.

It had now been about 20 minutes since Sylvain had left the room. I could spend a few hours awake in a lovely room without going mad. Of course I could. I would lie in bed and read *Don Quixote*! This was the perfect opportunity. Given how awake I was feeling I'd probably end up making quite good progress!

I opened the bricklike paperback, read about two thirds of a page and then quickly fell asleep.

Upon waking next morning, I reached immediately for my phone. Still no signal.

Eventually I managed to summon enough brain strength to get out of bed and went onto the balcony. It was, objectively, a bright and lovely day. A dozen or so people were walking out of a field behind the farmhouse with blue oblongs under their arms. The window faced away from the town but I could see mountains, Pyrenean vistas, of a kind I'd never IRL looked upon before. It was nice. It was nice. But I did want to be, in some way, online.

I sighed and tried to be mindful and went back inside to shower and dress. As I was applying my emollient, Sylvain knocked at the door and said he'd wait for me until I was ready.

As we walked out of the Eastern House again, Sylvain asked if I'd managed to get out and meet anybody the previous evening and I told him I had read and fallen asleep. He said this was 'cool' but in quite a disappointed way.

He took me to the communal kitchen and watched me eat some yoghurt and granola. Next it was to the swimming pool where one muscled, leathery man was doing a fast front crawl, and the Terrasse Ensoleillée on which a few people were dosing up on vitamin D and carcinogenic irradiance.

After this Sylvain showed me the gym, where a sign stated (in English) that guests were requested to 'refrain from using the exercise equipment for purposes other than fitness (checking emails, watching films etc.)'.

From there we went on to the Yoga Barn and finally the spa where, at Sylvain's gentle behest, I was booked in for a Warm Shell Massage – the least intimidating item on the menu of treatments – later in the afternoon. Sylvain suggested I should try a range of treatments during my stay – an Aromatherapy Dance, for example, or a Sofri Colour Energy Candle Bath, so that I could write about them all, and I told him it'd be a waste because I wouldn't appreciate it.

'It'd be like,' I said, 'getting some swine to try some pearls so that they could write about them!'

Not sure he *fully* got the wordplay – if that's even what it was – but he definitely got the sense of it and he received it chucklingly before turning quite serious to say that I should at least speak to some fellow guests so I could hear about the treatments.

This prospect made me itch slightly. Those I'd seen sitting around in the communal areas drinking juices and not using their devices looked older – if not, in all cases, in a very literal biological sense, then just in a sense of being more mature and/ or accomplished in bearing and demeanour, able to sit with good posture and good clothes chatting quietly, or simply alone, seeming content.

I felt sweaty and awkward and inexorably of that mindset that makes interacting with strangers seem an exhausting, cell-fatiguing effort.

But *then*, after I'd gone and sat on the patio for 20 minutes and spoken to nobody, Sylvain took me to the Meditation Barn and asked me to take my shoes off while inviting me to sit on one of about 10 cushions arranged, gridlike, on the smooth wooden floor, ready for a group meditation. Really the timing couldn't have been better, because the meditation, which had brought on a great, panicked internal howl when Sylvain mentioned it, transpired to be – look, I'm not going to say life-changing but definitely *afternoon-changing*. There was something surprisingly liberating and restorative about sitting and straddling a pile of cushions in a converted barn with long, blue-curtained windows permitting certain streaks of sunlight, in whose slanting glow dust particles moved against the dimness like gentle pixels. It evoked primary school and sitting in the hall for assembly – a remembrance I was surprised to find welcome and reassuring.

The cushions also made it feel kinda like school, though I can't recall often being given cushions to sit on, certainly not firm, torus-shaped ones with labels declaring them to have *Supima Cotton* outers and to be filled with buckwheat. Maybe there was like *one* old beanbag in the library, on which whoever was the saddest child in the class at the time might be allowed to sit, by the teacher's side. Unlike your school, where I imagine you were all given a personal, monogrammed velvet cushion stuffed with state-school children's hair.

Anyway, there was something very nice about sitting astride my own little cushion pile, in my own few-metre-squared space, and seeing others settling in around me, crossing their legs and closing their eyes and seeming more human and essential than they'd seemed out in the lounge and by the pool. More vulnerable, somehow. The muscled swimming man was here now, telling the woman at the front of the room, in a broad Midlands accent, that he couldn't bend his knee very well, and so she handed him an extra, smaller cushion to rest it on.

This woman – who I reckoned to be in her mid-forties, with long, slightly tousled dark hair – was in charge of the meditation, and sat facing the rest of us in a blue vest and those baggy, strappy trousers like the ones you used to wear at uni – hareem pants maybe? – and much wooden jewellery. She introduced herself as Chloe, before leading us on a meditation that lasted about an hour, but which was delivered so slowly and with so many meditative pauses that there were probably only about ten minutes of words spoken, short and hypnotic repetitions generally concerning breathing and bodily tension.

It was all done in English but the potency of the experience, or my experience of the experience at least, derived from the quality of Chloe's voice, songful and cadent and French-accented, more than what she was actually saying. External cares began to fade as her words and her pauses alloyed with the dimly defined space around me and made me feel quite safe and protected on my little cushion, my own happy isle, my own mountain peak.

I was brought back down to the familiar foothills of low-level mental disquietude almost as soon as the meditation finished, however, on account of my efforts to talk to the other guests. As I walked out of the barn, a few of them were lingering on a sun terrace, so I sat down to put my shoes on and, emboldened, I suppose, by mindful residues and heedful of Sylvain's desire for me to hear more about the treatments, I plucked up the courage to say to the patio at large, 'That was good, wasn't it?'

Only the woman to my immediate left seemed to hear me and she replied with a non-linguistic noise that made me feel like what I'd said had been quite facile. A few seconds later, perhaps aware of her effect on me, she offered a consolatory, 'Meditation is always good.'

'That was my first time,' I told her, pouring myself a grapefruit water and beginning privately to consider how long I could remain safely in the sun without protection.

'Wow,' she said, quite sincerely but with no follow-up.

She reminded me a great deal of Cindy – the same silvery blonde hair, the same majesty in her posture, the same healthy radiance in her general aspect that betrayed her years, except that I didn't actually know how many years either of them had. It occurred to me suddenly that she was most likely Cindy's sister!

'Are you Cindy's sister?' I asked.

'No,' she said. 'Who's Cindy?'

'The owner of the retreat.'

'No,' she said again.

With such a famous rapport established, I felt the time was right to ask her about the treatments. This ended up with me just listing the treatments from a menu brochure on the table and her just describing back to me in simple detail what they were.

'Hot Stone Massage?'

'That's a massage where they use hot stones.'

'Skin-Healing Seaweed Wrap?'

'Your body is wrapped in seaweed which heals damaged skin.'

'Colon Hydrotherapy?'

'I haven't tried that one.'

Finally she asked me why I was 'interrogating' her in this way and I told her about the job, the Featured List and how Sylvain wanted me to gain a knowledge of the range of treatments even if I didn't try them all myself.

'Oh right,' she said, lifting a wide brimmed sun hat from under her chair and placing it on her head. 'So you're reviewing the retreat?'

'No, not reviewing exactly. More like . . . celebrating.'

'Celebrating?'

'You know – just writing copy to celebrate all these different places and things that Urb have picked as their best in Europe.'

'But don't they all write their own promo copy?'

For a mindful person, she was very pedantic.

'Yes, but we're looking for a particular tone across all the Featured products.'

When did I start including Urb and myself under one pronoun? I looked around for other guests to engage with but they all seemed too spread out and otherwise engaged, either by each other or by the sunshine.

'So you're better at writing about places than those who actually run them or frequent them?'

'Well—'

'Even when you don't have knowledge of Wellness treatments for example?'

I was pretty stumped by this. All I could think to do in response was channel my inner Bethan Decker: 'I think it's very much about creating a tone of everyday authenticity, the insight of the non-expert. People are bored of professional reviewers.'

'Oh right,' she replied, seeming unconvinced.

At this point, the muscled man with the tight knee came over, nominally to pour himself a grapefruit water but apparently also having been drawn in by the conversation.

'So you're getting to stay for free?' he asked, before even saying hello or introducing himself.

I confirmed I was but reiterated this was a proper job of work and that the writing was not proving easy.

He told me how much he was paying to be there, which I'm not even going to reveal to you but I immediately felt very guilty for walking around feeling so out of sorts, and then I just felt confused about feeling guilty when I couldn't really help feeling so out of sorts and how it could be that I was feeling so out of sorts so expensively.

The man continued to tell me just how lucky I was to receive the treatments for free. He worked very hard to afford special experiences like this, in a job that had something to do with designing luggage. It was, he said, an excellent place to unwind. He said that was especially important for him since his wife died a few years ago, which I thought *quite* a heavy reveal so early in the conversation, but we were all mindful people here.

He seemed obsessed with the financial logistics of the trip. How much was each stage costing? Was I getting paid on top of that? What kind of expenses was I permitted?

The Cindy-like woman was still fixated on my qualification for the job. What had I really done that made me a suitable candidate to go around Europe sampling luxury experiences? They weren't all luxury, I told them. I hadn't really done anything, I told them. I was just an authentic person sampling, mostly, authentic places and activities in Europe. Was I saying that this place was in some way not authentic? No, I said. I wasn't.

I felt like I was being grilled. Figuratively, and in an increasingly literal sense by the heat of the sun, which I could now feel searing the ridges of my forehead. I made my pallid excuses and went back to my room, where I just managed to pick up *Don Quixote* again before Sylvain knocked on the door and told me it was time for my Warm Shell Massage.

Fortunately the warm shells were quite central to the experience, which somewhat allayed the anxiety I ordinarily associate with massages. Basically, the only massage I've ever had is the one your mum gave me for my 21st – as in she gave me a voucher, not a massage – which was a very generous gift and one I suspect she might have won in a local raffle or something, given that I had to travel all the way to a rural hotel outside York for it. That massage was the opposite of relaxing, on account of the fact that I was so preoccupied with becoming in some way aroused that I summoned all my energies to detach from the physical reality of the situation at hand. The poor old massage therapist kept bidding me relax, stop tensing, loosen my shoulders, which I couldn't do, and I think in the end she gave up trying with still about 20 minutes of pre-bought/won rubbing time to go.

The appearance of the shells, however, I'm glad to say, chased away any prospect of inappropriate physical sensation and I was left able to enjoy a decent 40 minutes of having some heated-up shells (I *think* clam) put on me by a fairly serious woman in a black tunic. It felt a bit like I was being prepared for burial at sea, which I didn't mind all that much.

After the shells, I returned to the farmhouse where, somewhat mercifully, Sylvain banged a gong to mark the beginning of the Silent Dinner, which he explained was intended to be a time for us to savour and contemplate the food we were eating (steamed snapper with fragrant coconut sauce served with coconut, ginger and black bean quinoa, with a bowl of frozen coconut yoghurt and fruit for dessert). So far, the dinner had mainly had me contemplating the apparent versatility of coconut.

It was also, Sylvain said, before striking the gong again to commence the silence, a time to reflect on the day. He said nothing about it being a time for older, more economically accomplished guests to gang up on innocent younger guests and ask them invasive, alienating questions, which I thought was a welcome touch.

Generally finding, as I do, communal dining experiences draining, I enjoyed the silent dinner. The only difficult moment came when I asked the leathery, bad-knee man, sitting a few feet away, to pass the pepper by miming shaking pepper onto my plate, to which he reacted with an exaggeratedly confused frown, as if it was bizarre that I was even trying to communicate with physical gesture in the first place. I then attempted to convey my meaning by pointing down the table towards where the pepper pot was, just to his left, but this too he failed to comprehend – deliberately, I suspect – and ended up responding to my increasingly indignant prodding gestures by doing things like scratching at the table where he thought I was pointing. Eventually I just got up and collected it myself, tutting as I went, which earned me a tap on the shoulder and a plaintive shake of the head from Sylvain.

After dinner Sylvain banged the gong again, permitting the

resumption of verbal intercourse, but it resumed so tentatively, and centred so much around the sharing of interesting, meaningful impressions and reflections experienced during the dinner that I couldn't bear it, so I went and walked around a bit outside. From the car park I could see the town resting happily in the twilight like an illustration on a red-wine bottle sticker. It was Friday night. Down the mountain there'd be bars open and quietly whimsical waiters carrying trays of frothy-topped beers to laughing people sitting at pavement tables. I sighed and went back into the farmhouse. The main room was almost empty now and I wondered where everybody had gone before I remembered that it was 7 o'clock . . . WIFI time!

I think I genuinely ran across the room, through the glass walkway and to my *chambre*, whence I collected the tablet and ran all the way back to the Devices Room like a child with a rugby ball and a surfeit of ambitious energy. The room was completely packed. On every buckwheat-husk-filled cushion, on every hand-hewn stool and bench, guests sat and studied their devices, some of which were leaking, through headphones, music and sounds at a volume that wouldn't be considered permissible in the quiet coach of an East Coast mainline train.

I stood in the middle of the room and started pawing at the tablet screen, feeling like a quantity surveyor or the maître d' in a very modern restaurant. I checked my emails and Twitter but there was nothing good there. Finally a serious-looking woman who'd been scrolling through Instagram got up and left the room and just as soon as I'd taken her vacated cushion beside the muscled man, he struck up an obnoxiously loud FaceTime conversation, apparently with his young son who was refusing to go to bed.

'You have to be good for Granny!' he said. 'Daddy can't go away and relax, knowing that Granny's at home getting stressed out by you.'

I couldn't take it. I felt as if I was in a desert and shimmering before me was some great, quiet lager-y oasis. The thought crossed my mind for a moment that being in this environment had revealed a psychological reliance on alcohol to deal with stressful situations. But then I reasoned that I wouldn't feel so stressed were I not in this situation in the first place. It was a perfect, self-sustaining loop of excitation and denial. And a bloody expensive one.

There was only one thing for it: I downloaded four episodes of *Ray Mears' Extreme Survival* and went to my massive bed.

In the morning I was woken by the sound of a rooster crowing like Chanticleer, somewhere within the compound. Twenty minutes later, as I was getting out of the shower, Sylvain was at my door inviting me to a 'Morning Mindful Croissant-Making Workshop'. I got dressed and made my way down to the kitchen where a few guests, fresh and groomed and excited to be awake were standing at a long workstation with sheets of floury pastry in front of them. Opposite them stood a man in a white tunic, presumably the baker, and next to him, Chloe, the meditator.

Sylvain introduced me to the group, telling them 'Mark might write about the Mindful Croissant-Making for Urb.'

The other guests didn't react and Chloe simply said, 'Well, now we are here to experience the mindful croissants.'

Then followed the soothing spectacle of the baker instructing us in French how to fold the pastry to create the croissant, and Chloe translating in that brain-melting voice of hers, with mindful flourishes such as:

'As you turn the sheet with your thumbs, think about how grateful you are for your thumbs.'

'This croissant will look the same as so many other croissants, but of course in its small intricacies it will be totally unique. Just as this day will be for you.'

'When you have folded the croissant you should breathe in deeply, then out again as you contemplate it. Try not to breathe straight onto the croissant as this will bring germs.'

We didn't even then get the satisfaction of being able to eat the mindful croissants, as they would now need two hours to rise, although as mine looked exactly like a dog shit, this didn't feel too great a shame. Instead we were invited to help ourselves to a selection of fruits, yoghurt, juices and herbal teas which, even in their abundance, didn't quite hit the spot like a coffee and something greasy would have done.

I sat out on the patio to eat breakfast, in the morning shade naturally. Sylvain came out and handed me the retreat brochure and asked me to consider what treatments or activities I'd like to try today. There was 'Yoga for People With Bad Posture' starting in half an hour, which perhaps I'd enjoy. I told him I'd have a look and let him know. He went back inside.

I didn't fancy the yoga. I didn't fancy anything. I didn't want to interact with anyone, and I didn't want to have to get changed again or get wet again or get oily or hot. I wanted to be left alone.

I heard the patio door open again and turned expecting to see Sylvain re-emerge onto the patio but was greeted instead by the baker.

'*Bonjour*,' I said. 'I enjoyed the croissant-making.'

'*Bfff*, is stupid,' the baker replied, lighting a roll-up. 'But it is . . .' he rubbed his first two fingertips and thumb in a universal gesture.

'How do you like retreat?' he asked.

'It is okay,' I said. And then said it again because I could think of nothing else to say.

'You feel . . . *comme on dit* . . . trapped?' the baker asked.

'A little.'

After a pause the baker spoke again.

'Sometimes the guests go to the town. The castle is . . . quite interesting. Bars are down there and some restaurants.'

'It's a bloody long way down though.'

'But you can take the taxi.'

'No phone signal,' I said ruefully.

'Sometimes other side of building on the . . . *comme on dit* . . . hum . . . La Plateforme de la Sérénité?

'The Platform of Serenity? The Serenity Platform?'

'*Je sais pas.*'

I didn't know either.

'Whatever you call it, is good place for your phone,' he said with a furtive air, as if he wasn't really supposed to be revealing this information.

With this the baker tapped out his cig on the farmhouse wall, put the dead end in his pocket and went back inside.

I looked out over the retreat. The buildings looked slightly unreal, like an artist's impression. Reluctantly I scanned the list of treatments and activities, and one did catch my attention and immediately offer some appeal: 'Solo Forest Bathing'. The baker had inspired a sense that it would be good to get out of the retreat for a bit.

Sylvain returned a few minutes later and asked if I had found something I'd like to do.

'Yes, I'd like to go Solo Forest Bathing,' I said.

'Ah,' he replied. I wondered if this had been a bad answer.

'Would that be okay?'

'Well yes, the Japanese have a term of "forest bathing" which means an experience of taking time in the woods, in nature, for a cleansing of mind and spirit.'

I already knew this. You don't work in a hot-desking office and spend half the weekend reading left-wing supplements for as long as I have without learning what forest bathing is. Plus it said almost exactly the same thing under 'Forest Bathing' in the brochure in front of me.

'That's interesting,' I said.

'But really this means just going for a walk in the woods,' Sylvain said, that doubtful lip protruding again.

'Yes,' I said.

'I mean it is a good thing to do for our guests who have been here perhaps one week, perhaps more. They have done lots of things here, they have met with other guests. They are ready to go into the woods to reflect . . .'

'Mhmm.'

'But perhaps you would prefer to stay in the retreat and try more of the other treatments and experiences first, meet more guests and hear their positive words about the retreat?'

'I think I'd really like to go forest bathing,' I said.

'Okay,' Sylvain said, clearly trying to stay mindful. 'I will show you a route, because if you go the wrong way you can arrive in Spain. Please give me a few moments.'

Victorious, I went back to my room, loaded up on factor 50 and put my cap on. Sylvain was waiting for me on the patio and smirked at my cream-pale face as I re-approached.

'Lot of cream?' I said, trying to show that I didn't resent his laughter too acutely.

'It is a lot of cream,' he confirmed.

It was a great moment.

I enjoyed the walk greatly, managing not to accidentally end up in Spain and feeling very . . . cleansed by the forest. The views were spectacular and I felt energised as I returned to the Together House, in time to see Sylvain overseeing the serving of lunch, flitting about like a ferry steward on a stormy sea. I was somewhat disappointed to hear that lunch wouldn't be silent and that, in Sylvain's words, 'intimate interaction' was 'very much on the menu . . . along with minestrone soup made with garden vegetables topped with spelt croutons.'

Naturally I found myself seated next to the Cindy-like woman and the leathery man and so steeled myself for another half-hour of seething interrogation – but it never came. They both seemed friendlier today, smiling as I sat beside them.

The man apologised that he hadn't properly introduced himself and said his name was Colin and that he was from Nuneaton, which partly dissolved his aura of unlikeability. The woman introduced herself as Indigo, from the Chilterns, which didn't do much to undermine the impression I had formed of her yesterday, but the amiable and genuinely curious tone with which she asked about my morning did. I told them about the forest bathing and made some wry observations about Sylvain. They both laughed gratifyingly.

Then Indigo said:

'God it'd be good to get out, wouldn't it?'

'Leave the retreat, you mean?' Colin asked.

'Yes, exactly.'

'Go for some forest bathing maybe?' he said.

'Yes. Or go into the town.'

'Do some town bathing,' I said. They both laughed again. They were now my best friends.

'I wouldn't mind a drink,' I said.

'A drink would be lovely,' Indigo added.

'A drink *would* be lovely,' Colin confirmed.

An hour and one visit to the Serenity Platform (a pagoda-like structure of ambiguous purpose, located atop of a mound behind the main building) later, the three of us were climbing into the same taxi that had brought me up here two days earlier.

The driver was still perplexed about the novel status of old Durand's *ferme* and Indigo, the most accomplished French speaker of the three of us, explained at length about the retreat and its buildings and treatments and selection of juices and teas, at the end of which I think he was still fairly uncomprehending.

Indigo and Colin had expressed a desire to go round the shops for a bit and to see if, in Indigo's words 'there were any wonderful little things to buy'. Having almost no inclination, and even less spare cash for this end, I arranged to meet them in a couple of hours in a nearby bar, right by where the taxi dropped us off, a sort of plaza, covered over by a grand awning accommodating some kids with micro-scooters, a beleaguered dog and an assembly of raffish middle-aged tinnie-drinkers, whose rowdy outcries punctuated the otherwise steady scene. In the meantime, I would take myself, naturally, to the château.

Seen from the castle gatehouse, terracotta roof-tiles formed a sea of soft waves and sudden angles, concealing a thousand Saturday afternoons, and nudged the eye upwards and beyond to close and distant mountains.

Within the château walls I received an enthusiastic crossbow and longbow demonstration from a thin, goatee-sporting lad of about my age dressed up as a medieval archer (him, not me). This might have been me in another life (and still might be in this one). I got to have a go with the two projectiles and received a '*pas mal*' on both counts.

Higher up the hill, in the castle, I joined a group tour and understood only the proper nouns. Nevertheless, I buzzed off this medieval fix all the way back down to the plaza where I found Indigo and Colin just returned from their shopping and both laden with, I assumed, lots of wonderful little things.

We found a tavern with half-timbering, gothic lettering and stained glassed on its façade and beautiful dark wood furnishings, smart brass bar fixtures, jolly yet debonair patrons within. N.B. I don't think it was in any way explicitly signed as 'a tavern' but in my fantastical would-be medievalist mind, bars had become taverns and will stay that way until I reach Barcelona. Here we, unlikely trio, drank together for several hours. After a few *demi*s for Colin and me and a few white wines for Indigo (and Colin as well), things became quite candid. Colin talked about his wife's death, though not so dolefully as to shift the mood too much; Indigo told us of her husband's affair with his personal stylist and her subsequent experiences with Guardian Soulmates. Feeling that I owed them an insight into my own tribulations, I told them about you and everything that happened. I didn't go into all that much detail, but simply being able to say some of it out loud for the first time in weeks was helpful.

My memories grow increasingly hazy after that point. Most of all I remember feeling relaxed, as if the last couple of days had been a psychological ascent and this were the peak from which I could now descend. I guess it shows the potential of travel – bringing new challenges, situations and people into one's ken – to spell personal change and new insight. And as the circumstances of this small epiphany show, perhaps you don't need to go to a luxury retreat for that. A mid-range, small-town bar will do just as well.

It was dark when the wiry-haired driver dropped us off at the Urb, and Sylvain was waiting for us in the farmhouse. He said he'd been very confused by our leaving but stopped short of telling us off, disarmed perhaps by our collective good spirits and all-round aura of Wellness. He simply asked us not to tell Cindy that we'd left the retreat and bade us *bonne nuit*.

Indigo and Colin both became, with equal swiftness and intensity, very tired and so headed off for bed. I, feeling rather well indeed, went to the Devices Room, empty now, and bashed out my copy. It came easily, as a result, I'm sure, of the beer and the general insouciance I'd felt about the whole experience.

Upon sending, I worried that it would come across as facetious and mocking, because it was, really, but Bethan Decker replied almost immediately to say she loved it. Things had worked out very Well indeed.

Before I left in the morning, I showed Sylvain the copy at his insistence. He said he found it 'very pleasing'. He liked, he said, the way I'd captured how 'accessible and fun and relaxed' the Experiences they provided were.

Colin and Indigo weren't at breakfast so I asked Sylvain to give them my best wishes before I stepped out into the sunshine again and threw my bag into the back of the Mégane.

I hope you enjoy my account of Foix as much as I've enjoyed writing it. It's certainly made the journey fly by! Perhaps I'll send reportage from Barcelona too, where I'll shortly be arriving.

Until then,

Mark

From: Mark Rosiello
To: Paris Rosiello
Jul 10; 11:21

Hola from Catalonia.

My final morning in Barcelona. You find me hungover but happy in the wake of three excellent, hot, humid days here and having just finished breakfast. An omelette. What else.

I've been drafting this email for the last couple of days but only just got a spare couple of hours to finish it. Everywhere I go, I keep seeing little things I think you'd find funny or weird or problematic. This has been the case in Barcelona especially, since the city has made such an outstanding impression on me and since I also remember you mentioning it years ago as a city you were especially fond of.

I want to tell you it might just be the most I've ever enjoyed a place. And I want to tell you also that it has given me better understanding of your criticisms of Urb.

Firstly, though, to begin at the beginning: I felt I was back in Bethan Decker's good books, or her Good Cloud-Stored Working Document, following all that happened in Foix, judging from the email she sent me just as I was arriving, in which she re-stated her apologies for the confusion at the retreat and told me my description thereof, basically written drunk in a fit of slightly mocking irreverence was 'bang on perfect – just what we're looking for'. This is turning out to be quite the rollercoaster.

Anyway, I arrived in the Catalonian capital on Sunday feeling, if you can believe it, somewhat trepidatious. And for that, you can blame *mi madre* – not, I mean, in the ineradicable Freudian sense, but in the very particular respect that she warned me to be careful in Barcelona. She is, as you know, not unquiet in her general mind but nor she is not unworldly. She teaches languages. She's seen the world. Well, she's seen northern France anyway. And so she's not easily given to the reflexive xenophobia that might collocate with a place like Barcelona in the tourist mind. She is, though, forever haunted by some anecdote about a university friend of hers being pickpocketed in the city in 1973. Of all the places I'll visit – young ex-communist capitals, economically subdued southern metropolises, sites of recent terror attacks – it was Barcelona and Barcelona alone that she, despite never having been there personally, felt it necessary to warn me about. She wasn't alone. A now habitual pre-arrival 'safety in [city]' Google search revealed a veritable subculture of people about to go to Barcelona and freaking out about the supposed dangers of pickpockets, bag-snatchers, muggers, swindlers, scammers, pimps, sex workers, drug dealers and more besides.

Naturally, there is also a counter-movement intent on quelling the hysteria and maintaining that Barcelona is utterly safe to anybody exercising ordinary levels of caution. I concurred with the assertion that 'you'd have to be an idiot to let a stranger teach you how to play football or dance flamenco in the street' (remember that detail) but, nonetheless, I did disembark at Sants station with a padlock on my big rucksack and my passport and debit card in my money belt, and my money belt high and incisive, around my midriff, and my head screwed on and my wits about me. But by the time I'd got off the Metro at Drassanes I'd realised that nobody else was being so self-importantly over-cautious and I decided to chill out a bit.

Writing copy now seemed a less onerous task, following the triumph of the Foix write-up. Clearly the key to meeting Bethan Decker's standards of *authenticity* was to not write very authentically at all, unless Barcelona proved itself to be more straightforwardly and sincerely appreciable. Judging from the Trip Pack, the Barcelona Home was an intriguing one. Listed as a 'Cool Apartment in the Gothic Quarter', it seemed from the photos like a decent but rather small and unremarkable flat to be touted as 'the coolest small apartment in Barcelona, with an awesome story!'.

That 'awesome story', I read, had to do with the co-Hosts, a couple called Marie and Bianka, who, my Trip Pack stated, actually met when the latter stayed in the former's Urb apartment, the very apartment in question! Once again, the place was listed as an 'Entire Home', though it looked from the photos reasonably 'lived in', i.e. resplendent with reassuring clutter piles (clothes, papers etc.) and a slightly haphazard decor scheme, and not like the kind of sterile, photogenically empty offerings the Entire Home label often attaches itself to.

Little more was said or shown about the apartment's coolness or the awesomeness of its accompanying story, however, so I supposed it would be my task to bring both qualities to the fore in the copy.

As well as that, I would sample and write copy for two Experiences during my three-day stay:

A Cycling Self-Tour (Day Two)

• This was not, as the name might suggest, some Jungian/Buddhist journey through my own past and present personhoods, but a bike tour which I would apparently conduct myself (with the help, naturally, of an app).

A Street Art Walk (Day Three)

• This seemed fairly self-explanatory and apparently *didn't* involve an app.

I was hoping also to do some things just under my own steam, get the measure of the famous city in as organic a way as possible.

I found the Urb easily enough, on a narrow lane, a few streets back off the southern end of La Rambla. The entrance hall, tiled on all sides, was dark and cool, in every sense a welcome reprieve from the pseudo-tropic air outside. As I climbed the several flights of stairs, I began to fantasise about the improved fitness and musculature of the lower limbs that all these 60-litre backpack-laden stair efforts might give me by the end of the trip. Needless to say, by the time I'd reached the fourth floor the fantasy had evaporated and I was left still thin-legged and panting.

A woman in her early 20s answered the door. She was tall with dark hair, some of which was tied up into a sort of 'ball', for want of a more technical term, while certain 'tresses', for want of a less weirdly archaic one, hung down to her shoulders.

'*Hola*, Marie,' I said.

The woman explained that she was not Marie but was in fact Bianka, Marie's girlfriend.

'I will do the Welcome,' she said. 'Because Marie is at work. She will come to see you tomorrow evening.'

I told her this was no problem before letting her show me around the small but decent flat with a dark tiled floor and art and plants and guitars and reassuringly cluttered kitchen. She seemed a little more relaxed than my previous Hosts, less nervously intent on impressing me. She asked if I would like to sit on the sofa and I said that I would. She sat to my left, in an armchair with her legs over the arm, which struck me as a cool way to sit.

We chatted for a bit. She told me she was from Belgrade, and that she first came to Barcelona two years ago on holiday, staying in Marie's Urb. They got on so well, she said, that she decided to move to Barcelona so they could be together.

I asked what she made of Barcelona and she said she liked it. 'At first I was overwhelmed,' she explained, 'because it is so busy and there is a fiesta every night and people take a lot of drugs but now it is okay.'

When I told Bianka I'd read online about this part of town being potentially unsafe at night she laughed. 'It is safe,' she said. Boldly, she added, 'Everywhere is safe.' I decided to take her word for it.

Standing up, she told me that Marie would speak to me the next day, and we walked out into the street together. When she said she was turning left, I arbitrarily replied that I was turning right, just so that I could be on my own, which was odd really because I was finding her perfectly pleasant company. An old reflex, I suppose.

I had a whole afternoon and evening of liberty and I felt strangely at ease. I picked my way through a few random alleys and lanes onto La Rambla, the city's epicentral boulevard, which I recognised from *Homage to Catalonia*, a book you first made me read when I was about 14 and too young to appreciate it really, in whose opening pages Orwell describes: 'this wide, central artery of the town' and its 'loudspeakers [. . .] blaring out revolutionary songs.'

I've just reread the first couple of chapters. These are his first impressions of Barcelona:

> *It was the first time that I had ever been in a town where the working class was in the saddle. [. . .] There was much in it that I did not understand. In some ways I did not even like it, but I recognised it immediately as a state of affairs worth fighting for.*

How far away I felt, making my first moves through the old proletarian stronghold, with my cap and factor 50, from the world in which you could go, on something of a whim, and fight for a cause you don't even fully understand. For a few seconds though, now and again, when wandering down some dusty and broiling backstreet, cloistered from the thunder of modernity, I could delude myself that I was Orwell, or Laurie Lee or El Cid, moving with real telos through a romantic, bloody age.

That first afternoon I walked about, channelling those old wanderers yes, but also channelling you, as I imagined what would be going through your head, what *did* go through your head when you first came to Barcelona, and I set about with a psychogeographical frown to get the measure of the city.

I'd gleaned from Maps that the northerly sections of the boulevard were lined by expensive hotels and high-street outlets, so I turned left towards the southern end, where photographic menu boards advertised 20-euro meals to tourists. I crossed a roundabout and came onto a wooden boardwalk. Maps told me that this was La Rambla de Mar, built in 1994, in the city's confident post-Olympics era. The walkway stretched out over bay waters towards the waterfront development of Port Vell (with mall, cinema and sea life centre). It was like being at Hull Marina, except I was warm and not sad about life's apparently unerring disappointments.

I did, though, feel dull in my head and slightly sick so I retreated into the slightly less frantic and tourist-overrun Gothic Quarter. Here, apartments were stacked high above labyrinthine and shadow-cool streets, each with their own small balcony, from many of which hung the red and yellow flag of Catalonia. You could probably stand on your balcony here and hold an intimate conversation with any one of about thirty neighbours.

On every surface were graffiti tags and vivid stickers. One sticker in particular caught my attention more than once, which bore skull and crossbones and the statement, in black upper case against a yellow background: 'Tourism Kills the City'.

The spirit of exploration deserting me abruptly, I sat in a

small square and drank a beer before going back to the Urb to nap.

In the evening I ate in a Greek restaurant on the excitingly named Plaça Orwell, and read up on the history of the square, and then went for another walk. After dark, people sat on crates and drank shop beers around the terrace tables. South Asian men were selling cold cans of Estrella to British teenagers for one euro (an improbably small mark-up on the shop price).

I bought one and wandered through the Gothic Quarter and back onto the Rambla, feeling almost gleeful in my solitary wandering, giddy at the slight madness of it all, the relaxed urgency of everyone and everything around me, the wide-eyed fervour of the thronging tourists, and the cool intensity of those who would sell their labour to them, the waitress, the rickshaw rider, the man endlessly launching some kind of luminescent helicopter into the air to no obviously forthcoming reward. But then I became aware of myself, apart from them all, the impartial observer, and suddenly felt uncomfortable, purposeless, no longer relaxed in my solitude. I wished you were with me. I wished Neevie were with me. I tried to call Neevie but got her voicemail, already in bed as it turned out, waking at six as she now does, living her best freelance life.

I sat on a fountain and watched the man with the helicopter launch and retrieve it, launch and retrieve it a while. When my beer was done, I went back to the Urb.

The next day it was time for my first Barcelona Experience, the Cycling Self-Tour whose administering enterprise, 'youBike', was housed in a large, glass-fronted building, not unlike a car showroom, just a few streets back from the beach. It was, unsurprisingly, full of bikes, stacked up neatly in tiered rails, mostly identical black city bikes, with a few mountain and children's bikes alongside. The place had that warm, leathery smell of tyres stored indoors that's pleasant then unpleasant then kind of pleasant again.

A young man in a green T-shirt greeted me. I told him my name and said I had been sent by Urb to cover the Experience and he went and got another man in a green T-shirt. This one had glasses and seemed to be, if not the boss of the other one, at least his senior in some way, given how insouciantly he relieved him, even flicking his fingers at him with the sort of shooing gesture an evil step-parent might reserve for a young protagonist in a children's film.

'Okay, Mark!' he said quite loudly and without looking at me, which made me worry he was going to be overbearing and performative. In the event, he wasn't so bad, just a little patronising perhaps as he showed me my bike and explained how the tour would work, after first taking possession of my passport in case I 'tried to steal the bike or died'.

'These are the pedals,' he began. He proceeded to explain what the pedals did and the brakes, gears, bell etc. with some suggestion of self-irony in his voice but not quite enough to redeem the fact that he was literally telling me how to ride a bike, even though I'd already told him I knew how to.

He then, however, in a manner at once hasty, nonchalant and slightly sardonic, explained to me the bike's locking system as if *this* was a standard component of bicycles, which was, *frankly,* an insult to have to explain to every idiot who came in the door, even though it was an extremely complicated mechanism involving a D-lock, a chain lock *and* a sort of wheel lock which seemed to be part of the inherent machinery of the bike.

Before I'd even thought of asking him to repeat the explanation about the locks, he had moved on to talking about the most distinctive element of the bike: the small video screen mounted on the handlebars. This, he explained, would relay 'the self-tour'.

'It's pretty easy,' he said, quickly pressing the screen about eight times to start the process in motion before coming to a home screen bidding: 'Welcome to Bike!'

'First we must choose your language, that's British,' he said, almost to himself, with a sort of lingering percussive emphasis on the 'sh' of British as he pressed a Union Jack icon, which yielded a text caption 'English'. 'English, sorry,' he self-corrected. 'English, British, I don't know!' he laughed, juggling his empty hands to suggest indecision. I laughed too. It seemed a reasonable thing to laugh about.

'Okay, now we have got to decide . . .' he said, clicking on a 'next' icon, '. . . who will be your guide.'

A smiling woman now appeared on screen, in the way profile footage of footballers might suddenly appear during the post-match analysis bits on *Match of the Day*, contextless, as if conjured by magic. The woman had dark hair and looked to be in her mid-twenties. She wore a bike helmet and had her hands placed on her hips. Around her navel a red text caption read 'Isabella'.

'This is Ramona,' the bike man said, swiping her away to the left of the screen and bringing in her stead 'Mateo' who had his big forearms folded and an absolutely huge smile. 'This is Mateo . . .' the bike man said. He kept swiping, bringing up more avatars, with more names, which he continued to reel off with a tone of bored comfort of a kind you might adopt to list which of your friends were at a recent birthday party.

'. . . Rafi, Simona, Al – he's British, I think – Pierro, Ramona . . . Oh yes, we had Ramona. That's all of them,' he said.

'Right. I mean, which is the . . . best?' I asked.

'There is no best,' he said.

'Okay,' I said. 'So what's the . . .' I moved my hands quickly in front of my chest in a sort of controlled doggy paddle-type motion which I hoped might ameliorate my not having any real notion of how to complete my question. The bike man just looked at me.

'So what is the difference between them?' I offered.

'There is no difference. They are all saying the same thing. They will all give you the same tour. But, you know, they have very different . . .'

'Different *styles*?' I said.

'Yes! Different styles. They have different . . . voice. Different face. Different, all different.'

'Okay,' I said, conveying a growing understanding, a growing enthusiasm. 'I think I will pick Al, he's British you say?'

'Yes, Al I think is British,' the bike man said.

'Wait, no!' I said, halting my forefinger's quick progress towards Al's rugged, rosy face. 'I want someone not British. Mateo, is he Spani— wait, Catalan?' I said.

'Er yes, I think he is Spanish, but it is all in English,' the bike man clarified.

'No, I know. I just would prefer to get to know a Spanish person,' I said.

'Oh,' the bike man said, I *think* picking up on my attempt at fun. 'It is a good . . . idea,' he said as if he was beginning to suspect his time was being wasted.

'Have you met these guys?' I asked, gesturing to the screen.

'No,' the bike man replied. 'So you would like Mateo?'

'Yes please,' I said.

The bike man tapped on Mateo's face and he was illuminated for a second. Next the bike man indicated that the screen now showed a satnav-style map on the left side and Mateo to the right. Mateo then said, impressively loudly, 'Click to start the tour.' These words also appeared in a text box before Mateo's navel, in a friendly font.

'Now we go outside,' the bike man said.

He pushed the bike out onto the pavement. Mateo kept smiling and blinking. Traffic rushed by. Sunlight crackled on the wide bay waters.

The bike man told me to get onto the bike and naturally I made a complete mess of it on account of being instructed and subsequently observed in the act. He could have asked me to just stand fairly still for five seconds and I would have embarrassed myself somehow.

'So, yes,' the bike man said when I'd eventually steadied myself. 'Now you're all ready to begin the self-tour.'

I didn't feel all ready to begin the self-tour.

'Could I have a helmet?' I asked. The bike man rolled his eyes and went and fetched a helmet, which naturally took me a whole undexterous minute to adjust and fasten.

'So now you are feeling safe, you can press "Start the Self-Tour".'

I looked down at the little screen. Mateo's text box now read

'Press START TOUR when ready'. I did as I was told and with only the briefest of glitchy transitions, Mateo unfolded his arms and began speaking.

'Hello!' his voice resounded through the speaker. 'And welcome to Barcelona! I'm going to show you the coolest places to see.'

'You can hear him?' the bike man asked. I nodded. 'Then off you go,' he said. 'We will see you in about three hours,' he said.

'Let's go,' Mateo now said. 'Ride to the blue dot.'

The satnav screen showed a flashing blue dot a few streets away with a snaking blue line mapping my route there.

'All right then,' I said to the bike man, who'd already turned to go back inside.

I began pedalling. It was very difficult to follow the instructions on the screen while also remaining aware of the all-too-real, all-too-dangerous world around me. Meanwhile, Mateo kept chiding me. 'Go to the blue dot,' he said, and then a minute later, 'Let's get to the blue dot.'

'Gotta get to that blue dot!'

I came eventually to the blue dot and found that it marked Plaça Orwell. I remained on the saddle and leaned against a piece of street art while listening to Mateo's monologue. 'This is Plaça Orwell,' Mateo told me. 'Named after the great English writer George Orwell. Locally it is known as Plaça Tripi. Orwell came to Barcelona to fight in the Spanish Civil War . . .' He proceeded to tell me a few things that I'd already found out from Wikipedia when I'd sat in the square the previous day. After a few minutes of this, the map marked a new destination with a new blue dot. 'Time to go to our next destination!' Mateo said eagerly.

I moved unsteadily through small streets where road and pavement were almost one. At the edge of the Gothic Quarter, Mateo told me we were nearly there. I came onto the Rambla and gave up trying to cycle through the crowds after just a few seconds, deciding to get off and push the bike lest I caused serious harm to myself or another person, or their photograph.

The blue dot, it now transpired, marked the Rambla.

'Welcome to the Rambla,' Mateo near-sang. 'This is the most exciting street in Barcelona.'

I'd sort of had my fill of the Rambla but as Mateo excitedly began to take me through a potted history of the celebrated boulevard, I figured that even if this felt about as far away as one can get from the 'real' Barcelona, I should hear my only slightly pixelated friend out. I have a curious mind, as you know.

I was fucking hot though, and in the rush of heading out that morning to make the meeting time for the Experience, I'd only had time to apply one whole-body layer of factor 50, which I now determined might be insufficient given the intensity of both the sun and my pallor.

I wheeled the bike away toward a quiet, well-shaded side alley, while Mateo exposited the Rambla's original life as a sewage-filled stream. I brought the bike to a halt. 'Go back to the Rambla,' Mateo said.

I ignored him and put the bike on its stand while I took off my bag to get the sun cream.

'Go back to the Rambla,' he said again.

'Go back to the Rambla,' he chirruped, well above the ambient sound of the city as I squirted some cream into my palm before rubbing my hands together.

'Go back to the Rambla,' Mateo continued to say, prompting me to fumble around on the device for the volume button – smearing cream all over the thing as I did – but I couldn't find one. Nor could I see any sort of mute icon on the screen.

'Go back to the Rambla,' Mateo repeated and repeated, increasingly strident in his tonal constancy.

The only icon I could see to press was a small 'x' in a square in the top left corner of the screen. First transferring as much cream as I could from my hands to my body, I pressed the x. A new text box appeared in the middle of the screen, asking 'Are you sure to want to EXIT?' I clicked 'yes', quickly prompting Mateo to disappear completely along with the map of his precious Rambla and environs.

I waited for some kind of settings menu icon to appear on the screen but it did not. Instead I saw the Choose Language screen again. I pressed the Union Jack icon to select English and then, out of some bizarre and probably unwarranted sense of loyalty, Mateo again. 'Are you ready to start the tour?' he asked. I confirmed that I was. 'Go to the blue dot,' he told me. I looked at the map and saw that it was pointing me back to Plaça Orwell.

I did not want to go back to Plaça Orwell. Nor did I want to go back to the bike shop to admit my total, sun-cream-covered incompetence to the men in green T-shirts.

'Fuck,' I shouted, genuinely shouted. I tensed and made my entire upper body vibrate as I sometimes do in such moments. The city around me seemed unaffected by my plight. Human life resounded in the Rambla. Traffic droned on. Waves broke distantly on the shore.

I sat on the kerb, tried and failed to cry and, soon feeling a good deal more relaxed, if not still a little surprised by the intensity of my reaction, I asked myself once again: what would Paris do?

You would not, we can be fairly confident, have got yourself into such a tiz in the first place. But indulging the thought exercise in the simplest terms possible, I decided that had it happened to you, you wouldn't have seen it as a situation to dry-cry about. You'd more likely focus on the fact that you had possession of a bike, and at least two and a half hours until it had to be returned. So I got back on the saddle and resolved to seek, I suppose, the real Barcelona.

Whether I found it, I don't know. What I did find was a dreamy sojourn towards the beach and then north, following the coast, along a decidedly Ballardian circuit, past beaches and casinos and superclubs and parades of restaurants, playgrounds, a marina, a Decathlon, a vast, ambiguous, unpopulated zone which might have been a level on Tony Hawk's Pro Skater where sound-checks for a music festival were heard, a nature reserve, factories, a power station which seemed like a remnant from a future that never came to pass, and luxury and non-luxury apartments, before finally I decided I'd gone far enough and it was time for a swim.

I tried locking the bike to a bench but I couldn't work out how to do it, which made the rage boil again for a few seconds before I regained my WWPD equanimity and simply, in the most mindful way possible, proceeded to slowly and effortfully drag the bike across the sand trying not to collide with any sunbathers, and finally dump it by the water's edge along with my clothes and bag.

The water was as warm as a half-hour-old bath. Three young Spanish boys were splashing around nearby and seemed to find me a source of interest. Eventually one of them, apparently the most cocksure, asked me something in Spanish. Or Catalan.

'*No entiendo,*' I said.

The boys laughed. After a few seconds the questioner came back and said, '*Anglès?*'

'*Si,*' I said.

'How old are you?' he followed up.

'30,' I replied.

'I am 12.'

They laughed and then huddled together giggling. This provided the structure for the ensuing conversation, them laughing for a minute before giving me quite a banal question or statement and then laughing at my answer.

'Where are you from?'

'England, London.'

(Laughter followed by discussion)

'Do you like football?'

'Yes.'

(Laughter followed by discussion)

'Do you like Barcelona?'

'Yes.'

(Laughter followed by discussion)

'Do you have girlfriend?'

'Erm. Erm . . . not sure. Possibl—'

'I have four!'

'That's a lot . . . Many.'

'Not for me.'

(Laughter followed by discussion)

Then followed a really long private consultation amongst the boys, at the end of which the young *niño* came back with: 'I am nice.'

The validity of this claim was undermined almost immediately as the boy emerged from under a wave holding a massive rock. He then held this up as if to throw it at me, from point-blank range. His friends laughed, almost disbelievingly. He then drew his arm back. From the look in his eyes I suspected that he himself wondered if he might throw it, as if he were encountering some terrible new potential within himself.

This is the real Barcelona, I thought: off the tourist trail 20 miles out of town, standing waist deep in the sea, about to be bludgeoned in the face with a massive pebble by a 12-year-old boy.

At last, with a snigger, he dropped the rock. I swam around for a minute, heart racing, and then got out.

'Goodbye,' the boy called. 'It was nice to meet you.'

I put my T-shirt and hat on, dragged the bike back to the pavement and rode off again, sopping wet.

When I got back to the Gothic Quarter my shorts were completely dry. My T-shirt proved sufficiently absorbent for wiping the residue of cream from the screen.

'How was the tour?' the bike man asked as he took repossession of the bike, not even glancing at the screen.

'Very good,' I answered.

'I am glad. I hope you will write some nice things.'

'I will,' I told him.

I'd written enough disingenuous copy in my time – in the last week even – to feel it couldn't really be so hard to write about an Experience I hadn't actually had.

After lunch I went to the Museum of Catalonian History where I spent too long on the early historical sections (as in Copper Age early; you might as well have been anywhere during the Copper Age) so failed to properly take in the thorough coverage of the region's modern history. But still I learned a lot about

Catalonia, its cultural distinction from the rest of Spain, its historically fraught relationship with Madrid, the brutality it suffered during the civil war, the doggedness of its many resistance movements, the centuries-long shaping of its identity, and the ongoing question of how independent it truly wants to be.

All of this left me wondering about the general political outlook of contemporary Catalonia, and, by chance, later that afternoon I read an article from a British news site (I forget which one) claiming that Catalonians are probably split about 50/50 between those who do and don't want independence from Madrid. These days, the letter claimed, it is a topic to be avoided for Catalonians during social interactions, as discussing it invariably leads to arguments. Reading this I felt aware once again that I'd had no meaningful interaction with any locals, excepting the mocking and near-murderous sea boys.

In the evening, at least, I met Marie. She apologised for not being around the previous day 'to do the Welcome' because she couldn't get the afternoon off her job in construction logistics (a role which seemed to belie her scruffy, artistic demeanour). She was a good deal shorter than Bianka, diminutive and spirited with short red hair. And she was, I decided, as she whirligigged around, shedding the accoutrements of the working day and apologising for points of inconsequential mess around the flat, immediately likeable. Like Bianka, she seemed less affected than my previous Hosts, less conscious of my supposed status as somebody worth impressing.

In our introductory chat, she told me she was French but visibly found my efforts at her native tongue too frustrating to deal with so continued to speak English.

Finally, she settled at the table, where I was positioned to make a start on the bike tour copy. She exhaled a sort of end-of-day relief and asked me a few questions about myself with an apparently genuine curiosity, or at least an admirable willingness to listen. In turn I asked her about herself and learned that she came to Barcelona eight years ago intending merely to stay for one summer. What was it about Spain that she liked so much? I asked.

'It is not Spain, just Barcelona,' she said. She hadn't seen much of the country otherwise and had no pressing plans to. I asked if she'd ever been to Madrid and she told me she hadn't, in the way a Glaswegian might if you asked them if they'd ever been to Yeovil.

As I was already in the copy-generating mindset and had my tablet out on the table in front of me, I figured it'd be useful to chat to her a bit about the apartment, her relationship with Bianka and their approach to Urb hosting. Truth be told she didn't react *that* well to this suggestion, as she became a great deal shyer at feeling herself, I suppose, being formally put on the spot in this way.

She told me, while staring at her hands, that Bianka had been one of her first Urb guests and that they had been together ever since. 'So you guys share the hosting duties?' I said.

'Yes,' she confirmed. 'Usually I try to be here for the Welcomes but Bianka has more freedom in the days so sometimes she will do.'

'Okay,' I said, noting this. 'And you guys live here or . . .?' I'd noticed a second bedroom, which Bianka hadn't shown me during the Welcome.

'I live here but these days I have a lot of guests so now we stay a lot at Bianka's.'

It wasn't exactly an awesome detail but I noted it down.

'And now you advertise the flat with your story of how you met?' I asked.

'What do you mean?' Marie said.

'As in: you and Bianka met when she was your guest. Do you use this story to advertise the Urb?'

It occurred to me that I did not know exactly where this detail from my Trip Pack had come from.

'No, no,' Marie said quite seriously. 'We do not advertise. I only received a message from Urb to say that they will choose the apartment for the . . . er . . .'

'For the Featured List,' I said.

'Yes, for this, and I think it is from the guests who stay. They always give good reviews and a lot of them will say in their comments about Bianka and me, because we have told them our story and now Urb has seen this and perhaps this is why they write to me. I don't know.'

'Right,' I said.

'Bianka is not so happy about them mentioning our relationship.'

'Why?' I asked.

'She says it is ours. It is a private thing and now they want to use it to make the apartment have more story for their own marketing.'

I doubly regretted my inquisition now. Clearly Marie hadn't expected it.

'I say it is fine . . . It is not such a big problem and if it helps to get more guests, this is good. Perhaps we can work less. She can do her studies with more concentration and I can work only four days and do my music. But she is not so sure. It is, how do you say . . . a tension.'

'That's a shame,' I said.

'Yes,' she said and looked quite doleful.

Neither of us spoke for a moment. I stared at the three lines I'd written on my tablet screen.

'Mark, I am sorry,' Marie said. 'After this day at work my mind is very . . .' She gave a fraught hand gesture by her temple.

'Yes, I understand,' I said, closing my tablet case.

'No, I would like to carry on talking,' she said. 'But would you mind if I smoke.'

'Course not,' I said.

'You wanna smoke?'

'Tobacco?' I said.

'No . . .' she laughed. 'I mean . . .'

'Oh,' I said, the thought occurring to me that it might not be all that ethical to use drugs with an Urb Host before realising that I had never conceived of having a spliff as 'using drugs' in my life before.

'Er yeah,' I said, 'yes, great.'

'Okay, that is good for me,' she said and disappeared into the other bedroom. This would, I told myself, probably help with the research, the story surely becoming all the more 'awesome' the higher we became.

Marie returned a moment later with a large Ziploc bag and, as she asked me about my initial impressions of the city and my plans for the remainder of my stay, rolled a spliff without much fanfare. She lit it and took a few drags before handing it to me. I found the first few drags rather harsh, having not smoked since probably that time you and I got stoned after the Lord's test. We passed it back and forth quite briskly and within minutes Marie had contracted genuine, old-school giggles. I can't even remember what she was laughing at. We'd just been talking some more about how she found Urb hosting and then she completely lost it at a story she was telling that I couldn't really follow – something to do with one of her Urb guests later going on to become Madonna's PA.

When she was composed again, I asked Marie about her mention of playing music. There were two guitars in the living room and one in the hall. Did she ever play for guests? I asked. She seemed to find the very notion funny, but then answered that she did sometimes. I asked if she'd play for me now and she shyly objected at first but then quickly allowed herself be persuaded, letting me hand her a red parlour guitar from behind the sofa, and playing a blues song that I didn't recognise and whose lyrics I couldn't quite catch. But she sang well and was, by my admittedly inexpert judgement, pretty good. I told her I thought so and that her voice reminded me of Björk's. This seemed to please her a lot, but I probably mainly said it because she had told me two minutes earlier that she liked Björk.

She played another song and then said that being a writer I might like to help her with some lyrics. Too stoned and swept up in the moment to explain that I'm not really a lyricist, I agreed, and Marie produced a print-out of lyrics to a song called 'Fire Rabbit' which her friend had written for her to play. She played it once through and it was genuinely quite good imho, seeming to evoke themes of generational anger at difficult-to-identify oppressors, and the importance of resisting apathy and resignation. It did, though, contain a few strange non-sequiturs, which might be a result of mistranslation such as: '. . . in that dark and secret place/ where we all have your face'.

I shared my thoughts and she looked a little crestfallen, saying she now thought she'd misunderstood the song because she thought it was about love. I replied that there could be no single, correct interpretation of good lyrics, which seemed to re-encourage her. I then offered a few edits, mainly focussed on bringing through the Fire Rabbit motif a bit more and skimming off the incongruous lines. Marie thanked me for these, but I'm not convinced she'll heed them.

The remainder of the conversation is a total blur. I scribbled a few notes as we talked but I can't now see how **'Guy Ritchie is England – melody – does 'burrow' represent prescription medication – Lionel Messi tax – upside-down Merkel'** will make for the kind of story Bethan Decker is hoping to read. Still, it was nice to have a relaxed, silly time with Marie before she headed off to Bianka's, and feel after a bit of a failed day that I'd had an 'authentic' evening of sorts.

Sure, it wasn't ideal that when I woke up in the morning I realised that I'd texted Neevie again telling her I was going to 'learn guitar so I could write songs about [her] and serenade [her] with them' but, mercifully, she'd replied with the laughing/ crying emoji and a 'sounds like you're having fun! Excellent x'. So no lasting embarrassment. And, with the fresh day came the next Experience, the 'Street Art' tour.

While waiting for the Experience Host to arrive at the meeting point (a large graffito of an owl wearing a cap) I got talking to a young couple from Wigan, whose names were Megan and Elliot. They were, if possible, even paler than me, but braving the sun with a kind of steely, hatless resolve, their sweat-drizzled brows furrowed above Wayfarer shades. They were staying in an Urb by the beach with, they said, 'a lot of cockroaches but very good aircon'. They'd gone onto the Experiences tab that morning, seen two spaces left on the tour and snapped them up. I asked them if they were graffiti enthusiasts but they said they weren't really.

'She's been getting into it on Instagram,' Elliot said. 'Showing me some proper nice ones, so we're looking forward to it.'

'The graffiti in Wigan is usually just people's names or random scribbles or drawings of dicks,' Megan added.

The tour started enjoyably and certainly felt a world away from British provincial street-daubings, as we ambled around the bright, humid streets listening to a man with an undercut, called José, explain the difference between 'guerilla art' and 'beautification', between 'pieces' and 'bombs', between 'throw-ups' and 'tags' (I don't really remember what most of those things are now, only that they are all different from each other). As we proceeded, José held aloft a large paddle, shaped like the kind of teardrop icon that marks places on digital maps, with his own tag stencilled on it. This, I suppose, was in case I, or Megan or Elliot, or any of the other dozen or so Urb Experiencers, who between us looked as if we'd never produced, or even shown more than a cursory interest in a single graffito in our lives before, got separated from the group.

I felt oddly comforted by the tour. The salve of the colours, the leisurely pace at which we moved, the rhythms of José's voice, the balminess of the day and the mentally tenderising effects of the previous evening's spliff and subsequent weird sleep – all these conspired to put me into a relaxed, if slightly addled state, and as we neared the tour's end, moving back into the familiar environs of the Gothic Quarter, I began to look forward to a little siesta.

My reverie was broken quite abruptly, however, by a growing clamour of shouts and whistles. As we crocodiled along one narrow street, a whole succession of people, seemingly not tourists, bustled past us. José stopped to let them by, frowning slightly. After a few moments he led us off again.

We came around the corner into Plaça de Sant Jaume, a fairly grand square a few streets from Plaça de George Orwell and found it completely packed with protesters. The crowd was stationary, deliberately so it seemed, and its energy was spirited, bordering on aggressive. To say there was almost a carnival atmosphere would be a cliché, but in this case a pertinent one.

José looked genuinely thrown now. I was about midway back in the group and suddenly found myself slightly separated, hemmed in by strangers on all sides. I looked to José for some kind of instruction but he was hardly visible, having become engulfed by the crowd. After a moment I saw him forcing his way back, receiving some help from a couple of taller tour guests who had managed to remain adequately self-possessed, unlike the rest of us who were all beginning to betray signs of panic.

I looked at Megan, who was looking at Elliot, who was looking uneasy and, by now, quite sunburned.

'Okay, we'll go back!' José shouted, his voice barely carrying over the surrounding roar. I turned and saw people at the back of the group, a quiet trio who seemed completely nonplussed. 'Go back!' I relayed loudly, trying to maintain at least some semblance of composure. 'Back out of the square!'

'We can't move!' one of the Finnish people shouted, the crowd behind them now becoming as dense as a thorn forest.

I turned back to José and found him at an even further remove and apparently in some kind of altercation. A group of people, about five or six men and women, who looked to be in their early 30s and not inherently aggressive, were blocking his path. He was trying to push past a tall man who wasn't having to do much but stand normally to block him. José gestured past the man and shouted something, apparently to communicate his urgent need to return to people in his stewardship. Two men were laughing at him and a striking woman in sunglasses was responding volubly, to his plaint. I couldn't hear much, except the word '*turistas!*' which she shouted a few times.

As the woman continued to scold him, José bowed his by now quite sweaty head for a moment, his brow visibly knotted, before rearing back up, lifting his paddle high in the air and barging past the large man. He'd almost slipped by when the big guy got hold of his backpack and dragged him towards his group again. The woman was right in his face now and, with her target completely disorientated, she grabbed his paddle and began whacking him with it, around the flanks mostly. Deflecting a particularly lusty blow with his forearm, José shrank back and quickly retreated into the dense crowd behind him.

Our leader ousted, we remaining graffiti tourists made our own respective surges for freedom. I was, I feared, about to be swallowed by the crowd, when I felt two hands grab my shoulders and I turned to see Megan and Elliot beckoning me to follow them away through a narrow channel behind a newspaper kiosk.

Right back at the edge of the square, Elliot swore loudly, to no one in particular, 'What the *fuck* was that all about?' Looking at him, I decided now wasn't the time to tell him his forehead had turned purple. I looked back at the melee. On a makeshift stage in the mid-distance, a man was yelling into a megaphone, although nobody in the crowd, which must have been at least 500-strong, seemed to be paying much attention to him. I studied the signs and banners held aloft. Most were in Spanish of course, or was it Catalan? Either way I couldn't fathom the collective agenda immediately. But after a few moments, and the apprehension of a few nouns, common and proper, a theme began to reveal itself:

'*BARCELONA NO ESTÀ EN VENDA*', read one.

'*POR LA ABOLICIÓN DE TODOS LOS PISOS TURÍSTICOS*', read another.

(I know the exact wording because I took photos on my phone.)

And now, as I scanned the merlon-like placards and signs some more, I found plenty enough written in good, clear English:

'MY BUILDING IS NOT A HOTEL'

'REFUGEES WELCOME TOURISTS NOT'

'URB – A DANGER TO OUR NEIGHBOURHOOD'

This last one, of impressive design standard, showed my employer's logo inside the red triangle of a traffic hazard warning sign. Another sign held a few feet to the right of this one, apparently by the same designer, also showed the Urb logo in a red triangle but this time inverted and rendered to seem like a pair of testicles which were about to be castrated by some scissors, rendered in Catalan colours.

In case the message needed spelling out, text underneath this image read, simply: 'CASTRATE GENTRIFICATION'.

'It's a protest against tourism,' I said.

'We can see that,' Megan replied.

We each stared out across the crowds for a while, blinking in the heat. Eventually, feeling ready to accept my pernicious *turista* status and having grown fond of my new pals, I suggested we go get iced coffees. Elliot said he'd prefer a beer and I wasn't going to argue.

Over cold *cerveza*s on a bar terrace several streets away from the chaos, we discussed the meaning of the protests. Elliot couldn't understand why people would be opposed to tourism.

'It brings money in, doesn't it?' he asked with a forceful lilt.

'I suppose the people who don't benefit directly from the tourist economy might resent their homes and communities being reshaped by it,' I suggested.

'Yeah, I guess if loads of people from all round the world all suddenly started coming to Wigan we'd be pretty pissed off,' Megan said.

'Why the fuck would loads of people suddenly start coming to Wigan?' Elliot asked.

Answer came there none.

'And what's the problem with Urb anyway?' Megan asked.

I hadn't told them of my purpose for being in Barcelona and now the strange thing was that my instinct was to offer the kind of sentiments that I imagine you would have, had you been there.

'Maybe Urb facilitates mass tourism by circumventing regulation in a way that hotels never could,' I offered.

Neither of them seemed all that impressed by this suggestion, so I steered the conversation away from the social ills of tourism for the remainder of the drink, instead asking them about their plans for the rest of their stay. They had three days left, which would be furnished with activities including paella-making, a tour of Camp Nou and, of course, the cycling self-tour. As they saw away their *cerveza* dregs they seemed upbeat enough and I bade them a good-remainder-of-trip on a street corner before setting off back to the Urb.

As I picked my way through the gathering crowds, I struggled to reconcile the scenes in the square with my experience of Urb in Barcelona. Were Megan and Elliot really a threat to the city, a young couple here to have a nice time and spend a few hard-earned (I assume; never actually asked them what they did for a living) euros? And how were Marie and Bianka in any way damaging the city as two young women, working and studying and contributing to its very fabric? Two women able to enjoy here a freedom in their relationship that they might not elsewhere. Whose business was it if from time to time they decided, in order to support their passions, to rent out one of their apartments to visitors? Visitors who would come and explore the city and contribute to it economically. Yes, of course there had to be regulation and compromise, but to rabidly condemn such a clearly in-the-grand-scheme *positive* force as travel seemed totally wrongheaded. It seemed an easy diversion from the real systemic problems that afflict cities, resulting from a broken global economic system. I understand that these people are angry, but they have surely missed their target by some distance.

Wasn't demonstrating against Urb *specifically*, given the larger economic background and all its systemic ills, somewhat akin to writing a letter of complaint to Estrella after getting a pint of it spilled over your shoes by a drunken idiot in a bar?

Maybe this was a strained analogy. I felt exhausted and started to wander back to the Urb for a siesta, until a reminder notification flashed up on my phone:

'STARTING IN ONE HOUR: SAGRADA FAMILIA VISIT'.

I had completely forgotten that I'd booked a ticket for the cathedral that afternoon. I had to see it, of course, weary though I was. What sort of a hipster pseud would I be going to Barcelona and failing to visit Gaudí's pinnacle achievement, even if it was unfinished and cost 25 euros to get in?

In the end, I'm glad I did. For one thing – as you'll no doubt already know – Gaudí devoted his life to it, before he was killed by a tram at the age of 73 with about a quarter of the construction completed, so as a monument to vaulting ambition alone, it feels worth seeing. It just about manages, in my book, to transcend its electronically ticketed, machine-gun protected, audio-guide mediated anchorings and inspire a kind of woozy terror with its stark depictions of Christ and co, and stem-like spires crowned with bulbous fruits. On the walk home, I suddenly saw Gaudí's influence everywhere in this strange city, in this modernista super-organism of unfamiliar, anti-geometric shapes, beguiling curves, swollen apexes, art nouveau forms and gothic borrowings suggesting flora, berries, fertility, growth.

Also, before I go, I have to tell you about something that happened last night – a ridiculous encounter that I only remembered as I sat down to eat just now.

So after dinner on a bit of a whim, I went on my own to a club just around the corner from Marie's place called Club Macarena. It was nowhere near as terrible as it sounds but actually a vaguely trendy, small-scale house and electro club, whose doorman initially wouldn't let me in because he said my ten-euro note was not crisp enough. Going into it, I mainly just wanted to be able to say I'd been clubbin' in Barca, and hardly expected to last two hours, but so delicious was the vibe and so scintillating were the grooves and so massage-like was the bass and so much (a tiny bit) cheaper than London prices were the drinks, that I stayed the course and emerged blinking onto the narrow *calle* at about five, whereupon I got chatting to a really friendly guy – whose name and general aspect I can't remember – about football! He was absolutely over the moon to hear I liked football too and asked me if I wanted to play.

'But do you have a ball?' I asked, blatantly fucked.

'We don't need ball, man, come on!'

He then basically rugby tackled me and, as he was much taller than me (that I do remember) I struggled to extricate myself from his grip and he merrily led us both down the narrow street for a good few paces before I managed to stumble free, right outside Marie's door.

'Well this is me, man!' I said. 'Have a good night, yeah!'

'You too, Mark! It was great to meet you!' And then, when I'd turned to go in: 'Oh Mark! Wait! Look, you dropped your wallet.'

I looked down and, sure enough, my wallet was on the floor in the middle of the street. I picked it up and thanked my new friend profusely for his vigilance and kindness. It was not a problem, he said, and went on his way.

As I was getting into bed, I did have a momentary prang about whether the lad might have somehow, in a split second and in the middle of a public street, have 'copied' my card. This immediately seemed paranoid even for me. *What would Paris do?* I wondered, *if he had somehow allowed himself to be roughhoused by a stranger in an alleyway.* 'Not much,' came the answer. Likely spend almost no time at all pondering it and certainly not cancel his card over such a minor theoretical risk. So I resisted doing so. I hope you'd be proud. Is this 'growth'?

I mean, just for safety, I did phone the bank in the morning to ask their advice and the guy on the phone said:

'Have you waited on hold for 20 minutes to tell us that a man held your wallet for three seconds?'

So, I'm sure it'll be fine. Guess the street 'footballer' took pity on me or maybe was just trying to teach me to be more careful or something. Tbh, even if he were trying to rinse my account, he wouldn't get very far, as I've regrettably now spent a good chunk of my first wage instalment. Or maybe *not* regrettably. I've had fun. And I will continue to have fun. Just on a bit of a budget for a while. Next, in Toledo.

Adios.

Mark.

From: Mark Rosiello
To: Paris Rosiello
Jul 13; 13:02

Hello Paris,

I write to you from the capacious, bracingly air-conditioned comfort of the high-speed Madrid–Marseille train, the 'AVE 9724', AVE standing for Alta Velocidad Española, but, according to Wikipedia, also meaning 'bird' in Spanish. How nice is that? You'd struggle to get any comparably satisfying acronym-pun in English . . . 'British Intercity Rail . . .' can't even think of an adequate 'd' word to complete it. 'Device?' Rubbish. No thanks.

In any case, you. just. do. not. get. trains. this. fast. and. comfortable. and. good. in. Britain.

Apparently this train's top speed is 7 mph faster than HS1's!

Fast as the train might be, it's still a long way to go. We've only just left Zaragoza. I should really work on all my Spain copy, especially as I need to embellish a large portion of it (the aborted cycle self-tour in Barcelona and now a tapas tour in Madrid, ruined by sickness). But I've got at least seven hours left of train time to worry about that. For now, let me tell you of Toledo . . .

While the heat in Barcelona was often humid and sometimes quelled by sea breezes, in Spain's 'holiest city', an hour or so from Madrid by train in the province of Castilla-La Mancha, it was dry and dead still. As in Foix, I found in Toledo a well-preserved old city surrounded by an expanse of modern urban sprawl, visible from the high vantage of the former element as a heat-shaken near-mirage of office blocks, car parks, roundabouts, billboards, and high-cabled bridges.

My purpose, however, was focussed mainly on the old city, specifically a view thereof, to be taken from my Urb, located high in the hills close to the famed Mirador del Valle viewpoint. The Trip Pack told me that this Home had been awarded the honour of **'Best View – Mid Spain – Other Cities'** by the company. Not to be confused of course with the **'Best View – Mid Spain – Madrid'** or the **'Best View – Mid Spain – Nature'**, nor of

course, with the **'Best View – Southern Spain – Other Cities'**
or the **'Best View – Northern Spain – Other Cities'**.

Yes, this simple-looking Urb – a one-bed flat, owned by a
woman called Diana (who had no profile in the Trip Pack save
for a small, grainy photo) – possessed, if Bethan Decker's notes
were to be believed, the best vantage point from any Urb Home
over a mostly urban scene, between Granada and Barcelona (not
including Madrid). For this, the Home was to be included on
the Featured List and, to boot, given a 'badge' in the form of a
small trophy-like graphic to be displayed on its listing page.

I would sample no Experiences in Toledo. It was, in Bethan
Decker's words, 'all about the view'. Toledo was not, she explained,
a particularly 'hot' destination for Urb's core under-30 demographic but the inclusion of this Home and the awarding of the
badge were an 'experiment' designed to see if targeted badges,
emphasising very particular, unique features of 'secondary cities'
like Toledo could pull travellers from bigger ones like Madrid.

Accordingly, my job would be to make the view sound as nice
as possible, which seemed simple enough.

Naturally it would require a great hill climb to reach the Urb
but, feeling well-conditioned after my Pyrenean hike and
Barcelona bike ride, I'd fully intended to walk there from Toledo
train station – a quite stunning Moorish revival building in which
elegant chandeliers, and horseshoe-arched windows and a dumb-
foundingly intricate wooden ceiling hung above a bored and
sweaty public. I'd barely set foot, however, on the Alcántara
bridge, a roman/medieval structure spanning the lean river Tagus,
when I had to turn back.

It was the hottest I'd ever felt in my life and I was close, I
genuinely think, to collapsing. Shocked and dizzy, I went back
and sat for a bit in the train station where huge, industrial fans
offered some mercy. I filled my water bottle in the loo and drank
the whole two litres in about five minutes. An older couple, a
man and a woman with caps, sunglasses and suitcases, both
seeming almost as red and overcome as I was, sat on the bench
next to me. The man, audibly American, asked if I knew how to

get into the town. It was too hot to walk, I told him, and that was all I knew.

'We're never coming back to Spain again,' the woman said.

No disrespect to them, but they looked as if time might not permit them another trip to Spain regardless of their wishing.

We established that their hotel was just down the road from my Urb, so we together joined the wilting queue of people, mostly other elderly Americans, at the taxi rank in front of the station, and shared a hot, silent ride up to the Mirador, after which they disappeared into the air-conditioned interior of their hotel, while I trudged up the road as Maps deigned. Worth noting here that I wasn't actually having a totally bad time in the heat. It felt somehow heroic to be so hot. Somehow, I suppose, *quixotic*. I was at the very peak of Toledo. But although it was just there, down the hill and over the river, that badge-worthy view, I more or less forgot to even look at it, focussed as I was on the task of getting into the Urb.

I rang the bell and was met moments later by Diana. More or less as soon as she'd opened the door and heard me greet her in English, she asked whether I could speak Spanish. I apologised that I could not, and she looked terrified, even though, it quickly transpired, she spoke English fairly well, albeit in a slightly hesitant, shy kind of way. She looked to be in her early 40s, with long, dark hair which she held back with a hair-band, and was by turns energetically curious and haltingly nervy.

I'd arrived slightly earlier than arranged on account of taking the taxi, and Diana hadn't finished cleaning the apartment. She apologised and I followed her through to the bedroom where I just fecklessly stood in the doorway and watched while she moved around the place. She asked me questions as she did so, seeming intrigued by my job and professing her own intellectual proclivities to be more scientific and mathematical. She used to work as a health and safety engineer in Madrid, she told me.

'But then the economy went . . .' she said, before crossing her arms emphatically and making a sort of *sorry, wrong answer* SFX. She lost her job and couldn't find another one in the same sector.

Now she worked as a science teacher, which she enjoyed, though it didn't pay as well as her old job. During the winter she used the apartment to give private tuition, herself living in a different rented property in the new town. I asked how she came to have the place and she told me she'd bought it 15 years ago and used to live here until she lost her job and a friend who'd become a full-time Urb Host persuaded her it was a good idea to move and rent the apartment out.

View aside, the apartment had nothing all that noteworthy about it. It was one of about ten flats in a fairly modern block, one of only three or four dwellings on the road. Inside it was clean, airy, quite bare.

'What guests love from this place,' she said, 'is the view,' and gestured towards the window. She hadn't been surprised when Urb contacted her about the badge.

'People always leave comments about the view,' she explained. 'To me it always seems normal. You don't notice the beautiful things when they are there every day.' This was probably true, I said. Sometimes, she said, she had to close the shutters during tutoring sessions to stop the tutees becoming too distracted.

'What do they say about the view in the comments?' I asked.

'They just say they like it,' Diana said. 'It is hard to put into words. That is the thing with a special view.'

I told her that my main purpose in Toledo was to write a description of the view to go with the badge. She puffed her lips and told me that would not be easy, before taking me out onto the balcony to get a better look at it. We both stared out at it for at least a minute, occasionally making approving noises, as if we were a couple whose awkward first date was being redeemed by the sharing of a tasty dessert.

'What do you think?' she eventually said.

Nothing came immediately to mind. It was a nice view, really nice. But other than resorting to cliché – 'sweeping', 'spectacular', 'breathtaking' and the like – I couldn't think of anything inter-esting to say about it.

'It is nice,' I said.

'Yes, it is nice,' she confirmed.

We went back inside. Diana wanted to show me some Toledo tips on a map on the dining room table. She asked me what I had planned during my stay and I told her I was looking forward the next day to visiting Don Quixote's windmills as I was a big fan of the book. I didn't think it worth revealing that I still hadn't finished it.

'You like Don Quixote?!' she asked, with some wonderment.

'Yes,' I replied, hoping she wouldn't infer from the brevity of my response just how few pages I'd read.

'But it is so boring!' came her actual reply.

'No, it's funny!' (I mean, I've heard it's funny anyway.)

'It is not,' she said.

Had she seen the windmills? I asked.

'No,' she said. 'I have no interest in windmills.'

It wasn't that she was anti-literary – as she poured juice for us both she spoke rhapsodically about Lorca and Shakespeare. It was just that, she said, Spanish kids have to read Cervantes in classical Spanish, which is really difficult, as Shakespeare is for English-speaking kids, I guess.

'In Toledo you have to see El Greco,' she told me.

'Ah, of course!' I replied.

'You know El Greco?' she asked.

I couldn't now admit to not knowing what El Greco was, having just said 'Ah, of course' at its being mentioned. *El Greco.* *'The'* something. I guessed it was probably a cathedral.

'Is that the big church?' I said.

Diana squinted at me. 'No, he was not a big church. He was a painter.'

'Ah, of course,' I said. It did ring a faint bell.

'One of the most famous painters ever to come from Spain. He lived in Toledo. Though of course he was from Greece. El Greco means 'The Greek'.

'Of course.'

I felt exposed. Not simply for not knowing who El Greco was or even for having sort of pretended to before being outed, but most of all for first having swanned in giving it the big one about Don Quixote as a precursor. I got that dull, self-loathing feeling I get from doing badly at *University Challenge* when playing along at home with other people.

I like to think of myself as a conoisseur of art despite regular reminders that I am not. If I could only accept my points of ignorance and be content to learn new things and not boil with inner rage every time someone mentions a painter who is considered famous but of whom I've never heard. It left me thinking that actually Alex's Cheeky Louvre Tour with its accessible airs and only occasional segues into complexity wasn't so asinine after all.

Diana showed me on a map where I could find El Greco's house, along with some of his other paintings. She also pointed out other sites of historic and cultural interest and certain useful amenities, the former all being within the high walls of the old city, and the latter all to be found in the wide, new yonder.

Diana gave one more extensive and eloquent apology for the quality of her English and left me to it, 'it' being almost giving myself whiplash rushing to log on to the wifi. And I had good reason to: I'd been expecting an email from Neevie (such seems to be my permanent state these days) and lo it had come!

Hey Mark,

Sorry for being useless at communicating. Have been manically trying to wrap up all the art fair stuff (successfully) and desperately trying to line up the next job (unsuccessfully). Bit annoying in the latter case but the good news is that means I'm definitely looking good to come to Athens like we discussed! I've booked a flight on July 22nd which gets me in at 5:12pm local time, if that works?

Hope you're having an amazing time. Been following your progress on the map. How did you find Barcelona? Did you go to Sagrada Familia? Also while you're in Spain you have to try Patatas Bravas! So basic but yet so good!

Sounds like you're having fun, which is great. Hope you're feeling okay in general. Heard much from back home?

Nx

My heart soared to read this, even the fifth time over. Neevie was coming to Athens! Neevie *is* coming to Athens!

Flushed with eudemonian gladness, I, after replying excitedly to Neevie's message, felt moved at last to take a proper look at the view, with the time and solitude necessary to give it proper regard and perhaps make a few notes too.

It still looked nice. The sun was low in the pink sky to the west now, creating pleasant glowing effects between the clouds, but that seemed a fairly temporary feature. It struck me again just how obscured any elements of modernity were behind the mounted old city – which might have been deliberately achieved, like with the protected vistas in London which mean you can't just toss up a big office building between say St Paul's and Hampstead Heath – but to actually *describe* this state of affairs seemed inherently conservative-minded somehow or even just prosaic, like, what would I actually write? 'The fine old city shrouds all the dispiriting trappings of the travesty that is modern civilisation' or just 'you cannot see anything new from this window – [thumbs up emoji]'.

I moved out onto the balcony as if this might *activate* the vista a bit more. It really was nice. It had a river and a big palace (Alcázar) and lots of little sandy houses and a pleasing number of trees and as I jotted all this down, I began to feel like a primary school child on a geography trip dispassionately listing objects on the horizon, so I stopped.

It would be far better to look at it with fresh eyes in the morning before heading off to the windmills. So I went out and drank *cerveza*s and read *Don Quixote* in four different squares, and got lost in mazy streets under high church towers and I felt excitingly like the protagonist from a cut-sequence of the kind of medieval strategy game we used to play on your PC as kids, as if I was about to follow some hooded and stooping figure into a tavern and hear him tell how he fought with El Cid at Valencia. I was, tbh, quite pissed. Later I stood on a rock on the hillside and saw the moon combine with the vivid yellow uplights of the Alcázar.

Early next morning I completely forgot to look at the view

before I travelled by coach to Consuegra, a small town 50 km from Toledo where TripAdvisor maintains – Diana's cynicism notwithstanding – 'Don Quixote's windmills' are to be found, a claim based probably on the fact the author lived briefly in Toledo and set his story in the region.

The coach, a commuter service, was almost empty, save for a few other tourists and an elderly woman who looked as if she might have finished an early cleaning shift, judging from her large carrier bag filled with cloths and sprays and the fact she dozed the whole way until abruptly waking up about a minute before her stop.

In the six or seven small towns the coach stopped at on the way, fascist and anti-fascist graffiti was visible, in about equal abundance. It was only mid-way through the journey that I noticed a swastika carved into the seat-head in front of me.

After the rolling wave of low-level dread upon seeing the insignia came a memory of, weirdly, your 30th birthday and sitting up with your parents and Danika after you'd gone to bed and my parents had cleared off home. We were talking about 'Europe', I think, your dad asking Danika about her work and travels, but using her answers mainly as a jumping-off point for his own stories and opinions. Danika, I'm guessing in search of some respite from this, had turned to me to initiate a two-way side-conversation, and from my asking her about Golden Dawn in Greece, who were pretty fresh on the scene back then, we'd got to talking about the presence of the far right in different European countries. As Danika was telling about the nascent movements in Spain in reaction to the migrant crisis, your dad butted in to say that Spain is effectively immune to modern far-right politics because it was so damaged by Franco's fascism. Danika said she found this assertion naive. She'd talked to lots of people who were Spanish and the signs were there. Your dad said he wasn't naive because he had actually been alive during Franco's reign. I, shamefully, told Danika I thought your dad was right because I'd read about it in a *Guardian* article (I suspect your dad had done the same). Why do I always try to seem an authority on things I have no direct understanding of? Anyway, your mum suggested we change topic and we just started talking about your dad's new ergonomic chair instead.

Cringing at that memory and staring at the bleak symbol in front of me, I suddenly didn't feel in much of a mood for the windmills. But then I moved seats and listened to Laura Marling again and felt a bit better.

The windmills ('*los molinos*') were, it turned out, only about 100 years old, as confirmed by a sun-bleached information board on the arenose road approaching them, so definitely can't be said to have inspired *Don Quixote* which Cervantes wrote in the early 17th century. Reasoning, though, that the fundamental nature of windmills can't have changed very much across that 300-year interval, I was satisfied by these smooth white cylinders with elegant black sails and conic roofs, that stood sentinel over count-less miles of dusty ground. You could forgive Quixote his mistake.

Trudging along a narrow ridge that reached out into arid fields like a jetty into a wide lake, I got as far as the fourth *molino* before the heat, only fractionally mitigated by the prevailing sandy gusts in the air, became unbearable and I had to turn back. None of the windmills were turning, their sails apparently braked. I saw few other visitors up there, just a few families and one coach party leaving as I arrived.

One windmill had been converted into a 'Gastrobar', and, after a diverting and shade-favouring walk around the nearby Consuegra castle, I paid my visit here, dragging a small table and stool a few feet into the shade of the structure. I asked the waitress for an English menu and from it ordered, in a fit of localism, the 'Consuegra Platter' of 'wine, olives and manchego cheese local to this place'. The waitress apologised that the platter was unavailable, owing to 'droughts'. I made do with a Kronenbourg and a bag of nuts.

I looked out over the scene. Some men were at work up high ladders, painting the windmills. If I had to do that, I thought, I would be dead within an hour. As I passed on my way back to the coach one bowed slightly and said '*hola*'.

Back at the Urb an hour or so later I sat on the balcony with my notebook, ready to have another tilt at the view but, whether owing to the heat or the afternoon beer, I found words would not come still. Not good ones anyway. I sat for an hour, staring, jotting down phrases, crossing them out. Staving off the familiar feeling of creative frustration, I resolved to come back to the view after writing about the flat's other features, producing 300 words on the generous storage facilities before deleting them.

I went out to drink beers and walk the ancient streets again but, stressed about the view, I couldn't relax and didn't enjoy it as much as the night before. When I got in I wrote something down but in the morning found it to be incoherent – *the Alcázar is the crown on the head of the old city, which the river Tagus frames like a watery beard* and so on – my judgement having been addled by drink and darkness. I hauled myself from bed, made coffee and went onto the balcony with the tablet. By the end of the second cup I had a paragraph:

> . . . *time seems to stand still here, over this hill which rises from the Castilian plain, rising like a mirage on the dusty, shimmering horizon . . . there can be few better places from which to view it than this apartment . . . you really could enjoy this celebrated city without ever leaving your balcony. And it's worth noting that with good wine, and good company, the view looks even better!*

I sent what I'd done to Bethan Decker and set out for a final day's exploration in the late morning heat.

At El Greco's house, where, as an information board points out, the painter never actually lived during his 37 years in Toledo, I strived to understand his paintings. Feeling initially that I was failing to get his brilliance, I couldn't help but see his supposed innovations as amounting to just painting everybody to look a bit long and sad and slightly murine, sometimes letting the primer or the canvas show through the paint.

Then I remembered a point Alex made on the Louvre tour –

'sometimes it is the things that look amateur which represent the biggest breakthroughs in art'. At the time I thought this a facile point but now staring at an almost cartoonishly zen, cross-bearing Christ with his big body and tiny head, then a morose St Peter, then an arrow-riddled yet quite relaxed-looking San Sebastian, I did begin to appreciate these works' brooding complexity, their various subjects' pervasive dignity and the painter's subtly reality-breaking mannerist breakthroughs a bit more.

By the exit there was a large print of El Greco's 'View of Toledo' (the original being in the Met in New York), a bold, undulous landscape of the city, which made it seem strange, the hills verdant and the river swollen, under a grey sky. I could hardly square it with the still city around me, parching under the high sun.

Toledo is renowned as 'the city of three cultures' and certainly Moorish, Christian and Sephardi Jewish elements all seemed boldly manifest in its architecture during my final walk around, often interlaced in stunning interplay: Moorish arches above Christian pillars; a mosque repurposed as a church; a synagogue re-purposed as a church (it was mostly stuff being turned into churches tbh). But the city's history, gleaned from its museums and tourist sites, as much as one of harmonious coexistence between the three religions, is also one of conflict, regular and often violent reconfigurations of power dynamics, during the Reconquista of course, with the gravest example being the issuing of the Alhambra Decree by Ferdinand and Isabella in 1492, demanding the expulsion of all practising Jews from Spain.

Now, the sacred buildings had all been adapted to the logistical demands of commercial tourism (which I guess is the true modern religion, amiriiite?) and, in the new town, I saw a graffito asserting that 'refugees are not welcome'.

When I got in, I found that Bethan Decker had replied to say she was happy with the copy but that she felt a lot of the detail in the description of the view was unnecessary. I could lose most of the paragraph, she said, and just describe it as 'really nice'.

I came to Toledo to write 'really nice' and I regret nothing.

Late in the afternoon Diana came to 'do the Checkout'. As I gave her back the keys, she asked me if everything had been okay. I told her it had been more than okay – very, very good in fact.

And how did I find the view? she asked.

'Really nice,' I said.

'Yes,' she said. 'That is a good phrase for it.'

As I left Toledo, the temperature was pushing 42 degrees C. The record for July here is 42.6.

I've just broken off for a train picnic of sardines and bread, to which I've become somewhat addicted over the last few days, and now I shall tell you of Madrid . . .

I arrived hot and sweaty into the city's Atocha station, the temperature still above 40 degrees.

At the Urb – listed curiously as 'A Dream in Cream' – I slumped down exhaustedly on the sofa, as soon as my Host, Iker (whose profile declared he liked 'fitness' and 'organising his life'), had shown me into the living room, which was wide and high-ceilinged and almost nauseating in its pervasive off-whiteness. Iker, a burly, nearly middle-aged man in a black Under Armour T-shirt, who looked not only as if he could lift me up with one arm, but as if he might, in certain circumstances, have wanted to, told me to stay off the couch until I'd showered because I was 'too greasy'.

He explained, quite superfluously I felt, that all the furnishings in the lounge were cream-coloured – 'everything from Buttermilk to Eggnog'. I couldn't tell whether I was on the receiving end of a bespoke patronising monologue – he being intent to influence my copy through outright assertiveness where other Hosts had sought to impress and flatter – or whether this was a generic spiel doled out to all Guests. Either way, I could see for myself that everything was cream and didn't really require a more specific description thereof, but I listened politely anyway, for what else will I ever do?

The Welcome became unquestionably bespoke when Iker deigned to tell me that he would like me to write in my 'story of the apartment' that people are not allowed to spill anything on the furnishings. 'This is very important,' the big man said with a look in his eye so cold that it could have air-conditioned the room, were there not already a machine working away quietly in an ivory-coloured casement above the doorway.

I stifled a chuckle: it would make for such weird copy telling people not to spill things on the cream. Not very Human Touch. Affecting an understanding frown, I reassured Iker that this didn't need to be in the promotional copy. First you want them to book, I told him, then you can tell them the rules. Most Guests will be very careful anyway. I promised Iker that I would be very careful myself. Iker looked at me like the owner of a newly trained puppy about to leave it alone in the house for the first time.

After Iker left I went to the bathroom (also cream-schemed, though this felt less remarkable) and showered as instructed, opting to use my own emollient rather than the 'Cream Crème' provided in a dispenser on the wall, lest it inflame my eczema.

Successfully abluted, I resisted still the allure of the sofa – deep, velvety, almost milky – out of fear that my newly applied emollient would vindicate Iker's worst fears. Instead, I took a second 'Baby Cream' towel from the shelf, and used it for prophylaxis against the bed, whereupon I took a siesta – if it wasn't too late in the day for a siesta, although in the globalised age, surely siesta time, like everything else, is in flux.

Upon waking, I put on my smart shorts (i.e. of the two pairs in my possession, the ones with the least visible sun cream stains) and set out, deciding to go out and walk around, '*flâneur*-style', to find a place for dinner. The city seemed lively and likeable but loud and fast with wide streets and tall, elegant, understated buildings, bestowing merciful shade.

It occurred to me that this was the first city I'd been to, perhaps ever, which I just couldn't get a steer on from a map; I could establish no sense of a centre, of a systematic 'order' along historic or economic lines. Perhaps because it was too big or just too hot, but I was happy enough just to drift around in it.

Many of the restaurants I passed were tapas places, bewilderingly astir, but, with a 'Tapas Crawl Experience' in store the following evening, I kept walking until I found a charming 'Vegan/

Bionic' restaurant on a quiet backstreet. A pavement chalkboard declared that the place was 'Just Open' and 'Half Price First Week!'. *Muy bien!*

I stepped inside to find it three-quarters empty, air-conditioned and more or less perfect in every way. I was greeted and seated quickly by an almost aggressively gentle thin, bald man in an orange T-shirt.

He gave me an English menu and a 'natural wines' list.

'Are these half price too?' I queried.

'Yes, it is all half price,' he said with a placidity that perhaps didn't fully mask a low-level resentment of this fact.

I ordered a carafe of tempranillo, which I managed to drink before the starter arrived. As the gentle man served me my '*tartar de tofu*'. . . I ordered another one (carafe).

'Another carafe?' he clarified with an ambiguous tone, which might have contained disapproval or at least surprise or concern at the effective loss of his wine mark-up in the face of my appetite.

'*Sí*,' I said. *Sí*, for it was only two euros; it'd have been a folly not to. And I now half remembered some article I had once half read about natural wine being less hangover-inducing because it didn't have as much of some sort of chemical or something in it. Or was that organic wine? What was the difference anyway? What did it matter? It was better than the usual shit I drink in corners of rooms at house parties in London to quell the gnawing sense that I should have stayed at home.

The second carafe came. The spinach lasagne came. *La vida era buena* . . .

Back on the street, in very good spirits, I simply couldn't believe how warm it was, and that's in the wake of its being very, very warm every day for the last week or so. It was more about the warmth of the night. I simply couldn't recall it ever feeling so warm, so late in the day; it was midnight and I was dripping with sweat. People, families, were still out on the streets, children playing in the little off-street playgrounds as if it were 10am.

Feeling it would be wrong somehow to go to bed while all this was happening, I found a cheerful, no-frills bar and drank a large *cerveza* at a plastic pavement table. The patrons were of all ages, including yet more lively children, and all seemed local and friendly with one another. Or is that just an effect of being a lone outsider in an unfamiliar place that you assume everybody else knows and likes each other? Good vibes all round anyway, here. One thing I've definitely noticed is that people in Spanish bars seem to be there primarily for the purpose of being with others – talking, laughing, all that stuff – and secondarily to drink. In Britain, I tend to think, the motives are usually inverted.

Of my own purpose for staying out, I'm not exactly sure. Probably both the drinking and the being with those enjoying being with others, in equal measure. I felt supremely happy in this anonymous state. The copy would write itself and tomorrow I'd get to enjoy some renowned art. I considered approaching a nearby table of strangers who looked about my age, but on reflection I didn't feel the need to. I was happy enough in their proximity, enjoying their energy, their synergetic aura. Also, if I'm honest, I still felt awkward about doing that sort of thing.

Nobody paid me much attention anyway, which was fine by me. Comfortable in this anonymous, limbo state, I sank a couple of *cerveza*s and eventually ambled off to bed, still sweating profusely.

I'd wanted to make an early start next morning, to write up my copy about the apartment so that I could visit the galleries before the tapas crawl in the evening. But it was gone 10 when I found myself shuffling, tablet under arm, to the glossy and – naturally – cream-coloured living room table. As I sat, making very slow progress (struggling mainly to find enough synonyms for 'cream') my gaze was drawn to a church visible through the locked window – a slightly frilly, neoclassical number with square columns and a grimy façade. In a high niche stood, without the benefit of legs, a small Madonna, holding an even smaller Christ. I assume it was Christ anyway. She could have been holding someone else's baby, as she was, apparently, the nicest ever woman. Her head, half veiled, was tilted towards the babe. Classic Marian stuff.

I glanced at her a few times, trying to focus on something real and hard in the world, to break the fog that had amassed within me. After a while I forgot about her and just got on with trying to put words on the page, which proved difficult, and soon found myself breaking a long, hard-won abstention from porn, loading up Pornhub, stopping only momentarily to consider whether Iker, untrusting as he seemed, was likely to check over the internet history of his Guests and if he was, how likely he was to tell Bethan Decker of any indecent discoveries. But just as I was about to roll the cursor over the first thumbnail that caught my eye, I felt Mary's gaze upon me once more. Sure enough she was still there, and looking sadder than ever.

I stood up to draw the cream curtains and, abruptly realising that I was concealing myself from a statue in order to masturbate, I abruptly got a grip of myself and sat down again. I just couldn't bring myself to work. I couldn't focus on the screen and began to feel dizzy. I moved to the sofa where I lay horizontal. I was, I had to admit, somewhat queasy. I considered going back to bed but, determined to make something of the day – going to explore Madrid and visit the Prado and Reina Sofía galleries (to see Goyas and Guernica!) – I decided to press on, resolving that I was simply hot and dehydrated and would feel right soon enough.

Just as I stood to gather my tablet and keyboard from the table, quite without warning (except the warning of having felt sick for half an hour) I threw up. All over the cream sofa and rug.

How? How could I have let this happen?

After a brief lachrymal grimace, I assessed the damage. Most of the sick had gone on a throw over the sofa and on the floor rug. Not a bad outcome all things considered, you might think. I checked the label on the throw and, with some googling, ascertained that it was machine washable. The rug seemed trickier though. I googled whether rugs are machine washable and found that cotton and synthetic ones generally are. I checked the label and found this one to be 'Indian Jute'. The internet was less clear on what to do with this, offering a great number of suggestions from WikiHow, including using, variously: bleach, baking soda and white wine vinegar (of a similar shade to the rug). The unifying consensus was that such rugs cannot be machine-washed.

Overwhelmed, I had another dry cry and pulled myself together. I looked at the sick on the throw, already crusty and vibrantly orange against its creamy background, and took it into the kitchen to put it in the washing machine only to discover that there wasn't one. Only blank cream units and a smell of Dettol (or whatever Dettol is called in Spain). So I took it to a nearby *lavandería*, on the way stopping at a corner shop to pick up the recommended white wine vinegar, baking soda and detergent for the rug, while the shopkeeper watched on with a look that seemed to suggest he knew exactly what I was up to.

At the *lavandería*, I put the throw in to wash, adding detergent to the machine and only then noticing a sign stating that the machines add detergent automatically. It looked very soapy indeed in the drum. Only after I was convinced that the machine wasn't going to spew a soapy effusion all over the floor, and feeling slightly better for having achieved something, I went to a nearby café and ordered *patatas bravas* – as satisfying as Neevie promised – and a Coke, which I don't think I've had since I was 12, all of which went down just right.

I returned to the launderette to find the throw perfectly clean, and then to the apartment to find the rug apparently clean too, the wateriness of the sick having, I can only assume, allowed it to simply evaporate away. Inspecting it closely, I found a slightly dark hue still visible in certain patches, but basically indistinguishable from the pattern.

Feeling rather chuffed, I hung the throw to dry and skipped off, taking the shady route wherever possible, to the Prado and the Reina Sofía for a lovely air-conditioned cultural excursion.

There was an exhibition on about 'Cubism and Bourgeois Interiors'.

As I progressed through the gallery it struck me that I've seen a lot of different 'bourgeois interiors' in the last few weeks. For isn't that what Urb represents, the commodification of the bourgeois interior? The properties are, in most cases, tremendously comfortable spaces to inhabit. Not just in a literal, physical sense, but also in a psychological sense, in their provision of an atmosphere of homeliness when you're not at home – something hotels by their nature fall short of.

I remembered a detail from Freud's 1919 essay 'The Uncanny' – perhaps the only detail I remember from that essay, having probably not even thought of it since uni – specifically the examination of the German word which is equivalent to 'uncanny', *'unheimlich'* (literally 'unhomely') and resulting assertion that uncanniness is a feeling of the familiar (the homely) suddenly seeming unfamiliar (unhomely/uncanny) and thus frightening.

On the way home I, as habit determined, picked up some nice bread and tinned sardines, satisfying but not too heavy before the tapas crawl – I didn't want to be sick again! – and once back at the Urb, I put the now-dry throw back over the sofa. This done, I sat down with my tablet and snack, and reckoning myself simply too worn out to do copy just then, I decided just to watch some Netflix and generally chill before I had to set out again.

I fetched a plate and sat at the table to tear up the bread and then opened the tin of sardines, which proved immediately a bit tricky. It was a ring-pull mechanism and the metal tin lid juddered as it opened. Standing and stepping away from the table to give my arm enough room for the action, I now managed, in one determined, fluid motion, to pull back the metal lid, allowing, at last, the contents to go flying all over the throw and rug.

I looked down. There was a small sardine fillet on the sofa and another on the rug. But that was not all. The sardines were, as it turned out, covered in tomato sauce.

I collapsed on the rug, head next to the thick red stain and I began to weep. Real tears this time.

After a few minutes I picked myself up and made a plan – a

hopeless, futile plan, but a plan all the same: vinegar and baking soda on the rug and back to the launderette with the throw.

Forty minutes later, I returned to the Urb, exhausted, holding an only fractionally less soiled throw, looking down at an only fractionally less soiled rug and finally accepted defeat.

I would have to use what little money I had left in my account to pay for the presumably very expensive rug and throw, and ask Iker not to tell Bethan Decker.

There was nothing else to be achieved. I couldn't write now, not even a message to Iker. The only thing I could do which wouldn't make things worse for myself was to go on the fucking crawl and interact with strangers and eat a shit load of tapas just a few hours after being sick (the nausea had returned) and be enthusiastic about it too.

I looked up the meeting point on the map and found it to be a 15-minute walk away; it was already gone ten to seven. And so, un-showered, with a belly full of *bravas*, I ran off to the meeting point, only realising halfway that I hadn't even cleaned my teeth after being sick earlier in the day. What an abysmal first impression I must have made to the other tapas crawlers, improved in no way by my extended near-sprint through the sweltering rush-hour city to make it on time.

I don't think I'd ever actually had tapas before, not in its authentic form anyway. Certainly I've had small plates, perhaps even of a pseudo-Spanish variant, but served expensively and confusingly in a Soho restaurant to a group whose general acquaintanceship was not improved by the experience. But I felt, as I jogged through Madrid's bustling streets, that the real, the *authentic* thing – cheap, casual, delicious, bonhomie-inducing and served with cold wine on the thick wooden tabletop of a cool, ancient restaurant – would surely be more my bag.

And yet, like so many things, the reality, even here in actual Madrid, is less wonderful than you imagine it to be, the fault being all mine of course. Tapas is what it is; it can't help what it is any more than the sea can help being the sea – it is for the sailor to adapt. But adapting, I realised, as soon as I arrived on the heaving street terrace and struggled to pick out the large group of laughing, young-ish people I was supposed to be with from countless other groups of laughing, young-ish people amassed there, would not be easy. Finally, I spotted one that looked notably less together than the others, slightly more feigning in its conviviality and I knew it to be mine.

The Tapas Dudes – Alvaro (a toned man with a sparkling smile and a stern eye) and Jada (a toned woman with a sparkling smile and a stern eye) seemed genuinely concerned for my welfare, at least initially, late and red and gasping as I was.

'We have waited for you,' Jada told me and, as I assured them I was fine and was just a little queasy from the heat, their concern seemed to take on a more admonishing, less empathic edge.

'The crawl is delayed now,' Alvaro told me, smile disappearing. 'People will have to rush the *gambas*.'

'This is not good,' Jada added.

'Will you be able to enjoy the tapas and write about it in a happy way in your condition?' Alvaro asked.

I would, I assured him, fighting down a wave of nausea. And so the physically and mentally stressful sojourn of tapas-tasting commenced.

In the first bar – where 15 of us crowded around a small barrel – we had the aforementioned *gambas*, which were indeed rushed down, along with baby octopus, tostadas, olives, and sangrias, and I, between straining hard to stomach the food and, by unhappy positional accident, having the responsibility of pouring everyone's sangria, failed to offer any sort of enthusiastic audience for Jada's chat about the company and the bar and the food and the city and all the other things she thought might be informative for the copy.

In bar number two – a tiny deli-like outlet with minimal pavement space – I stood with my face in someone's armpit and had to apologise to Alvaro for not being able to eat any of the tapas he had ordered for me because it was all meat.

In bar number three, a dim and sweaty establishment of which I remember basically no visual details, I ate nothing and ran to the toilet to throw up again having to wait 10 minutes in a queue and pay a euro for the privilege.

In bar number four, it all became too much and, seizing the opportunity when Alvaro and Jada were occupied in loud badinage with the proprietor, I fled. Any worry about what the Tapas Dudes might tell Bethan Decker was eclipsed at the relief at simply being out in the fresh air and free from any imperative to eat.

I stumbled home, downed a pint of water and collapsed into the bed.

I finally roused myself just before ten with a start, my first waking thought being about the stains. I trudged to the bathroom, delaying going back to the scene of the crime to assess the final damage. There would be no time now to message Iker with any sort of convincing excuse or explanation, as he was due to arrive for the Checkout in a few minutes. I would just have to go get cash out of the ATM and hand it over to Iker as soon as letting him behold the ruined wares.

But upon stepping into the living room I was shocked: both stains were completely gone. Completely. Not a trace. I almost rubbed my eyes with clenched forefingers, Warner Brothers-style. I got down on my knees and stared at the rug. There was possibly a very, very faint dark patch where spillage had been but even this might have been my mind or the window-mediated light playing tricks.

Utterly dumbfounding tbh. On my knees on the rug I stared out of the window and saw Madonna looking down upon me. I sat frozen like this until the sound of Iker coming into the room behind me brought me to my senses.

'Good morning. Are you okay?' he said, sharply.

'I am praying,' I told him.

I could think not only of no better but really no other possible explanation.

'Ah,' Iker said quite acceptingly, before proceeding to move around the flat inspecting every surface. I lingered for a moment and then went to pack up my things.

Once Iker was satisfied with the integrity of his creams, I checked out and made my slow, sweaty way back to Atocha to take the train to Marseille.

Well that helped pass the time. We've just got to Perpignan. Perpignan. Who'd ever have thought I'd be in Perpignan? Not me.

Salutations.

Mark

From: Mark Rosiello
To: Paris Rosiello
Jul 16; 10:15

Hello Paris,

Another train, this across the French-Italian border, as I head towards our ancestral village in Tuscany.

I've just left Marseille where I arrived the day before Bastille Day. The lateness of the hour – in strange, urban-gothic symphony with a lad trying to sell me hash the very second I stepped out of the Gare St Charles and a man scowling at me from his car as I crossed the road and the slightly sketchy dimness of the two or three streets between the station and the Urb and, let's not forget, my naturally skittish tendencies – was a bit disquieting.

Worse, my Host, Romain – an 'artist and social worker who wishes you to be welcome' – would not be there to greet me, being instead away on his summer holiday, somewhere in the Alps, for which he had sent, via Bethan Decker, an incredibly apologetic missive, explaining that this was the only chance he and his partner had for a holiday all year and that if he did not go away he feared he would 'turn mad'. In solidarity with the man, I determined to brave my lonely arrival.

Upon entry to the apartment, a few floors up a steep spiral staircase which served as an atrium for the many-levelled utilitarian tenement building, the air was still and warm, and it was heavily dark. I found the switch and the apartment's suddenly over-lit characteristics revealed themselves: somewhat pokey, a little untidy and furnished in a basic, even homespun way, with bricks and planks for bookshelves and tatty little curtains instead of cabinet doors. For all of this though, it was not 'unhomely'.

I quickly discovered that Romain had more than mitigated for his absence with countless handwritten notes stuck around the place, the first of which read 'WELCOME HOME' and hung from the arm of a male mannequin with a cowboy hat, boxer shorts and a ripped torso, daubed with blue paint, standing directly behind the door in the hallway.

The apartment, according to the Trip Pack, offered the chance to 'stay in a real artist's studio!' Aptly, there was no living room, just a large open space, skirted with worktops and shelves and boxes of tools, paints and materials. Strewn across a large desk were pencil-drawn design sheets, apparently for sculptures and installation pieces. On one wall were painted humanoid figures, men as if seen via an X-ray-type device, with, it looked like, large (literal) boners.

I pottered around, discovering the rest of Romain's notes, denoting: my room, his room, the bathroom, the toilet, the kitchen, the fridge, how to turn the gas on, how to turn the gas off, the wifi details, and several other useful points of domestic information. At no stage in this (or in any other) feat of communication, however, did he say anything along the lines of: 'btw my flat is quite weird'. And, in the end, why should he?

I sat down to carry out my 'safety in Marseille' Google search, having neglected to perform this important duty in Madrid, and quickly discovered a familiar kind of forum-mediated consensus: the city centre is pretty safe, save for a few streets around the station, which are better avoided at night. One poster suggested that women might not wish to dress up nicely and walk around in the evenings as they could be mistaken for prostitutes. Another had it that the city is run by gangsters and the police serve only an 'ornamental' presence. More consensus came with the observation that the Quartiers Nords are the most impoverished parts of the city and that it might be dangerous for tourists to go there, but, as one poster asked, 'why would you bother if it's so far away from the centre?'

Further reading revealed these cautionary notes to be the tip of an iceberg of reportage into Marseille's endemic, institutionalised poverty. One article suggested that the city is 'more like Britain than Paris' in that social housing is contained within the city itself rather than being shoved out to the suburbs. But many others talked of Marseille's outer *cités* being damaged by underinvestment and effectively being cut off from the rest of the city by the Metro and tram lines.

But these anxieties and my own first impressions of Marseille (quiet, too quiet, and a touch sinister) were belied as soon as I stepped onto the Boulevard de la Libération, which was filled with people, people strolling and people sitting and people standing, outside bars and restaurants and on benches and on fountains. Trams shoved through the happy crowds, which swelled still more as I joined La Canebière leading to Le Vieux Port. Here was L'Église Saint-Vincent de Paul, standing gravely above the merriment, there an art-house cinema, vomiting hipsters all over the pavement.

That night, in Marseille all seemed well on the streets. More than well, blithesome in fact. The crowds surged around the old port. The lights of the bars, restaurants and the big Ferris wheel played on the water, and everyone was smiling.

The next day, determined not to further rinse my depleted cash reserves, I decided to find inexpensive activity ahead of my first Marseille Experience that evening, a 'VIP View of Bastille Day Fireworks'.

A walk up to the Basilique Notre-Dame de la Garde cost nothing and afforded not only stupendous vantage over the city and surrounding coastline but also quite a fun chat with four 18-ish-year-olds, originally from Tunisia. When I asked them whether they now consider themselves French (a latent, reactionary 'integration not immigration' thirst at work here??; also with my limited French I couldn't think of many other questions to ask them) they emphasised their being '*Marseillais! Pas*

Français!' It's not unusual, I later read, for Marseille's immigrants to feel this way.

Their group dynamic felt somehow reminiscent of the little crews who'd wander around the Hull suburbs when I was young: three lads – one cocky and loud; one more polite and nervous; another reserved, almost catatonic – and one girl (girlfriend of the confident one seemingly), apparently brighter than her male confrères (in this case, the best English speaker anyway) but also prone to giggling self-apology. I felt no less self-conscious and inferior now than I had as a nervous child and approached by coveys of cooler kids.

They rolled a spliff and I asked if they weren't worried by the presence of several armed soldiers patrolling only a few metres away. 'They are only here to shoot the terrorist,' the confident one stated bluntly. I half hoped they'd offer me a toke but they did not. They did, though, tell me I look like Wayne Rooney.

'*Parce que mon visage est très blanc?*' I asked.

'*Oui,*' the leader replied, '*et très rouge.*'

The 'VIP' view of the fireworks turned out to be just the same view as everyone else was experiencing, except I was standing on the terrace of a restaurant behind a red rope, demarcated from the rest of the happily watching crowds.

I was greeted by our Host and the restaurant's owner, Didier, whose slicked-back hair, two-button-open white shirt, and general testosteronic, early middle-aged vibe gave him the air of a nightclub-owning quasi-villain from *Hollyoaks*. He looked only temporarily perturbed by the scruffiness of my old jeans and battered trainers, which certainly stood out against the far more impressive presentation of my fellow guests. But he plastered his smile back on to pat me on the back and usher me onto the terrace, to where he said it was 'safe and nice'.

A young service staff delivered champagne and vol-au-vents – small pieces of salmon on small pieces of bread; olives; some sort of chicken bite, which I declined. Bottles of water were free; cocktails and beer at a price. Didier looked smugly over things, standing sentinel at the threshold to his roped-off kingdom, a couple of times turning away, with a great lack of humour, those who innocently tried to enter the terrace. He seemed very taken with the exclusivity of the whole business and would occasionally walk over to where I was standing next to an artificial shrub to gesture out at the crowds and say things like: 'They must all wish they were in here, behind this rope, with a bit more space' and 'I think they wish they had a glass of champagne' and 'No calamari with a nice sauce if you are them.'

To me the people on the other side of the rope seemed pretty untroubled by their supposed privation, cheerful and voluminous as the crowd seemed, made up of families, exuberant teenagers, cool squads on mopeds, shabby solitary old men – all happy and unified enough.

Compared to standing around awkwardly next to uncharismatic local businessmen and moneyed tourist couples, it looked blissful, which is why, when Didier had stepped inside for a moment to attend to a dispute over cocktail measures, I – feeling that the champagne, calamari and general hauteur had given me fodder enough for my copy – took the chance to slip away and become lost in the smiling throng, just as the fireworks began to explode above the Ferris wheel, over the harbour, lighting up the entire bay in midsummer glory. Once again, I felt a slight pang of guilt at perhaps not properly fulfilling my obligations as an Experiencer, but how hard could it be to imagine what it would have been like to have viewed the same fireworks from a slightly different viewpoint, except behind a rope, in order to entice the kind of suckers prepared to pay 100 euros for that sort of privilege?

I enjoyed my newly regained liberty by buying a couple of Cans for Mélenchon and watched the remainder of the free spectacle from the vantage of a side street off the Vieux Port, where I had a conversation with an old guy who also happened to be drinking cans in the street. I say 'conversation', but it was really just him saying '*Ah, c'est beau! C'est beau! Bravo Marseille!*' over and over again and me saying '*oui*' and smiling. He offered me a cigarette and looked heartbroken when I declined – but freewheeling liberty has a limit. When the fireworks were done, I made my way, through the joyous crowds, to bed.

Another day, another Experience: a luxury boat trip, this time, to one of Marseille's famous 'Calanques', which are narrow Mediterranean coastal inlets with very nice beaches in them. The boat, *Liberté 2* departed from the city's harbour, where it gleamed so brightly that it was, at close quarters, genuinely impossible to look at without sunglasses. The warm and personal insinuations of the Host moniker seemed particularly far-fetched here, primarily because there was no actual 'Host' to speak of, just a small crew of young workers who scanned tickets and served champagne – more fucking champagne! – on the wide, white deck, looking almost militaristically alert.

The other guests seemed unbothered by the lack of formal welcome and began immediately stripping down to their swim-wear to recline and sunbathe and drink champagne and grin toothily at each other and at everything around.

Not really up for performing the full body factor 50 applica-tion in front of these strangers, I kept my shirt on and my collar up and sat around the side of the boat away from everyone, reading the paper. By the time the vessel was way out to sea and the view of the land was luscious and slightly indistinct in the marine mist, I began to feel quite content, for who would not feel content under a vast Mediterranean sky, rushing over clear bay waters, the gathering wind redeeming the rough heat of the day, even if there are large speakers virtually right above your head blasting out generic EDM?

Twenty minutes later we rounded the coast and came upon a bay, sparkling and mobile in its blueness. Above it stood the limestone horseshoe of the Calanque and, in between, a busy beach. As the boat drew closer, the beachgoers became discern-ible in their happy activity. Children splashed in the lapping waves. Families threw balls and rowed dinghies. All seemed to rejoice in this state of lively peace.

But then, those same happy people began to look our way, like a crowd in a midway scene of a disaster movie. As we drew closer, balls and Frisbees dropped, and soon we were close enough to see the giddy vaulting of waves ceasing too. The sunkissed reverie of the scene had been definitively broken.

The boat now came to anchor – or at least its loud engine was switched off – right in the middle of the bay, its giant speakers pointed directly at the beach like land-attack missiles, allowing the still more enervating music to thump at the shore and echo in the inlet as in a great amphitheatre. Apparently oblivious to the upset which our arrival had caused, the other *Liberté 2* Guests now set about leaping from the side of the vessel, before, as a rule, climbing straight back up the boat's ladder and jumping straight off again, naturally shouting and screaming and laughing all the while.

After taking my trainers off and putting them into my rucksack. I jumped off the side of the boat too. But I did not climb back up the ladder. Instead I asked one of the twitchy crewmates to chuck me down my bag before, fully clothed, swimming and then wading over to the beach, just about managing to not completely saturate the rucksack and its contents in the process.

Only when I arrived on the beach did I begin to question the wisdom of jumping into the cold water with all my clothes on. But, within five minutes of rumination under the hot sun, all regret was extinguished and I was, at worst, refreshingly damp, and covered with an almost crystalline sheen. Newly relaxed, I saw fit to eat an ice cream and then retreat into the forest behind the beach. I had a very vivid memory of our holiday to La Rochelle circa 2003 in which you and I scampered ahead of the rest of the family and shared a joint under the cover of the pines before scrambling over what felt like acres of rock pools, which all seemed full of magic and possibility as life itself did then too.

Here in Marseille, I stood in a similar forest as I watched a dog take a shit under the eyes of its yawning owner. I applied the factor 50 before making the circuitous hike up the road which led away from the beach and through the woods, signs warning me of the imminent threat of wildfires at every turn, and eventually reached the road where, after a dehydrating wait, I got on a bus back to the city.

I even treated myself to an Orangina on the way home, outside a bar in Notre Dame du Mont, which, with its chalkboard bars and cafés, large rectangular plaza covered with colourful awnings and wall-to-wall upbeat graffiti, is surely the Shoreditch of Marseille. Notice that I've so far managed to resist identifying 'The Shoreditch' of every city I've been to, but here it was just too irresistible. Needless to say, the prices were a good 20% cheaper here than in Shoreditch. And sitting with my ice-cold, corporate-branded soft drink on this sultry evening I began finessing my Take on Marseille, reckoning the city to be Up There With Barcelona as My Favourite of All the Places I've Been To So Far. I could picture myself living in Marseille, perhaps bombing about on a little moped with a shoulder bag full of hash, Neevie on the back, smoking in Adidas flip-flops. Or, more realistically, it'd be me on the back. Or, even more realistically, sitting alone outside the *salon de thé*, reading *Le Canard enchaîné*. In any case, a happy picture.

Later, my copy written and furnished with a great many lies and inventions about what a cool time I'd had in the private bar and on the boat, in my search for further inexpensive occupations, I found a free 'Corbusier Tour' online, which entailed a visit to the French-Swiss Architect's iconic *Cité Radieuse*, the modernist residential housing estate built for families displaced by bombing after the Second World War, considered the first great achievement of Brutalism. The tour guide, a bearded and bespectacled postgrad student called Henri, outlined to me and an audience of five or so other skinny, pale men with sunglasses and small beards that the building was meant to lay a blueprint for a new kind of egalitarian, communal urban living. Now, we saw through our very own designer frames that the building seems to be populated entirely by upper-middle-class professionals, whom we watched freely wandering around with their tote bags and eating salads on their balconies and generally seeming the quiet beneficiaries of a confused new century.

Seeing this monument juxtaposed with what Henri described

of the housing available for the non-affluent majority in Marseille – which, in many cases, represents a kind of cheap, bastardised version of the Corbusier design template, i.e. the sort of communal social housing familiar in the UK too – I couldn't help but carry back to the Urb an acute feeling that the modernist 'machine for living in' philosophy of residential building has failed, in Marseille, in London and in so many other places.

That evening, I finally met my Host, Romain, a friendly, tall and nervous man, verging on middle age, who turned out to be every bit as thoroughly polite and helpful as his post-it notes suggested. Just returned from his Alpine retreat, he apologised for his weekend's absence.

'It is my only chance to escape this place,' he said.

'*Pas de problème*,' I told him.

'I hope my signs have been helpful to you.'

I assured him they had.

I asked him about his life and work in Marseille and he told me he was an artist, working with the media of 'paint and the body' but for a day job worked as a social worker in a prison.

He asked me what my own job entailed and when I explained my summer's assignment, he seemed astounded.

'You have the dream life!' he exclaimed.

I hadn't thought about it like that before.

'You are so lucky,' he told me, absent-mindedly peeling a post-it note saying 'Bin' from the bin.

I tried to change topic and ask him about Marseille but he seemed a bit down on the city. 'When I came back from the Alps,' he said, 'I thought to myself: oh why do I have to come back to this place? But, you know, that's life.'

He smiled a quick, tired smile and began removing post-it notes from inside the fridge.

That's the reality I suppose I'm fleeing from (and occasionally being reminded of), as I dart around Europe on my mega-holiday: people coping (with varying degrees of success) with dissatisfaction, repetition and the sense there's something better out there, in some inaccessible elsewhere.

I went to bed in Romain's apartment that night with, at least, a renewed sense of gratitude, a suddenly much starker awareness of the degree of privilege underwriting this trip. I was aware also though, as the hours crawled forward and sleep came on slowly, that I didn't have Romain's sense of what he truly wants to be doing. There was a man who knew what mattered to him and who was devoting himself to it in his spare time, with little financial reward. Perhaps I have a duty to try harder to work out what that is for me, instead of just mildly resenting my job in London and solacing myself with the thought that I probably could be doing something else if I set my mind to it.

These were heavy, difficult Friday-night-into-Saturday-morning thoughts. But by the time I finally did drift off I'd managed to resolve that in the nearer term, the most important thing is to remember how lucky I am and to enjoy my trip more.

Onwards to Italy.

Mark

From: Mark Rosiello
To: Paris Rosiello
Jul 20; 19:42

Paris,

This email comes from the deck of the ferry from Bari (Italy) to Patras (Greece), assuming the 'superfast sea wifi' connection, for which I have just paid seven euros and which took 20 minutes to load the BBC Sport homepage, actually allows me to send it. Not that I'm in any particular rush. I'm sitting in a deck chair – not like a *deckchair*, more just like a metal chair, which is on a deck, screwed down to it in fact – eating biscuits and watching the sun set over the Adriatic. Could be worse.

I have *a lot* to offload, though, since I last wrote from Marseille, my passage to this point having revealed some things – not necessarily good things – about my character and the extent to which it might accord with a presupposed Italian national character.

More than anywhere else so far, I missed you here. Not just because your fluency in Italian would have been most helpful at times, but also because I could have done with the company at points, especially company wonted to provide steadying counsel during moments of panic.

Things started agreeably and relaxedly enough. My first days in the country held no working purpose as I had a few days off, during which I would visit, as I've always threatened to, the village of Sommocolonia, our ancestral seat in the Tuscan hills. I'd be staying in the nearby town of Barga where I'd meet up with Dyson, who, only a week ago, finally got back to my message to say he would join me in three days, fresh from his latest job in Budapest. Classic Dyson. But I was looking forward to seeing him. With him I'd travel to Florence for a couple of days before journeying on alone to Bari by train and then by boat to Greece. It would be an exacting schedule, a lot less straightforward than Bethan Decker's original plane-based plan. But it would be worth it. Lying in wait was adventure, discovery, pasta. And, best of all, Neevie in Athens.

I was determined for my maiden visit to the *patria* to be one of open-eyed, open-hearted discovery and edification. Genoa in the country's North-west region was my first port of call – literally as it's a port city, still Italy's busiest. This is where, my dad once told me, Great-grandad Domenico set sail for England around 1924. Another time, however, your dad told me he left Livorno in 1922, whereas Grandad Al said that his old man had in fact crossed the Alps by mule and then walked most of the way from Germany, though he (Grandad Al) was pretty senile by that point.

Admittedly I was only in Genoa for a few hours, as a stop-off on my way to Sommocolonia, Great-grandad's birthplace, amongst the valleys of my – well, of *our* – origin, where I was sure I'd feel my spirit lifted like the butter-tired protagonist of an Olivio advert.

I sat looking over the port, historically one of the most important in the Mediterranean. Did you know that the English

'St George's Flag' was essentially rented from the Republic of Genoa in 1190 to provide English ships with protection from the Genovese fleet? Actually, that is probably the kind of thing you'd know.

Whether Domenico departed from here or not, it struck me suddenly what it must have taken for a young man to completely abandon home and everything he knew in such a way. Here I was, a head full of romance, in a city of ramping tourism and Instagram backdrops, and there he'd been, a century earlier, desperate, presumably, to get away from his homeland, from Mussolini and who knows what other miseries.

After a strange series of connecting trains (on one I sat next to a woman with a sack containing, quite audibly, an alive chicken), I arrived at Barga, the nearest large town to Sommocolonia, a place that I remember Grandad Al mentioning from time to time. There was that Christmas my dad gave him some black and white photographs of Barga that he'd found at the library and Grandad put his glasses on and spent about half an hour looking at them, just peering at these two indistinct images of a small hill-town skyline, and saying 'Well . . . would you look at that? . . . Now isn't that something to look at . . .' He'd like to visit someday, he said. He said that often. But he never made even the most provisional plan to do so.

'Well, we should go! We should all go!' your mum would say, every time he mentioned it and we'd all say 'Yes! Yes, we should!' But we never did. Except now I was going. And I'd texted my dad and he replied to tell me he couldn't wait to see photos.

The bus from Barga station, when it came, was more like a large van, already containing about 12 people, mostly elderly, most hauling groceries. I held out some euro coins to the driver and said, '*Quanto costa?*', having practised enunciating the phrase solidly for the last half-hour, but he just waved me on and so I took my seat, sweating among the unruffled locals, trying to hold it together as the small vehicle lurched up the hill's winding roads, until finally I got off near my hotel, a century-old villa that was like something out of *The Godfather Part II*. Or perhaps it was

just a regular Italian villa, *Godfather Part II* being my only exposure to said. It was nice anyway, pretty cheap for what it was
really and rather unexpectedly run by a friendly Scottish couple
who were retired and, I gathered, living out their own ancestral
fantasy here.

The view from my room pissed all over the Toledo view, quite
frankly. It might have been the best I've ever seen – those lush
hills, somewhere up in which Domenico Rosiello was born. I
went to bed early ahead of the morning's pilgrimage and Dyson's
arrival in the afternoon.

Next morning, I set off for Sommocolonia just after dawn.
Dyson still hadn't messaged to tell me what time he'd be arriving,
and his phone went to voicemail so I left him a message with
the address of the hotel and told him I'd be back early afternoon.
Then I set out on a two-hour climb up a winding road with no
footpath, along which cars came irregularly but fast in both
directions, beeping their horns as they approached the bends,
giving you just enough time to jump towards the vertiginous
roadside as they passed.

By the time I'd reached the narrow and cracked village road,
beyond the last turn-off for other hill towns, the traffic had died
altogether. As I marshalled my energies for this last stretch I
thought about Great-grandad Domenico.

Few stories have come down about him. There's always been
a shared notion about the 'Italianness' of the family, of how
Great-granny Millie kept his spirit alive with marketplace paintings of Lucca on the living room walls, Paolo Tosti records, and
spaghetti bolognese, decades before it became a commonplace
dish in Britain. But this familial mythos is pretty specious really.
We have no real claim to a meaningful heritage from the man,
chiefly because we know so little about him. He was born in
1892, settled in Clerkenwell after his voyage over, worked on the
docks, met Millie at a dance in Leicester Square in 1925, married
her a month later before moving with her to Hull to work on the
docks there. He smoked constantly, and died in 1937, when
Grandad was six. Beyond that . . . *niente*. In terms of what

personal, human traits we might share with him, we have basically nothing. I certainly haven't inherited his presumed complexion or ability to withstand heat and altitude; I was sweating profusely as I reached his hailing place.

I don't know what I was hoping to find up there. Certainly I'd built the moment up in my head for weeks, envisaged it as some kind of homecoming into a bucolic dreamspace of exotic personal meaning, as if I might find an old man who looked like Grandad snoozing on a porch; or an old woman like Granny Elsie kneading dough and singing a *canzone* to the birds through an open kitchen door; or my dad huffing as he cycled with a pannier of vegetables along a cobbled path; or your dad pouring a glass of wine on a *terrazza* while our mothers frown at him and beat a dusty rug in the background; or you, perhaps, in a small workshop, concentrating hard on some important artisanal task; or myself, even, glimpsed abed with Neevie, through an uncurtained window. Instead, what I found was a small village comprised almost entirely of unoccupied holiday homes.

After walking for a couple of minutes and seeing no signs of life, only cute garden ornaments and breeze-ruffled patio umbrellas, I reached a crumbling but apparently still operational church. Certainly, its bell still clangs away in the cuboid belfry on the hour, but there was no sign of any human campanological presence therein. I was hoping to discover here a graveyard (and, perhaps, a baroque Rosiello family tomb withal), but there wasn't one. There were, however, several war memorials knocking about, and engraved on one I found two Rosiellos: Alfredo (*civili*), and Venanzio (*milita*).

Mildly excited by discovery of possible, very distant relatives, I texted my dad and then found yet more war memorials. The place was one big hilltop shrine to the Ultima Guerra. On cue, dad (blates just sitting on the 15-year-old family PC googling away furiously) replied to say these were probably the casualties of the 'Battle of Garfagnana', Christmas 1944 – a key engagement of the German assault on the 'Gothic Line' – which he reckoned could make a good film, as it has, he said, 'everything: ordinary people, suspense, action, hand-to-hand combat, prejudice [from the locals towards the African-American troops stationed here] short-term defeat, but ultimate victory.' Later one of my hoteliers told me that Spike Lee had already beaten him to it with *Miracle at St. Anna*. Didn't have the heart to let Dad know, as it would only represent another dream down the pan, along with the home beer brewing (it tasted bad) and the conversion of the back garden into a 'permaculture forest' (slugs).

I also sent a photo of the war memorial and a couple of shots of the village to your dad and he replied to say it looked 'marvellously unspoiled' and that it was good to hear from me and that he and your mum hoped I was having an 'illuminative trip'. After replying that it was 'fascinating to be up here' and that I hoped they were both doing okay, I wandered around the church grounds. In the shade of an apple tree copse were a small wooden bar and some plastic chairs, set up for a party that might have happened 20 years ago.

I then followed the narrow road to the farthest end of the village and just when I was about to give up any hope of encountering human presence, I heard voices. Following the sound, I passed along a high coniferous hedgerow, emerging at the end of a driveway to see a large family group eating lunch in a garden. There were at least three generations, maybe four – from a small baby under a parasol to a wise-eyed old woman in a wide brimmed hat, and between them at least a dozen other gregarious people of all ages, laughing over mismatched garden tables, laden with huge dishes of pasta, meat and salad.

'*Ciao*,' a few shouted as I passed by the gate. Here was the real Italy, what I'd ventured so far from the prescribed path for, authentic Tuscan life as it was still lived, by a happy few, up here in the hills.

'*Ciao! Ciao! Buongiorno*,' I shouted back, bowing slightly out of respect for the nobility of their way of life. My spirits lifted, I walked on towards a stile at the end of the lane. A few yards beyond the garden I heard a voice call 'pass the ketchup, Andrew!' in a broad Scottish accent.

I'd now reached the end of the village. Ahead ran a narrow path between the hillside and the last garden wall of the empty settlement. This was signed as 'Via Buffalo', a reference to the name of the US army division stationed there, upon whose story Lee's film is based. Another signpost showed that the path led eventually back down to Barga. I sat up on the wall and looked back over the village whence we, in a sense, came.

As I said, I don't know what I'd been hoping to find here. Not exactly rustic doppelgangers of our family but, at least some sign of life, of continuity with a past that our ancestors once knew. And the fact that I found only empty holiday homes and war graves and a mechanised bell needlessly parcelling out time forever and a Scottish family – who, it must be said, were very friendly – was disappointing. I don't mean their being Scottish disappointed me, or rather it *was* their being Scottish that disappointed me, but not in a sense that I have anything against Scottish people. I couldn't help being disappointed to discover a Scottish family, and only a Scottish family, *here,* like me, I assume, reconnecting with some ephemeral sense of heritage or historical belonging. Clearly they'd made their collective peace with what they'd found – the desertedness, the absence of community, the sense that regular life had just got up and marched off downhill many years ago and that all that was left now were curious half-memories and an uneasy quiet – better than I was able to. Perhaps they were, unlike us, genuinely an Italian family in some meaningful way, in more than name only.

I tried to force some sort of substance, some sort of meaning into my contemplation of the village; to somehow bring Domenico to imaginative life as a young man here, but I had nothing. I could barely even remember what he looked like in the photos. Everything felt truly flat now.

I'd obviously built the moment up too much, expecting it to be some kind of apex of my trip – a rich, wholesome, emotional experience that would somehow make sense of the last few months, one that would result in me understanding myself better, in a kind of deep, essential way that would help clarify and even strengthen my relationship with my family, including you.

So to come and find nothing but locked houses and learn nothing except that war once devastated this place and that, even before then, people had started to leave and were now long lost to the rest of the world was dispiriting, as if I'd been denied some long-promised release.

It made me question the whole enterprise of writing to you like this. Is it really worthwhile? Is it really helping me enjoy or appreciate or make sense of my journey or to deal with its petty frustrations and challenges? Is it helping bring the two of us closer in any real way? Or is it just . . . mad . . . to keep firing off these endless missives and receive no reply?

Okay. Just had to have a short break there. That all got a bit much. Also wanted to go and get a beer. Getting dark now and hardly anybody else on deck – very atmospheric! Anyway, where was I? Ah yes, Sommocolonia. Well, it wasn't all bleak.

The walk back down the hill did me good, I think, following an upliftingly wild route, taking in sweeping hill views, rushing streams and terrifying, snarling dogs held back only by thin wire fences. I arrived back into Barga tired and a little cheered, resolving (once again) to pull myself together. Hereditarily affirmative catharsis or none, there was still enjoyment ahead. In just a few days, I would be with Neevie in Athens, which of course will be the real apex of the trip; Sommocolonia was only ever going to be a kind of anticipatory sub-summit. So in the end it didn't really matter if it was a bit of a let-down. And, what's more, in the even nearer term, I had Dyson's arrival to look forward to – in just a matter of hours, in fact, the old lad and I would be settling in with a couple of *birras* on some elevated patio overlooking the hills.

Except we wouldn't, because as soon as I got back into signal range a text came through from Dyson to say he had been held up doing 'reshoots' in Budapest, meaning he wouldn't make it to Italy until the morning and so would meet me in Florence around lunchtime.

It was a mark of how out of sorts I was feeling, I suppose, that I didn't immediately sprint back to the hotel to start looking online to work out how I was going to get to Florence next day without Dyson to drive me. Instead, in a fit of weary apathy, I elected to leave that issue for – to quote the young Jerry Seinfeld – 'Morning Guy' to deal with and just trudge back with no sort of urgency, failing to shake my resentment at Dyson for the situation. Not really about the added cost or inconvenience of having to make my way to Florence by public transport, but because I'd looked forward to the drive to Florence, it being both the only chance of a proper car journey taken on my trip and the closest I'd come to the Kerouacian vision of travel.

Once again, I'd had a clear image in my head about how things were supposed to play out. I saw Dyson rolling up in front of the hotel in an Italian drop-top – an affordable one obviously, like a Fiat Spider, say, rather than a Lamborghini (even in phantasy, I've one eye on costs) and myself sauntering out and down the hotel's Palladian staircase, with sunglasses and cigarette of course – even though I don't smoke and rarely wear sunglasses – to chuck my holdall into the back and jump, literally jump, into the front passenger seat, whereupon I'd manage to connect my phone to the car's Bluetooth at the first attempt and sit back as Dyson negotiated treacherous mountain bends with impressive, almost native ease, as *DAMN* blasted from the car's mid-range speakers, until we hit the *autostrade*, disturbed air banging off the windscreen as we sped onwards, like Virgil and Dante flying from the undergloom of hell. But it wasn't to be, alas.

So no beers with Dyson that night. Instead I walked to the highest point in the town, the Duomo di San Cristoforo, a hard-edged Romanesque mini cathedral in white marble. The sun was cresting over a distant peak, turning the valley and its chestnut forest a deep blue. The small, square lights of the hill villages were constellating all around, drawing giddy appreciation from the dozen or so other tourists standing nearby on the wide marble platform. I stared out for as long as I could, itching with melancholy. When the sun lowered beneath the far hilltop I walked back to the hotel and to bed.

Over breakfast the next morning, I established that Florence, aka Firenze, (which is perhaps the most *tonally* different native city name from its English name of all encountered so far), was three hours and only 15 euros by train.

And so I continued my journey, writing up a few Italian reflections for you, then reading a few pages of *Don Quixote* before falling asleep. I'd paid little regard to what was expected of me in Florence, having only skimmed over this section of the Trip Pack back in June, so I glanced over it as I walked from the train station to where Dyson had texted to say he was waiting, in a bar near the Urb. The Home's chief feature was its location, on a quiet side street just a few metres back from the Piazza del Duomo, which looked to be something of a touristic epicentre.

My brief was to sample Florence's 'essential' tourist experiences, which were all within spitting distance of the Urb, on my own terms, enjoying the 'Essential Florence Home', which I was to use (and of course describe) as a kind of ideal pad from which to . . . [dynamic verb] this [enticing adjective] city. In her notes Bethan Decker had written to 'forget *authenticity* and *hidden gems* here. Nobody goes to Florence for the unseen Florence: they go for the *seen* Florence, the famous Florence. It's the city of the Grand Tour. It's Heritage City *non pareil,* so give it to them.'

The Home looked pretty swanky from its pictures, with high ceilings and expensive furniture, but it was only a one-bed, so my plan was that Dyson would take the sofa and I would go and meet the Host – Magda, '53, Swimmer, The beautiful life' – while he waited covertly nearby and then once she'd cleared off, I'd text him instruction to join me.

In the event though, I was so excited to see Dyson on a bar terrace a few doors down from the Urb that I completely forgot this plan. The mere sight of the bastard with his Peroni and his Cheshire Cat grin, looking every inch the international man of adverts in backwards baseball cap and fashionable trainers, put me, finally, into a long-craved good mood. As he gave me a strapping, back-slapping embrace, and said 'what a joy to see you mate' about six times, I felt flushed with relief at his being here, the first friend I'd seen in weeks, the only person, save for Neevie, who'd actually wanted to come and meet up with me.

Obviously if it'd been you sitting there tugging on a roll-up and soaking up the Italian sun, I'd have been a great deal happier. But as a next best thing, Dyson's arrival, characteristically relaxed and tardy, wasn't bad. It struck me as I sat with him and necked a quick half Peroni, that for all his faults Dyson was a committed, enthusiastic friend, and one I was very glad to see.

And so of course I forgot all about the plan to hide him and, after slamming my empty glass down on the *terrazza* table, just hurriedly bade him follow me up three flights to the apartment, whereupon he somehow ended up standing in front of me in the doorway and thus greeting Magda before I managed to, loudly shouting '*Bongiorno! Bongiornio signorita!*' in his gravelly voice and kissing her, I think, a total of four times on her two cheeks. She received us with a neutral demeanour and ushered us quietly inside.

What's worse probably is that I didn't even really explain to Magda who Dyson was. I just completely forgot myself and carried on like I was a regular Guest checking in for a fun mini-break and trying to hurry through the Welcome process as fast as possible. There's a chance she inferred simply that he was my partner, as it would of course be perfectly normal for someone to bring a partner on a work trip like this. But, thinking about it now, it's more likely that she read the situation exactly right: he was a boisterous *amico* whose purpose for being there was definitively not to assist in the marketing of her apartment, this loud unexplained man in a backwards baseball cap asking for recommendations for bars. In fact, it was only after Dyson had pecked her a few more times and bade her *addio* on the doorstep, and I'd stood behind him to assure her that I did have her number and that I would call her if I needed to, and that I did understand everything and that I did know everything I needed to know about the apartment and would leave my keys on the table upon departure, did it occur to me that I hadn't managed to ask her anything to help give substance to my copy.

By this point though, writing about Hosts and Homes and Experiences from a place of imagination and invention has proven so easy and effective that I wasn't too worried. I didn't need Magda to tell me how close her apartment was to the Uffizi or the Accademia or the cathedral. I would be able to discover all of these facts easily enough for myself.

When Magda had gone, Dyson and I sat around for a while. He lay back on the sofa, still with his cap on and told me a few stories from the fortnight he'd just spent in Budapest, such as when he got drunk and nearly missed his cab to the first day of filming or when he got drunk and nearly missed his flight. In fact, most of the stories concerned him getting drunk and nearly missing things.

We then went back to the bar at which we'd met and sunk a couple more Peronis. It was only now that Dyson saw fit to reveal the real reason he'd been late to meeting me: he'd logged on to Tinder in the customs queue at Bologna airport and within 40 minutes was at dinner with an American woman who was doing a PhD in European Law at the university. 'One thing led to another . . .' Dyson said. A gnomic catchphrase I've heard him use many times before.

He smiled and became absorbed by his phone, specifically by Tinder.

Was he actually intending to arrange a Tinder date while here in Florence for all of two days?

'Nah man,' he replied with a weary laugh. 'It's just a great way to get local knowledge.'

'What sort of local knowledge?' I asked.

'Tips on shit to do,' he said. 'The genuine, authentic stuff rather than the tourist shit.'

'Ah. I think I am quite committed to the tourist shit. Y'know. For work.'

'What sort of stuff?' he asked, frowning as he looked fleetingly up from his phone and glanced at the waitress as she passed over the terrace.

'Well, the big sell of the apartment is that it's so central,' I began explaining, and seeing that I had already lost him. 'So I need to sample all the classic central Florence stuff: Santa Maria, Uffizi, the Accademia—'

'Nah, you don't wanna bother with all that, man,' Dyson cut in. 'Let's find some real shit to do.'

Tired after travelling and probably tipsy after three bottled *birras*, I didn't quite have the mettle to tell Dyson that I had no choice but to do all the aforementioned, non-authentic stuff so that I could write about it and also write about how good it was having a nice flat to go back to and lie down in afterwards.

Instead I just asked how the Tinder interactions were going. He said he was now having a good chat with a 'nice German girl' called Hannah who, he said, spoke better English than me! She was in the city for a couple of days for a wedding. How this interaction might yield incisive Florentine lore I didn't bother to ask. Instead, I busied myself composing a breezy text to Neevie asking how she was getting on with work and stuff and telling her I was having a great time with Dyson (attaching a picture I'd taken of my beer for good measure). I almost said 'can't wait to see you next week' but stopped short for fear of seeming too keen. She replied quite quickly with the grinning emoji and a bunch of kisses, which was sweet, if a little unimaginative, though I know how busy she is, and we'll have plenty of time to catch up properly very soon . . .

Dyson apparently sated by his Tinder session, and I sufficiently rested, we deemed it time to explore. For a moment I considered suggesting going to one of the big tourist sites from Bethan Decker's list before closing time but, out of fecklessness and a desire not to cause a disagreement with Dyson, I decided to wait and make a proper fist of it the following day.

One of the women Dyson had been talking to had recommended seeing the sunset from a viewpoint called the 'Giardino delle Rose' ('Rose Garden') which Dyson relished saying over and over again for the entire half-hour it took to walk there, along with various other Italian words and phrases plucked from nearby signs and adverts.

We passed the cathedral, 'Il Duomo'. It seemed somehow subtle and naive at once, the decorative tone of the building pleasingly linear as if, I remarked (more to myself than Dyson, who was back on his phone), a reasonably artistic 10-year-old had drawn it with a stencil. (A later Google search revealed that the building 'exemplifies an early Italian Gothic style, ornamented with the characteristic inlaid marble panelling of Tuscan-style Romanesque architecture', which is more or less what I was driving at.) The square around the cathedral was full of tourists, as were the ensuing streets where people ambled, brandishing cameras and smartphones, many seeming woozy and blank-eyed in the evening haze.

The rose garden turned out to be a not-especially-authentic recommendation, at least using as a measure of authenticity the quantity of people sitting down on its steps with backpacks tucked securely between their knees. Unless, of course, Dyson's Tinder match had also matched with every tourist in Florence that day.

'Fuck's sake,' he muttered as we crossed the terrace stretching between the stairs and the dusty garden, whose roses seemed to have fallen victim to the ever-hottening summer. Here stood a line of *polizia*, casually toting machine guns as if they might at any moment spray down the hundreds of people sitting idly before them.

Dyson and I found space on the steps, by which I mean Dyson loudly asked a man to move his selfie stick, which he (Dyson) called '*il sticko*'. Dyson spotted an ice-cream van and went off to see if they sold beers, which I found a ridiculous speculation until he came back a couple of minutes later with two large Morettis.

Authentic or not, this was a cherishable experience, providing probably the best visuals of any Friday night session in living memory. The dome of the cathedral was prominent against the cityscape, which seemed to shake slightly in the heat. It could have been 1653. The low sun burnished the river. It seemed the afterglow of Europe, as if the last of the continent's light were burning out in some sad, romantic fire.

After a second Moretti, I raised the question of dinner. Bethan Decker had recommended a place near the apartment doing 'traditional Florentine cuisine with a global village twist'.

'Could be good,' Dyson said. 'I'm actually meeting Hannah at 9 and she doesn't want to go into the centre tonight because she needs to just chill before the wedding tomorrow.'

I privately marvelled at how familiar a sense Dyson had already gained of where this Hannah was and what she wanted from her evening. He didn't expand immediately on what this state of play meant for my dinner proposal but it transpired to determine that I, in a sort of unquestioning daze, ended up in a restaurant two miles away from the Rose Garden and even further from the Urb, with Dyson and with Hannah, who was friendly, with a round, oft-smiling face that turned mournful sometimes in the candlelight.

Dyson asked her all sorts of questions about the wedding and the other guests as if he really knew them:

'And what time will Johannes be getting there if he can't get away from work until 10 tonight?'

'Is Lenke going to be drinking after what happened at Tove's wedding?'

'I bet you hope you're not sitting next to Walter again, don't you?'

At just how rich and involved a preceding hinterland of Tinder conversation these questions implied the mind boggles, but Hannah didn't seem at all fazed and she answered them with a mildly fretful, mildly amused tone, the two of them becoming more and more tactile as the evening wore on. By the time my tiramisu dish was cleared they were openly getting off with each other at the table.

I decided to make my exit and drew a warm but rapid goodbye from the pair of them after I'd confirmed with Dyson that he had the address of the flat, though I guessed there was little chance he'd need it. Not tonight anyway.

Slightly jittery from overeating and the gently alienating dining experience, I felt too wired to sleep and so decided to walk for a bit.

At the Ponte Vecchio – a medieval arch bridge from whose picturesque sides hang small lodgings and shops – I saw a night walking tour and decided to surreptitiously join it, hanging back a few yards and pretending to be on my phone facing in the opposite direction to where everybody else was looking, so that the guide, a theatrical young man who seemed part Puck, part pirate, might believe, if he were to see me loitering, that I was some guy who just happened to be holding a smartphone near his tour group at every single one of its stopping places.

In the end I think my ruse was a little too cautious as I was generally too far away from the guide to get a coherent sense of what he was saying, catching only a series of half stories about renaissance patriarchs murdering their love rivals for no real reason and an extended account of Gian Gastone de' Medici, the last ruler of the dynasty, who, prone to 'being lonely' would spend 'hours each night drinking alone and looking at the moon'.

I was glad of the distraction anyway and returned to the apartment sometime after midnight, very much ready for a long sleep in the big bed.

Carrying my bags through from the living room I heard an unexpected noise coming from the bedroom. As I drew closer it was revealed unmistakably to be the sound of people having sex, either Dyson and Hannah or a couple of very, very louche intruders. Too tired even to become privately angry, I went back to the living room where I closed the shutters and collapsed on the sofa.

Many hours later I awoke with a flailing start, which brought me abruptly off my velvet sleeping place. I scrambled around like a lowly beast to find my jeans and my phone and then discovered that it was gone noon already.

I drank two pints of water, and, while I showered, resolved to make a quick exit, devour a *pannino* and coffee and then bomb round the Accademia, the Uffizi and the cathedral before they all closed. Not an ideal way to experience these famed establishments and even less so a way to sample the perfect well-balanced Florentine day, centring around my oh-so-convenient Home. But no matter. I was well capable by now of innocently and imaginatively embellishing half-realised tourist experiences.

Before heading out, I went down the corridor to check on Dyson and, to my mortal shock, found that the reports of intimate congress were *still* resounding. Or at least they were resounding again, resounding anew, it being unlikely, I suppose, that they had continued unabated for 13 hours. Though you never know with Dyson. Rest intervals enjoyed or not, I was surprised that this, this general state of affairs, was still on-going. Wasn't Hannah supposed to have left for the wedding already?

Quite miffed at Dyson's conduct by now, I hastily applied my factor 50 and got a great deal on my T-shirt and shorts. With no time to change, I bounded downstairs and made do with a bad cheese sandwich and machine coffee from a kiosk, which felt like some sort of sacrilege here but a necessary one given the growing time pressure.

Polystyrene cup in hand I made my way first to the Uffizi Gallery. There I saw I think genuinely the longest queue for anything I have ever seen in real life, outside of Alton Towers.

I walked around the building a bit just in case all these hundreds of people just might not have bothered to check for a quiet side entrance. After making a full circuit and accepting that the main doors represented the only way in, I went to the front and spoke to a lad in a red polo, no older than 18.

'How long does the queue take?' I asked.

'It depends where you stand?' he replied, quite ingenuously I think.

'The end,' I said.

He squinted through the bright afternoon to the back of the queue: 'Over two hours.'

I couldn't wait for two hours. Not, primarily at least, because

I didn't have the patience but more because I simply wouldn't survive standing in the sun for so long.

'Is there any way to get in quicker?' I asked.

'Yes you can buy online for a skip queue tomorrow,' he said.

This wasn't an option. I had to be on the train by 9am to stand any chance of making the ferry to Athens.

Accepting defeat, I went instead to the Accademia, where, amongst other hallowed works, Michelangelo's David lives and which surely would be enough of an Experience in and of itself. Lo and indeed behold, however, I found exactly the same scenario queue-wise – i.e. a queue as long as every lunchtime Post Office queue in a single London postcode put together.

I huffed an incredulous huff. They should warn people, I thought. Advertise the fact that queues might grow to such inordinate lengths during summer months, advise people to book online. It was at this point I saw a huge sign on the outside of the building warning, in several different languages, that queue times may be long during summer months and that visitors are advised to book online.

This was less than ideal. Wondering whether the two inaccessible galleries offered some kind of 'virtual tour' facility for me to call on when falsifying the accounts of my visits, I picked my way back through the madding crowds, to Il Duomo, which would have to serve as my only *actual* Essential Florentine Tourist experience. Naturally, when I got there, I found it closed for maintenance.

'Is there no chance of going in?' I asked the attendant who was standing there, completely unshaded beneath the afternoon sun, in a dark woollen suit with an astonishingly thick weave.

'You can go to Mass at six o' clock,' he said, the direction of his gaze obscured by sunglasses.

I thanked him and moved away.

In a shady corner of the Piazza I studied Maps to find at least one tourist opportunity in the vicinity that might, even at a stretch, be said to represent an 'Essential' Florentine experience, reasoning that just 'eating a pizza with an egg on it' probably wouldn't cut it.

The best shout seemed to be the Botanical Gardens, Google-listed as 'Giardino dei Semplici – the Garden of Simples, a botanical garden maintained by the University of Florence.'

Perhaps the slightly odd-sounding name might yield some sort of fun reference to the interminable Meerkat of the advertising realm, a jest which might appeal to a younger, more dynamic demographic than the one that might naturally gravitate towards a botanical garden, it being exactly the sort of place our mums would want to go on holiday, to everybody else's quiet exasperation. Still, I thought, Bethan Decker and Urb Family Members at large might appreciate the whimsical curveball quality of the inclusion. It would show initiative on my part, I thought, and playful discernment.

Sure enough, the gardens, tucked away on sleepy backstreets behind the Accademia, felt pretty inessential, deserted as they were and with most of their plants apparently dead. Perhaps there was nobody to look after them outside of academic term times.

Would an empty garden of dead plants cut it as an essential 'Heritage' experience? Probably not.

I had *niente*.

How much did it really matter though? As I traipsed back to the flat, I reassured myself Bethan Decker didn't really need *me* to go to all these well-known tourist sites. As she said herself, the point was that they were generic. I could easily repurpose the publicly available information about them and pass it off as drawn from my own lived experience. It was mainly about describing the convenience of the apartment, and the apartment itself, which I could capture in more intricate and genuine detail, though perhaps I'd make an omission of its apparent suitability as a love nest.

Satisfied that the day hadn't therefore been a total disaster, I made the short walk back to the Urb to get started on the fabricated copy. Nothing seemed to have moved since the morning. The kitchen shutters were still closed; my towel, now bone dry, still hung on the back of a kitchen chair; Dyson's bags remained scattered around the living room. That he must have gone straight out and not yet come back is what I concluded before I heard shuffling from the bedroom.

Dyson emerged a minute or two later, looking not as sheepish as he might have.

'Morning, mate,' he said.

'It's 5pm,' I said.

'Yeah. I meant figuratively, I guess.'

'So Hannah stayed over . . .' I said, with smile enough to imply agreeability without full-blown lasciviousness.

'Yeah,' said Dyson, mock-coyly. 'Sorry about taking the bedroom, man.'

'No problem.'

'Basically, there was like, five girls in one room where she was staying and she was worried that if she stayed there she wouldn't get enough sleep, so . . .'

I hadn't been looking for an explanation, especially not one premised on the notion that it had all been for the sake of Hannah getting a good night's sleep.

'It's fine, mate, honestly.'

'Cool,' he said, turning his head back towards the bedroom at the sound of footsteps in the corridor.

'Wait, is she still here?' I asked.

'No,' said Dyson.

'Then wh—'

Before I could finish the question, a woman who wasn't Hannah stepped into the living room. This woman had dark hair and looked like the sort of person who could make a living posting selfies to Instagram if she so wished. She was naked save for a towel.

'This is Chiara. Chiara this is Mark,' Dyson said.

'*Ciao* Chiara,' I said.

'*Ciao* Mark,' Chiara replied, in a broad Geordie accent. 'I'm just gonna get a shower,' she said, ruffling Dyson's hair.

'All right, babe,' he replied, smiling after her as she went.

Hearing the bathroom door close I gave Dyson a look of bemusement.

'Yeah, sorry about all the coming and going,' he said.

'Who's she, then?' I said.

'Chiara,' he said, as if I might have forgotten learning her name 30 seconds earlier.

'How did you meet her, I mean.'

'Oh,' he said, 'well, Hannah had to go somewhere.'

'To the wedding,' I said.

'Exactly yeah, so I got up, but you were out, so I went on Tinder just to talk to people about the city and try get some authentic tips. And that's how I got talking to Chiara.'

'Right,' I said.

'And one thing led to another . . .'

'Isn't she English though?'

'From Gateshead, yeah.'

'So why would she be able to give you authentic local tips?'

'That's a very close-minded attitude Mark. You don't have to be from a place to know it.'

'True.'

'She suggested,' he said, with a slightly proud tone, 'the Uffizi Gallery. Appar—'

'I just tried to go there,' I said. 'Queue was massive.'

'How massive?'

'Two hours.'

'Fucking hell, that's like Nemesis!'

'Yep.'

Chiara now returned querying the whereabouts of Dyson's shower gel.

'Mark says the queue at the Uffizi is two hours long!' he told her as he scoured the floor for his wash bag.

'Woah. That's like Nemesis!' she said.

'Exactly,' said Dyson.

'What are we gonna do, then?' she asked, water dripping from her hair onto wooden floorboards.

'Dunno. What are you thinking, Mark?'

'There's Mass at the cathedral at six,' I joked.

'That sounds great,' Chiara replied. 'I'll just go get ready.'

'Is she serious?' I asked Dyson as she disappeared again.

'Think so,' he said. 'She's very Catholic. Although only in a spiritual sense.'

I pondered in what other sense it might be possible to be Catholic, but not aloud.

'I think we should respect her religion if she wants to go to Mass,' Dyson said. I said nothing, having no better ideas.

And so it was that I took Mass at the Duomo with my old friend Dyson and my new friend Chiara.

It's quite pleasant, attending Mass at the Duomo. If you're able to suppress every screaming moral objection that erupts at the mere countenancing of this deeply rotten and hypocritical institutional ritual of sin-forbidding, you might, through the healing power of catastrophic boredom and strange Latinate cadences, manage to shake off some of the annoyances that have been dogging you for hours, if not days.

It would even go some way to providing some authentic experiential content for the copy, which would, I now accepted given the lateness of the hour, have to be written on the train to Bari the next morning. At this stage, all I wanted was food. And so I found myself accompanying Dyson and Chiara to dinner, which was an uncannily similar experience to the previous evening's, with Dyson talking to Chiara as if they were partners of seven years and me feeling like their teenage son, sullenly slurping up my *pappardelle* and speckling my big white napkin with sauce.

Chiara was perfectly pleasant as it turned out, a model originally from the North East, now living in London 'at least four months a year', she'd been working in Milan and had come to Florence to just be on her own for a few days. I opted not to ask whether spending the whole day with Dyson didn't somewhat undermine her plan, since they seemed so happy together, laughing away in the candlelight. I almost felt awkward and lonely as their third wheel, but knowing that in just under 48 hours I'd be enjoying a similar experience with Neevie gave me solace.

She told Dyson that she wanted to 'stay at his' again, so as we all walked home together, I nipped into a chemist under the ruse of buying deodorant (in reality earplugs).

The plugs were, if anything, too effective because I slept through my alarm, set for seven, and awoke just after eight, an hour before my train was due to leave. I decided to forsake showering and breakfast and even the most instant of coffees, conscious that if I missed this train I wouldn't make it to Bari today, meaning I'd miss the overnight ferry to Athens and be late to meet Neevie which would leave her there on her own and potentially with nowhere to stay. Besides, I'd also end up missing the Experiences scheduled for the morning, which would spell trouble with Bethan Decker.

After downing a pint of water and doing a perfunctory tidy of the kitchen, I flung my scattered belongings into my bag and had just started spraying on sun cream when I remembered Dyson and Chiara.

I went down the corridor to the bedroom. No need to tell you by now what I heard. I knocked loudly – they'd had their fun. The sounds of the enterprise within swiftly stopped but there came no reply and so I knocked again.

'Hello?' Dyson said with the querying tone of a man surprised at the very notion of another human being even *existing. She's all states* . . . and all that, I suppose.

'We need to go, Dyson.'

'Two minutes, mate.'

I returned to the living room where I took out my train tickets, printed a month ago in London, and put them on top of my bag. Then I put them back in my bag as there was such a thing as being too prepared.

After assuring myself I was as ready to go as I could possibly be, I sat on the sofa arm and made a great effort not to be the guy who sullenly resents other people's romantic, or at least erotic, fortunes. I was merely, I told myself, a man who was at risk of missing a train. And a ferry. And work appointments. And a romantic engagement of my own that could, quite seriously, amount to be the difference between the rest of my life being good or bad.

It had been at least five minutes now. I went into the corridor and found Dyson striding towards me, naked but for a towel, which was not even properly wrapped around his waist but merely held pinched with his hand.

'So when do we need to be out, mate?' he said.

'I need to go right now!' I half shouted.

'I just mean what time do we need to check out,' he said in a mollifying tone.

'We all need to go now.'

'But we could stay unt—'

'*No*,' I said, turning on my heel.

I heard Dyson return to the bedroom and lamentingly give Chiara the news.

Feasibly, I could have left them there and trusted that they would leave before the 10am checkout time, but I wasn't feeling generous. Also I feared what would happen if Magda came in and heard what I'd been hearing. And so, I put my bag on my back and stood by the door and waited a further five minutes for them to finally emerge, both looking effortlessly attractive in virtually identical outfits – white vests and dark shorts revealing intricate tattoos; caps, shades and new trainers. Were I not mono-maniacally focussed on just getting to the train I probably would have felt extra unfashionable and more middle-aged American tourist-like than ever.

'Really sorry for the wait,' Chiara said. 'We slept through the alarm.'

'No problem,' I said.

On the street I gave them both a rushed hug and had already started running while Dyson was still mid-sentence in instructing me to give Neevie a big hug from him even though he'd never met her.

I ran through the already densely peopled streets, which I knew, with the heavy bag on my back, was barely quicker than walking and made me look stupid, but dignity, like everything else, was out of the window now. I had seven minutes to make a distance that Maps estimated to be a ten-minute walk. At least three times I collided with the most undeserving of people: an elderly man, a small child, a street performer pretending to float on a magic carpet. But in the end, against, if not all then at least the majority of odds, I made it, haring through the dim station and throwing myself onto the hulking train just before the doors beeped to a terminal close.

I found my seat where I downed my water bottle and sat gasping for several minutes, to the visible annoyance of the man sitting next to me who was looking at spreadsheets on a leather-bound tablet. Within half an hour we'd reached Bologna, where I changed, bought a *pannino* and made my next train with minutes to spare.

From here it was just one train to Bari where, all being well, I'd have at least four hours' clearance to make the ferry, and enough time to get the copy written.

This train, a 'Tren Italia' service (not to be confused with an 'ITALO TRENO' one) had compartments instead of rows, a seating format I always relish as it makes the journey feel exciting and sophisticated and also as if somebody is going to be camply murdered. Determining, however, that there were no obvious intimations of elaborate lethal intent in my six-person carriage, I settled in, feeling almost content. I was going to make it to Athens on time. Once again, I felt slightly ashamed at having panicked at all. Now, with all my thoughts fixed on Greece and Neevie, I took out my tablet, relaxing with the prospect of having a few uninterrupted hours to work on my copy and notes to you.

But this would not be a six-hour train journey. Around 2pm – not very far into a fictive description of the statues room at the Uffizi, my only knowledge of which I was drawing from a slightly blurry photo on the gallery's website – the train came to a rumbling, unscheduled halt.

I thought nothing of it at first but after a few minutes, I began to worry, cued by the passengers around me from whom I gathered, via the universal language of bodily perturbation and loud, repetitive conversation, that something was up.

Do you remember when Grandad gave us the lesson in Italian hand gestures? I don't remember any of them distinctly, only his assertion that for Italians a vast range of meaning can be conveyed by manual expression alone. They were along the lines of:

fingers pinched as if holding some fresh herbs; wrist tilted towards head and wagging

= intense, emphatic interrogation, e.g. 'what the hell is this big pink Blobby man on TV every day?'

hand held up at shoulder height, thumb and fore finger pinched as if holding a lentil

= good, e.g. 'mmm, wine'.

There was no mistaking that the gestures being thrown around in the carriage were those of 'annoyance at the stoppage of an intercity train without contextualising explanation' or perhaps, more generically, just 'annoyance'.

arms cupped in front of the hips as if holding two melons
and
lots of head scratching

(which might be less an intra-nationally coded gesture and more just a reflexive, natural symptom of confusion).

Eventually a tannoy announcement came, seemingly given live by the conductor, lasting about two minutes. I waited for the English translation to come but it didn't. The train now slowly chugged into motion again, prompting no ostensible gladness in the compartment. Certainly, there were no gestures to that end anyway, lentil-holding or otherwise, and a few minutes later we stopped again, this time at a station where all the other people left the carriage, save an old woman whose stoic expression and thick cardigan implied her to be a lot less troubled by the delay and the heat than I felt.

When I realised the train wasn't preparing to move again, I turned to her and asked '*Parla Inglese?*'

'No,' she said with a look of contrition.

I nodded and set about constructing the requisite Italian

sentence in my head, assuming I would be able to say 'what is the problem?' in any romance language.

I swiftly realised that I could not. I didn't even know how to start the sentence. I wasn't confident that I knew a single Italian interrogative. I just stared at the old woman and shook my head, which unsettled her further. She said a long sentence in Italian, and I just shook my head again and sat back in my seat while she continued to speak, not necessarily to me, but apparently, about the regrettable nature of our lack of common linguistic ground.

After a while the conductor walked past the door and the old woman called to him. He came into the carriage and stared at me as she spoke to him. I heard them say '*Inglese*' a few times but not a single English word was spoken. The conductor then went off and the old woman said something else to me, at which I just screwed up my face in a kind of sad smile, intended to convey my gratitude for her efforts.

A few moments later the conductor returned, this time accompanied by a younger woman in a blazer with a *Tren Italia* pin badge who looked at me and said '*Inglese?*'

'*Sì*,' I said, quite proud of myself for merely knowing how to say 'yes'.

'The train is delay,' she said. 'There is fire on track.'

'Fire on the track?' I clarified, with a tone of mild alarm.

'Yes,' came her matter-of-fact reply.

'How long will be the delay be?' I asked.

She appeared not to understand.

'When will train move?' I said.

She held her arms half aloft with palms to the heavens – another clear enough gesture – and added, slightly tautologically, 'I don't know.'

The conductor and the woman in the blazer left and my helpful carriage-mate offered me a biscuit, which I accepted gladly, really quite hungry by now.

I tried and failed to distract myself – with my copy and my notes and books and newspapers and podcasts and crosswords

– from worries that I would miss the ferry to Athens and leave Neevie stranded and then miss check-in at the Urb and miss the first Experience. An hour went by, during which time the old woman's head moved hardly an inch, her beatific smile showing not a twitch.

I envied her quietude, assuming that, for her, the further delay of the train didn't represent the potential ruination of her entire summer.

Things were going about as badly as they reasonably could be. And then I got an email from Bethan Decker:

Mark,

I would have called but am currently in Lima at a conference event on eco-luxury hotels so can't really speak. I'm sorry to say I have three bones to pick with you. Well actually, two bones but the first bone is in two parts, so there are two sub-bones to it really: in Marseille you apparently left the VIP Fireworks event before midnight and thus *before the fireworks* and then in Madrid you *ran away* from the Tapas Dudes?? And this comes after another bone, which is that you did not complete the cycling self-tour in Barcelona but apparently just rode to the beach in completely the wrong direction! To be honest, that bone would probably have remained unpicked were it not for the emergence of the second bone/ sub-bones. Obviously the bike thing isn't that big a deal. When the guy called me up to try to explain it to me I'd just got off the plane and I had to ask the taxi driver to speak to the bike guy and try to work out what he was saying and even he couldn't understand it – something to do with the bike's inbuilt GPRS and a man called Matteo who lives inside the bike?? Something obviously got confused between dialects. Clearly you got lost or something. But the point is you should have told someone – either the bike company or me afterwards. And the stuff in Madrid is just . . . bizarre. Were you feeling alright? Are you ill or something? What's going on, Mark? I haven't heard anything from any other Hosts yet. Elisabeth in Paris said you were very polite, which is obviously good, but I now feel I have to check in with the others to make sure everything's been satisfactory. You must tell me as soon as problems come up in future. How are you getting on with your Florence copy? I was expecting it last night.

Don't mean to nag but after the bones I'm starting to worry!

Bx

Not good. Though at least it took my mind temporarily off the fact the train was still inexplicably stationary, the fact of Bethan Decker's dissatisfaction and the prospect of what might happen once she'd checked in with the various other Hosts whom I'd annoyed/ fobbed off etc. managing to eclipse my existing immediate worries. But then I had the train problem to take my mind off the Bethan Decker problem. When thinking about one became too much, I just thought about the other one, which is a sort of weird upside to having two big problems going on rather than just one. Sort of like 'every cloud has a silver lining' except more like 'every cloud has another cloud near it', which is truer in a way.

Beginning to feel as if my head might explode with guilt and worry and clouds and bones, I decided to get off the train for some fresh air – or at least, some very hot, dry air. Stepping down from the carriage side, as soon as my bare leg found sunlight it began to bristle with heat. I hurried towards the mid-platform shade and surveyed the scene. There was a remarkable stillness over things, which, given the context, was pretty annoying. Several of the other passengers had taken to the platform too. A few were smoking, some alone, others in conversive groups. An elegant woman with fine jewellery and high heels chatted good-naturedly with a scruffy man with a neck tattoo and I felt for a second as if I were in some GCSE anthology poem about social disruptions bringing about unlikely kinship. One guy had taken off his shirt and was lying flat out on the hard ground sunbathing. Another had produced a deckchair and sat watching something on his phone with headphones in.

Why was nobody furious? That no other person was showing even the remotest desire to leave this limbo I found personally offensive. The station sign reading 'Termoli' stood in front of a wall so high as to preclude sight beyond it. Vision the other way was denied by the big train and the station building. The most extensive view available was along the one-point perspective of the train tracks, whose tangling complexity got lost at a vanishing point made blurry by heat.

There seemed no likelihood of us moving any time soon, so I called Neevie a few times to relay the bad news, but it just kept going straight to voicemail. At the third or fourth attempt I decided just to leave her a message, a message so rambling and over-serious and humourless that I'm still cringing at it hours later.

It was genuinely like:

'Hey Neevie, how are you? Well, obviously you can't answer cos it's a voicemail, but hope you're good. ***huge weird noise that was like a laugh mixed with an inhalation, signifying nothing*** Erm. So yeah. Bit of an update, bit of an issue here. Here being Termoli, which I don't know where it is. I'm in Italy basically, but basically, I am on a train and it's delayed. Because of a fire on the track. I can't see a fire, but I believe there might be one somewhere. I have no idea when we're going to move. Anyway, the long and short of it is – I hope you're well by the way. I already said that. Sorry I'm not used to leaving voicemails. Who leaves voicemails these days? Does anyone listen to them even? I hope you do. Erm the point is, I just tried to call a couple of times and couldn't get through and I don't know when I'll get the chance again, although, by the looks of it, I might have all day here. Anyway, yeah, we're stuck and I hope we'll be moving soon. Just thought I'd let you know. Erm yeah. Speak to you soon. Best wishes.'

BEST WISHES! I actually said 'best wishes'. *And* I didn't even say the thing I was supposed to say which was that there was now a chance I'd be late to Athens. I called again and left another message clarifying this and apologising for the first message, which meant that the second message ended up being even longer and more rambling.

I looked around again and the air felt hotter and everybody on the platform even more serene and it was here that I snapped. Seeing the conductor step off the train and light a cigarette with the casual ease of someone slipping out the back door for a post-supper fag, I decided to confront him for some answers.

'Excuse me,' I said as I approached, apparently forgetting completely that I already knew he spoke no English.

He just looked at me.

'When will the train leave?' I asked and, when he made no attempt to answer, I asked again, almost shouting, '*When will it leave? You must have an idea!*'

He stared back at me, which I now accept was a perfectly normal reaction for a man being shouted at in another language. In the moment though, I read his blank and perhaps slightly amused expression as an antagonistic one. I did not, I'm sort of glad to report, continue to berate him but, if anything, I embarrassed myself more in doing what I did, which was turn away, giving a rasping, prolonged grunt like a tired 13-year-old and throwing my cap to the ground in front of me. There was laughter and a general ferment of surprise on the platform all around me as I stepped forwards to retrieve the hat.

Next, quite suddenly, I felt my legs give way – or perhaps, more honestly, I felt my legs weaken, a slight buckling of my knees and that jelly feeling you'd get at the end of a cross-country race and, probably relishing the mounting melodrama of the whole moment, I let myself collapse to the floor, where I grasped my cap and slapped it on the ground a couple of times as I thrashed around for a few angry seconds, like a suffocating salmon.

On the ground I felt sick with a dozen unhappy emotions: just to be conscious, just to be alive in that moment was an awful thing and then I felt a great final wave of anger rise and crash in a red flash before my vision.

And then calmness. It was like all negative emotion had burned out.

As I lay on the hot ground, I thought about a thing that happened to me when I was young, 15 or so. I'd been smoking weed with my friends, wearing about five layers because it was winter and then we ran, halfway across Beverley for some reason I can't remember, and we stopped outside Roy's shop, the newsagent outside which we'd sit most nights, to rest up on the wall and suddenly everything went strange, like the world was the image on an old TV set decaying into white noise and I could hear my friends saying 'Mark', 'Mark, are you okay, mate?' and so on. Next thing I knew I was on the floor, my mate Robbo's jumper beneath my head and as I opened my eyes I saw the three or four of them staring down at me, all quite scared.

'We thought you'd died,' Robbo said. 'Are you all right?'

I thought about it. I was all right. I was more all right than I had ever been before. I felt fresh, pure. Like I had just been reborn or had gone wild swimming.

I hadn't thought about that incident in years, but I remembered it now lying on the platform, because it was as if the very same thing had happened. I felt totally at ease for the first time in months and I was quite happy to just lie there, foetal in the public realm. It sounded now as if nobody was paying me any attention anyway, judging from the resumption of casual conversational noise all around.

After a moment I felt a gentle hand on my shoulder and looked up to see it belonged to the old woman, still wearing a cardigan and a beatific smile.

She said something in Italian and suddenly I understood her. I understood every word as she bade me stand up and ushered me back onto the train and into the carriage, where she insisted I eat four biscuits in swift succession, and, this done, suggested I take a small nap, which struck me as a good idea and when I woke again half an hour or so later, the train was moving and she was gone.

I arrived in Bari a couple of hours ago, allowing time for a tantalisingly brief wander before I had to check in for the ferry.

The place is not unlike Hull – a port city that has known better days. As I walked to the port for my ferry, I saw a newsstand relaying *La Republicca*'s headline:

'ARRIVANO IMMIGRANTI AL PORTO DI BARI. LA CITTÀ SI MOBILITA PER ACCOGLIERI'

('Immigrants arrive into the port of Bari. The city gets ready to welcome them' – you don't need me to translate obviously, I'm just showing off to you that I managed to.)

Half an hour later, with this echoing in my mind, I (all too easily) boarded the sumptuously appointed, high-speed ferry to Patras. Soon enough, I was up on deck watching Italy disappear, stewing in remembrance of the childhood holidays and school trips to France and lads' weekends to Amsterdam of my youth.

I then sat down here with a beer to write the copy, realised quickly that loading up complex photo galleries from over-designed museum websites would be a non-starter on this wifi so spent 10 minutes trying instead to convey the incredible price-quality ratio of Magda's apartment and then started emailing you.

I should really go in now. I've been the only soul on the deck for about half an hour and it is, I only now realise, fucking freezing, having been too absorbed by writing all this out to notice. That's probably what you call a flow state.

I feel a lot better now. Still some abiding worries of course: about Bethan Decker's ongoing dissatisfaction (god knows when I'm going to actually get the fake Florence copy done, let alone what the other Hosts might say when she asks them about me); about the job in general with the protests and everything; about you and all that happened and everything that's been left unresolved, churned up so messily in Sommocolonia; about the climate, as I've just read about wildfires breaking out in Greece, not far from Athens (he writes, beneath a great chimney billowing black exhaust invisibly into the night sky). About everything.

But I know that seeing Neevie will help appease all these worries, even the climate ones, as she's far better than me at not letting serious, rational concern collapse into nihilistic abandon.

Right, I think I'll go find some food that isn't biscuits and somewhere to charge my phone as it has now died and I haven't yet actually reassured Neevie that I am on track. And thereafter, I'd better find somewhere to sleep, as a cabin was three times the price of a regular fare. Everybody else has brought pillows and sleeping bags. I have nothing. For once in my life, I am definitively underprepared. It's actually quite thrilling. I hope the experience gives me a kind of intrepid, happy-wanderer air which will impress Neevie and not just a kind of 'frugal, under-slept man with neck ache' air, which will probably not impress her as much. Only time will tell.

Until Athens,

Mark

From: Mark Rosiello
To: Paris Rosiello
Jul 25; 21:17

Hello Paris,

I had an amazing time with Neevie in Athens, the travails of Italy now seeming a lifetime ago.

In the end, I slept long and well on the ferry, across a bank of airline-style seats and awoke to see the sun climbing over the Ionian islands.

Passage from the port of Patras to Athens, 200km over the Peloponnese, which might have been tedious in the midday heat, proved straightforward. Off the ferry, I was straight on a shuttle bus to the port entrance, and from there, straight onto the town bus to the coach station, then straight onto the Athens coach. Then came a delicious two-hour drive with a window-scape of violently blue coastal vistas. The fates were smiling . . .

Their lips straightened slightly, however, when I reached the bus station in Athens and found myself utterly discombobulated. The deep pertinence of the (possibly xenophobic) idiom 'it's all Greek to me' became apparent as I looked around for general signage or indeed any sort of intelligible linguistic marker. Whereas in France, Spain and Italy, I'd been able to infer, deduce and guess my way through the semiotic landscape, here, now in the Hellenic realm, I was utterly impotent. The Trip Pack simply said that my Urb Host, Karelina, would pick me up by the station entrance, but the station had at least three entrances and I couldn't even be sure I was at the right station!

A quick phone call to Karelina, who mercifully spoke good English, righted everything and within 10 minutes I was in the passenger seat of her car, heading to the apartment she hosts (and, I suspect, doesn't live in). She had the kind of smile that hits you like half a Valium and was immensely charming and helpful as she showed me around, before leaving me alone in the apartment, the *penthouse* apartment, the *penthouse* apartment overlooking the Acropolis, in an area called Koukaki, which, as you're likely well aware, is one of the most rapidly gentrifying neighbourhoods in the city.

Once again therefore, the less said about this place the better, it probably epitomising for you exactly the kind of decadent social cleansing I know you're prone to lamenting. I don't know whether the fact that the place costs about a fifth of what a comparable apartment would cost in London makes it better or worse. Probably worse. I shan't dwell too long either on the copious anti-Urb graffiti stencilled, in helpful English, all over the neighbourhood.

WAGE 500 PER MONTH
RENT 600 PER MONTH
FUCK URB.

Not the most elegant construction but I got the message.

What offset, if not completely nullified, my guilt was that I would be staying here with Neevie. I had a higher purpose: the pursuit of love.

I know you have forsaken your principles in the name of love in the past at least once – namely when you went into McDonald's in Bristol after a night out because the girl you fancied wanted nuggets, and you even ate some over-processed cadaver pieces from those poor over-bred chickens yourself, for example (shouts to Danika for telling me that one when I was biggin' you up at the fundraiser). Even the most hardened ascetics have their Achilles heels, their guilty pleasures, which they must carry an extra burden of guilt for, under the assumed weight of hypocrisy.

Meanwhile, I, hedonist (of a chronically neurotic and low-key stripe), generally just do more or less what I want, within a mainstream, liberal, consumer-capitalist ethical and economic frame *but* with a constant, mild sense of guilt. I do what I like most of the time and I feel low-level bad about it most of the time too. Except here I did not feel a pang of guilt, no familiar, steady chug of cortisol and adrenaline, but just lightness and ease and joy as Neevie and I sat together on the roof terrace and swam together in the otherwise empty communal pool and cooked together in the ultra-modern kitchen and lay together in the California King-size bed and looked out through our open balcony doors, the soft curtains illuminated, over the Acropolis and two thousand years of human reaching. Because that's what love does, especially new love: conquers all.

On the bus on the way to the airport, I'd grown nervous that the chemistry Neevie and I had might be lost, any amorous vibe that had developed between us across those four great dates, might now have dwindled by our being apart. But it's true what they say about hearts and absence and all that and I knew as much as soon as I saw her stride through the doors at Arrivals, resplendent in shorts and T-shirt, already more tanned than I was, absolutely beaming, positively glowing with clear gladness to see me. I was glad to see her too. I've hardly been gladder of anything.

I was worried that she'd think me cheap when I suggested we get the bus back into the city but she seemed to delight in the excitement and authenticity of the experience and high-fived me when I told her we'd saved 70 euros by not getting a cab and not making our own contribution to the local pollution. Anyway,

I'd brought champagne and proper champagne flutes from the apartment, so it felt extravagant in its own way.

At last, also, I'd been paid my second £1,000 from Urb, and swiftly spent a fairly inordinate chunk of it on provisions at the supermarket and so – both of us absolutely against waste, alimentary and financial – we attacked with relish the olives and the salads and the cheeses and the breads and the crisps and the roast cod and the wine and the beers and everything else besides. We then lay around the apartment for hours talking and watching rubbish on YouTube and doing everything you'd expect a new couple, one month separated, and now alone in a state of sultry luxury to do.

The next day we ate breakfast on the balcony before going up to the Acropolis, a fairly transcendental experience involving standing as long as possible before those deeply familiar and yet somehow disarmingly Ozymandian monuments, before the heat became unbearable and flight shade-wards necessary.

In the afternoon came the first Athenian Experience: a 'Cat Tour' of the Monastiraki neighbourhood, affording a chance to meet a very sociable colony of cats who live in a park. So. Much. Fun.

We ate dinner in Exarcheia, the anarchist neighbourhood supposedly lost to tourism that you repined at the fundraiser, although I can't fully acquiesce with your assessment that the neighbourhood has lost its edge: there are still riot police on patrol at its boundaries, if that's any consolation to you. The central square of the neighbourhood seems to function as a kind of support hub for refugees and other marginal groups, with a few guys muttering about cocaine to passers-by at the edges. There's graffiti everywhere and music and energy, and if a few fairy lights and trendy bonhomie in the bars and cafés represent social cleansing to you, then I have no answer. Neevie and I felt happy enough anyway as we drank ouzo and played dominoes with old Greek men, Neevie naturally being the one to start the conversation, even using a few Greek phrases she'd acquired from childhood island holidays. Their English, in turn, was good enough to tell me that I was bad at dominoes and also a '*very good-luck have man*', presumably for being with Neevie.

Next morning came the second Experience: a 'Romantic Boat Trip for Two to Peacock Island' – a private boat trip (yes another one; and this one just for two people arranged specifically by Bethan Decker when she learned Neevie would be joining me here!) to a remote islet called Agistri, 40km from Piraeus port, whence we rushed over the blue waters of the Saronic gulf, sitting close together on a blanket, our boatman Otis at the transom occasionally smiling down on us. As we approached the islet, Otis slowed the boat down, bringing the motor to a low rumble over which the sound of the waves' easy lapping could be enjoyed.

I can't recall ever having been to an islet before, and I wasn't disappointed – Agistri easily living up to its Trip Pack billing as 'A Haven of Peacocks', with the special-feathered specimens wandering freely and providing delectable visual accompaniment to our Greek salads and fries and bottles of Mythos beer. Neevie, I think, remained amused and not too perturbed by my neurot-icism over sun cream application and concern about swimming too close to rocks.

In the evening, Otis came to pick us up like a smiling dad at a school disco and we chugged back through the gulf at sunset, hues of gold and red pervading the sky. As we sipped our retained beers, the lights from the islands began to pierce the gloom. You can see how he might have dreamed it all, Homer – whoever he or she or they was/were – Saronically drifting, the impressions of islands in darkling layers on the horizon flanking channels and suggesting that untravell'd world, whose margin fades forever and ever . . .

Next morning, on Neevie's final day, we awoke before the dawn and climbed Mount Lycabettus, the limestone hill that juts above the city, apparently dropped on Athens by Athena herself as she travelled overhead and became enraged to the point of distraction by some bad news told to her by a crow. At the peak we found an Orthodox chapel with a paved platform, yielding more Homeric transcendence via a panoramic view of the city, pink in the dawn light. As jocund day stood tiptoe on the misty mountain tops, Neevie held my hand and, as I turned to look at her, she said: 'I'm really glad I'm here,' with a tone that told me that this was actually gonna be a thing.

And that's sort of how I hoped the last few days would play out. That's what I fantasised about, anyway, as I walked around Athens on my own.

Neevie didn't come.

I should have predicted it really. I mean, predicted isn't even the word. More accurately I should have clocked that she never *actually* told me she was coming. She intimated she was coming, yes. She heavily suggested, to an extent which, to me, felt as good as a confirmation, that she was coming (she'd even booked a flight for god's sake). But no *absolute promise* to that end did she ever make.

Here's what actually happened: labouring under the misapprehension that she was getting in to Athens in the late afternoon, I'd told her I'd come meet her at the airport, and then, having not heard back from her since before those voicemails at Termoli, dropped her a text just as I was going to sleep on the ferry to confirm that I was on track and would see her at the airport at about half five.

I awoke on the ferry, from a long and decent sleep across a bank of seats, to see the sun climbing over the Ionian islands and to find a voicemail from Neevie.

It was along these lines, (and this is probably not far off a direct transcription given how many times I've listened to it):

'Mark I'm so sorry! I've messed up massively! Basically, I can't come to Athens, which is obviously gutting. I really wish I could. Erm, and the reason I didn't let you know sooner is because even until, like, this afternoon, I was planning to. Like I'd booked the flight obviously and I even went and got currency the other day. *But* I'd been waiting to hear on this job, at the Edinburgh Fringe doing like marketing stuff for this venue. I applied for it ages ago and had given up on it really. And then they just called me this morning and said the person who they'd hired has fallen ill so it was mine if I wanted it. And I've just been debating in my head all day because I really wanted to come to Athens but I think I just can't afford to turn something like this down at the moment and it is quite a cool venue and it'll be good for contacts and my CV and all that boring stuff and the job starts Monday and I'm not prepared at all for it. I basically just need to spend the weekend reading press releases and trawling through emails and just trying get my head round everything. It would have been so fun just hanging out with you in Athens! Oh man. I mean I'll see you when you're back. It's my 30th in September so you've gotta come to that! I'll text you the date and stuff when I have a plan. Have an amazing time in Athens. Have an ouzo on me and . . . I can't remember where you said you go next, but have a really great time! I'll obviously be following you on the map. Do you care about the map? Am I just very sad? Probably. Oh and if your route comes anywhere near Edinburgh definitely give me a shout. I mean it probably doesn't but just in case, you're very welcome to come and stay. Okay I better go because I'm probably distracting you from lots of exciting things. I'm really sorry again for the fuck-up. I hope everything's okay back home as well. Like I said, give us a call if you wanna chat. I'm free any time. Well not any time. But I can make time. Take care! Bye!'

I couldn't resent her taking the job; if she was going to make the freelance thing work, she had to take whatever came up. I had to accept that. But it wasn't the thing from her voicemail that'd spun me out most, the thing that was causing me to go to back and listen to it over and over. That was the small detail towards the end of the message (this bit I have certainly memorised):

'I'm sure I'll see you when you're back. It's my 30th in September so you've gotta come to that.'

Obviously she'd see me when I was back, which she knew

would be in late August. The way I'd envisioned it (1,000 times over) was that she'd come, brandishing her summer-worn map, running into my arms at St Pancras telling me how much she'd missed me, having in Athens sworn many oaths of love.

Even if this were fanciful, I expected I'd at least see her before her birthday!

'See you when you get back from your trip; I'll invite you to my birthday party, whenever that is' isn't what you'd say to someone you're in a relationship with, however new and undefined. It's more like something you'd write to an old colleague whom you got with a few times and now don't really have any romantic feelings for but are keen to remain friendly with . . .

The ground shook, as if a distracted god had thrown down some mighty landmark in a fit of rage. On the coach from Patras I listened to Neevie's voicemail three times over and tried to settle on a calmer, non-catastrophic reading of things. She had to take the job at the Edinburgh Fringe, that was beyond question, but it nevertheless upset me that she wasn't coming. The prospect of her spending the whole summer in close proximity to hundreds of louchely self-confident theatre types while I traipsed around Europe on my own didn't exactly thrill me either.

So, what did happen in Athens? Well, I was welcomed by Karelina, who was charming and did have a nice smile but who also made a point of including in her Athens recommendations a beach, which, she said, was not 'full with Albanians and Pakistanis' unlike other beaches near the city. A detail I obviously omitted from my fantasy replaying of events.

Instead of meeting Neevie at the airport, I spent that first night lying around on my own in the bedroom, watching YouTube videos from my 'Watch it Again' list with the balcony doors closed for most of the evening, because of the acrid fumes from wildfires burning just outside the city which blew into the room when the wind was up.

Darkness fell and the wind died down and it felt as hot as it had in the afternoon, so I went up to the roof for a swim. But the pool was occupied by another group of about a dozen people from the adjoining penthouse, French, I think, and quite possibly another Urb party, judging from their coolness and youthfulness and the unconcerned manner in which they were throwing kitchen equipment into the underlit water.

I mustn't be perturbed, I mustn't be intimidated, I told myself. It shouldn't stop me from wanting to swim just because there were other people and a colander in the pool. And so I placed my T-shirt on a sun lounger and strode over.

Who knows, I thought, as I stood on the edge, assessing the pool's depth, dive-safety wise, I might even get talking to them, make friends with them. Perhaps a bit of wet and wild abandon was exactly what I needed tonight, as well as a chance to put my perhaps improved French to the test. It was at this point that I felt a shove in my back, and I flopped face first into the water, narrowly missing an impressively buoyant frying pan.

Resurfacing, I heard shrieking laughter all around and hardly looked up as I swam to the edge and clambered out, only glancing at my pusher, a boy hardly older than 18, grinning his apology. It wasn't, I realise, the greatest assault on my personhood, to be pushed into a pool only seconds before I intended to jump into it anyway. But the incident and the ensuing laughter were too much for my already tender ego to take and I gathered up my T-shirt and marched drippingly to bed.

Next day I did see the Acropolis and I was glad I did, but so indescribably hot was it that even though I was covered completely in factor 50 and wore a cap and a long-sleeved shirt with the collar up and had drunk four litres of water by 2pm and only left the shade for a maximum of 30 seconds at any time, I contracted something close to sunstroke.

After the briefest of looks at the Erechtheion, I could take no more and hurried downhill to the mercifully air-conditioned Acropolis Museum. About a third of the way round, as I stood wearily trying to study the supposedly reality-bestowing qualities of the sculpted folds in a statue's gown, I was approached by an attendant and asked if I required first aid, so overtly red and slumping and wan was I. I didn't, but I did quite quickly retire to rest for an hour or so in the air-conditioned café with iced waters and the pipe puzzle game.

The cat tour was actually boring and one of the cats scratched me (I'm still not fully convinced by the guide's insistence that it's not deep enough to merit hospital attention).

Next day I went on the Romantic Island Boat Trip for two, alone. Otis was perplexed that I had arrived on my own and when I, too defeated to offer any sort of dignity-preserving lie, told him what had happened he seemed even more upset than I was, shaking his head in uncomprehending dolour. When he finally brought the boat to a low-rumbling scud before the islet, he muttered 'she did not come' at least five times while staring into the algae-shadowed waters beneath.

In truth I saw no peacocks on the Peacock Islet, their 'Haven' apparently being confined to the hidden depths of the pine ridges above, from whence their plaintive notes warbled, as if to say: 'I wish all you fucking pricks on your sun loungers with your Greek salads and your small Heineken cans would get off this island'.

Here I swam a bit, read a bit, and thought about Neevie a lot, as I watched the members of the many present couples cuddling and rubbing creams and oils into one another's bodies. After two beers, Otis ferried me back across the gulf at sunset, and I did my best to cheer him up about Neevie's absence. He even managed a small smile as we bade each other goodbye at Piraeus.

Next morning, I didn't see Athens from the vantage of Mount Lycabettus at dawn because I slept in. In fact, I didn't manage to get up there until lunchtime when the air was dusty and sweltering and the platform crowded with tourists. I queued for 10 minutes to get a view that was, though slightly obscured by the backpack of a tall man in front of me, clear enough to reveal black acres on surrounding hills where the wildfires had burned.

In saying all this, I don't mean to sound down on Athens, which is unquestionably a brilliant city, a city of good and affordable restaurants which serve dips and wraps and salads that are the envy of the world; cypress-shaded backstreet bars, where the beers are a couple of euros and the savoury snacks are free; busy terraces in graffiti-covered neighbourhoods where fairy lights hang like pirate jewels; and of wonders of art and democracy, both ancient and modern.

That I knew all this to be true didn't make it any easier to focus on. All I could see was the sad truth of things, or a sad version of the truth anyway: the overwhelming number of home-less people on almost every street in the city centre; the acrid smell of the far-off fires that haunted the air, burning forests and crops and homes; of the frustration-borne graffiti to be found at every turn, much of it targeted at the EU, much of it targeted at Germany (a huge 'N€IN' festooned with yellow stars; a chain gang of prisoners carrying a stack of 100-euro bills; Angela Merkel with Mickey Mouse ears etc.), but much more of it targeted at tourists, like me.

And whenever I managed to relax for a minute and enjoy my cheap beer or my cheap dinner or my plush private apartment, I was hit with a tingling suspicion that the cheapness of my leisure experience came at the expense of an entire nation.

So, all things considered, I wasn't in the best state of mind for volunteering.

The initial arrangement had been made by Danika, following her off-hand comment at the fundraiser that I should come and help out at one of the charity's sites in Greece if I had the time while I was away. She was possibly just being polite but I took her at her word and, to be fair to her, she followed up quickly saying that even if you wouldn't be there, I should still come if I could make it work, and make it work I determined to.

Bethan Decker was fine about it back in June, the Golden Days when she still liked me and wasn't full of conspicuous doubt about my ongoing aptitude for the job. In fact, she was very happy, she said, to 'jiggle things around', because taking a week to go and work with 'the world's most unfortunate people' was exactly the kind of going-the-extra-mile that was 'so much a part of the Urb Human Touch', which meant we all wanted 'the places we love to be for everyone, from any background'.

And so it was that I arranged to go and do a week in Thessaloniki at the charity's warehouse. I wasn't able to volunteer in the camps themselves as that would have required more training and thus a longer commitment, but this, I told myself back in June was still Very Good of Me.

I have to admit, I'd been nervous about it all summer. The suspicion that I was perhaps not the brave, generous, enterprising volunteer hero that I've always quietly self-defined as was already creeping in, even before the Athenian catastrophe. By the time I was on the train leaving the capital, the feeling of aversion had become almost unbearable, manifesting now as a procession of intrusive visions of just how ill-suited for the coming experience I would be. I didn't know what exactly volunteering with displaced people, at the edge of a largely unwelcoming continent, on the cusp of a troubled hemispherical crossroads, would entail but I probably wasn't, my instincts told me, especially cut out for it.

Still, I had to do it now. I'd rented an Urb in central Thessaloniki, a small, private room in a shared apartment at the more affordable end of the spectrum – whose host, Sukie, an instantly very likeable woman in her early-fifties, welcomed me with measured and slightly nervous jollity. I apologised for how much I was sweating and asked to refill my water bottle as soon as we entered the kitchen. She told me it was fine: she herself had drunk six litres of water that day.

'In my ex-life I must have been a frog,' she joked.

'Yes, or a fish!' I added.

'No, a frog because I can be out of the water, I just like water,' she said, and that was the end of that riff.

I inferred that she lived on the income from renting out her two spare bedrooms on Urb, which seemed a logistical stretch given that I also met her son and daughter – both well into their twenties and who both came into the living room as I was talking to Sukie, acknowledged me briefly and politely in English, spoke to their mum for a few moments in Greek and then disappeared back into other rooms, of which there were seemingly only two.

So just their two bedrooms and 'my' room, in the rather cramped flat (with an admittedly spacious balcony). If the Human Touch, that supposed measure of domestic authenticity, was in evidence anywhere it was here.

The next morning having woken early and entered the living room, I found Sukie sleeping on the sofa. She awoke abruptly and insisted she had fallen asleep there unintentionally.

In terms of organising the volunteering, since those initial interactions with Danika, I'd mainly been in contact with a woman called Ilana, who apparently was 'more on the ground in Thessaloniki', insofar, I suppose, as she was literally *in Thessaloniki* and so necessarily *on the ground* there, whereas Danika was/is, I assume, in London. Ilana, whom I gather you've met, had told me to get to the warehouse some way out of the city itself for 10am and told me what buses to take.

Feeling not especially rested despite the long sleep, I took the two buses to the industrial near-wastelands which fringe the city and had breakfast – an instant coffee and microwaved *burek* – in a petrol station next to the warehouse.

At first look, the site seemed long-abandoned, its front yard littered with the rusting carcasses of vehicles and other unidentifiable machines. It was in better shape than the other buildings that lined this unholy stretch of road, however, many of whose company gates had rusted into illegibility, or whose roofs were collapsed or whose entire structures were burned virtually to shells. Inside, though, it was entirely functional, welcoming even, a warehouse space, which was a hive, as the cliché goes, of activity: dozens of people, of many ages, busily working away, moving, lifting, carrying within a matrix of stacked foodstuffs, clothing and various other provisions.

This is where you spent a lot of your time in Greece, isn't it? I could totally picture you here. Absolutely in your element.

Indeed, off to my right, three or four guys of your ilk – tall, long-haired (tied up for safety ofc) and obviously impressively competent at manual work – were toiling away. With my sun cream and cap and backpack I felt like a tourist invading a realm of actual purpose, which is of course what I was. I asked the closest person who happened to look the least currently engaged in serious machine work where new volunteers were supposed to go, and he directed me upstairs – without taking his eyes off a nearby man's efforts to cut a plank with a circular saw – where I found a dozen or so mostly young, mostly female volunteers sitting around a large table. I took a rickety office chair which squeaked as I sat down and looked up and smiled in case anybody had found it funny, which they hadn't. There was a bit of chat around the table, people sharing stories of relevant previous experiences – I kept silent, having nothing to add.

Now, Ilana, who struck me as 'strapping' if that makes any sense, large and healthy and focussed, came upstairs, wearing a polka-dot bandana and telling us that she'd be 'sorting us out'. She asked who was here for the first time today and only four of us put up our hands. She told the returning majority to go downstairs where Tom would direct them.

'Which one's Tom?' someone asked.

'The guy with the long hair,' Ilana replied.

'Which one?' someone else quipped and everybody laughed, and I laughed a bit too.

Ilana now asked the remaining four of us whether we'd volunteered before. Two had and the other hadn't, which made me feel slightly less alone in my lack of self-confidence, until my fellow debutant described herself as 'a yoga teacher, just trying to do my bit, ideally but not necessarily through yoga'.

'Hopefully there'll be a chance to do some yoga in the camps,' Ilana said, 'but it won't be the top priority.'

'That's fair,' the yoga teacher said, closing her eyes with some solemnity.

Ilana now turned to me. 'You're Mark, aren't you?'

'Yes,' I said.

'Paris's cousin, right?'

'Yes,' I said.

She paused. 'Okay. Thanks very much for coming. It's really good of you.'

Ilana gave us each a form to fill out, which included a box we ticked to say that if we died during the volunteering, we wouldn't try to sue the charity. Then we watched a video on Ilana's laptop about the charity and the work it does and the sorts of things we'd be doing during our time here. I struggled to take it all in, which was probably for the best as I likely would have found it even more upsetting if I had.

Ilana then led us downstairs to meet Tom, who turned out to be the man who'd earlier directed me upstairs. He gave the others the task of sorting huge sacks of donated clothes, and me that of preparing a pallet of foodstuffs to be delivered to one of the camps, taking an order sheet listing requested items (flour, sugar, cooking oil etc., requested by the 10kg) and retrieving the requisite amounts from the stockpiles.

This to me seemed an agreeable enough task. What I'd feared, I suppose, was being pushed beyond my comfort zone, either through exposure to human suffering unlike any I'd ever had to personally experience, or simply being required to show actual initiative, but this task, fetching items and stacking them on a pallet was well within my wheelhouse. It was fairly reminiscent in fact, and not necessarily in a bad way, of a summer job I did during my first year of uni, packing boxes of frozen chicken dippers near Gatwick. It might not have been trekking in the Andes or kayaking on the Amazon or whatever it was you did during your summer breaks, but it was (acknowledging I was only doing it for a few weeks for beer money and didn't have to try to live off it) strangely tolerable, almost pleasant at times: on hot days, when the temperature in the big freezers was a mercy and on hungover days when my mental fug would render the quiet, repetitive action strangely comforting.

Now there was no respite from the heat and no protective layer of post-crapulent fuzziness but still the task was, to begin with anyway, helpfully distracting, absorbing even – steady, unvarying in a calming way, with tangible and, ultimately, benevolent effects. Or it was until, after the packed crate had been lifted onto the van and dispatched and I was well onto my second order sheet, Tom came up to me to say instead of packing 200kg of flour and 50kg of sugar onto the last crate, as requested, I'd *in fact loaded 200kg of sugar and 50kg of flour* 'which was fucking helpful,' he snorted.

He then proceeded to explain to me the difference between flour and sugar and why it should have been obvious that flour would be required in greater quantities in the camp, as if I was a privileged Londoner who had no idea what I was doing and wasn't a proper volunteer, which really, really rankled despite being all too obviously true.

It was at this point that I snapped, which is a statement I now realise I've used more than once in the last few weeks. Maybe you can just snap and then snap again and then just keep snapping, perhaps infinitely for the rest of your life. Perhaps you just get used to snapping after a while. Snapping and snapping and snapping again, without increasing deleterious effect, might just become *my thing*. I'll be like one of those snap-on wristbands we had as kids which unfurled into a kind of stiff band, but, upon hard contact with the wrist, curled abruptly into a kind of bracelet.

'Fuck off,' I said.

Tom looked at me a moment, and then shook his head with a kind of wincing smile before walking away, back towards the large warehouse entrance where the van was being loaded. I feel almost as embarrassed about this outburst as I feel about what I said to you at the fundraiser, it being obviously less charged with personal emotion but no less pathetic in its mindless belligerence.

What really hurt was the feeling that I had failed. My one trivial attempt to do something good, something selfless during this entire summer of indulgences and I'd proven myself woefully incapable. What's more, I suppose, was the fact that this had been an effort to do something that *you would approve of*, to redeem myself in your eyes. Perhaps I'd thought of it as a tribute of sorts; I should have predicted it would go badly.

And so, when Tom had disappeared out of view I went back upstairs, picked up my bag and walked out of the warehouse, through the yard and onto the road towards Thessaloniki. As I passed along the railing at the front of the yard, I heard someone shout after me from the building entrance and turned to see that it was Ilana. I raised a dismissive arm and then kept on walking.

After about two minutes, I realised that even if I could remember the way back into the city centre the walk would take about six hours, so I traipsed back towards the warehouse to the bus stop opposite the one I'd got off at, a derelict, litter-ridden, shadeless structure by the edge of the busy road. 'I bet I'll have to wait the full 20 minutes for this bus,' I internally grumbled, for that was, my planning had revealed, how often the bus came. And in the event, I did wait 20 minutes. And then another 20 minutes. And then another. Cars and lorries appeared, shimmering on the horizon like beads of hot oil, before roaring by uncaringly, but no buses.

This was the perfect metaphor, I decided. For everything.

Me standing in this graveyard of South European industry, getting a taste of the reality faced by so many in this region who know a very different Europe to the one I know; people whom, I'd finally learned, I was incapable of helping or engaging with in any real sort of way, so morally and psychologically vitiated was I by a lifetime of conformity to the bankrupt credo of decadent individualism. I couldn't even put a few fucking sacks of sugar onto a crate without messing it up. I might as well, I thought, give up on everything as I'd given up on the volunteering.

And then the bus came.

Back at the Urb, I sat on my bed and tried to make sense of things. I'd messed up with Bethan Decker and the job (or at least I soon would have – once she'd heard from my various aggrieved Hosts). I'd messed up with Neevie. And now I'd messed up with the volunteering. They'd never let me go back now following my tantrum – if I couldn't hack receiving a mild telling off for messing up a simple job in a warehouse, what use could I be to anyone?

So the summer is, to all intents and purposes, over. The adventure is anyway. The Grand Tour, the epic journey, via which I was supposed to redeem a wasted youth, occasion a brighter, more fulfilling future. All brought to a bathetic end with one final cowardly, sulking act of retreat.

I feel like you'd be telling me 'I told you so' – that this whole enterprise, undertaken under Urb's sterile aegis, would feel ultimately too unrewarding and wearing to complete – were you actually to read this, that is; if you're actually able ever to read this; if this ever becomes more than just a futile exercise borne out of a probably futile hope that you'll fully recover; if you ever do reach a point where you're able to read again at all.

But I now don't know how likely that is. I'd really hoped I would have heard something by now, something more than that you continue to be stable and show 'basic reflexive responses' but they can't say how long it'll be until you start to show any sort of awareness again, or whether you ever will at all.

So this will be my last email, I think. Before I finish, I just want to say sorry, for making you angry that night. If you weren't so wound up as you cycled home, it might never have happened. Whatever people tell me about the accident, I can't help but feel this was a factor and that, being the last person you spoke to that night, the one who upset you, I bear some important responsibility for what happened.

And I want to say I'm sorry too if it seems like I've abandoned you. I almost didn't come on the trip. In those couple of weeks after the accident, I took my remaining holiday, told nobody at work what had happened and came to the hospital every day and sat by your side. Why didn't I tell Bethan Decker what had happened and that I couldn't do the trip? Genuinely, I thought you were going to wake up. I now appreciate how misguided a phrase 'wake up' is. How Hollywood a notion of brain injuries and subsequent recoveries it betrays . . . as if you might suddenly, after lying unconscious for a week, have opened your eyes, blinked for a few seconds, shouted 'where am I?' before jumping out of bed to high-five us all.

But the doctors gave us little to go on. Once a patient's in a coma, recovery can be very slow, they said, people either

advance to a conscious state, or . . . things can be more complicated.

Why shouldn't it have been the former? You're relatively young,
they said, the nature of your injury wasn't as severe as it might
have been . . . they induced coma quickly to prevent swelling on
your brain. You had a lot of factors on your side.

Surely, I thought, or hoped, at least – we all hoped – you would
return to consciousness quickly, and make a fast recovery and
that life would go on exactly as planned: we'd apologise profusely
to each other for what was said that night, you'd give me your
blessing to go on this trip and by the time I was home, we'd be
in the pub toasting to a very strange summer.

And then you went into a vegetative state and I couldn't fucking
take it. I couldn't take seeing you lying there, hooked up to
machines, with a now even less certain idea of what would happen
to you. I couldn't stand to see your fingers being squeezed with
pens and your face pressed and to ask what you might be feeling
and get no clear answer.

You might still recover, they said. You might even still make a
full recovery. But how likely was it? And when would it be? No
telling, no knowing.

So I decided to go.

I went to the Eurostar in a daze that morning. Things had
never felt less real. The rush-hour crowds at King's Cross were
a blur and the station noise was dim. This probably sounds
ridiculous or really dramatic but I knew I had to be out of the
country before things could make any sense again. Like the
unfamiliarity of things elsewhere – of language, and images, and
all the minute customs that define a place – would shock me
back to full consciousness somehow.

I hadn't, I only realised as I waited in the departures lounge
at St Pancras, told anybody in the family I was going. So I drafted
an email to my dad explaining things, about what had happened
at the fundraiser and how I'd been feeling since, and saying that
I just needed to be on my own for a bit and that I didn't want
to be contacted unless there was actual, significant news. I deleted

my Whatsapp so I wouldn't have to see any more messages in the family group saying 'he seemed well today but no major news' or 'he almost smiled' or 'doctors say brainstem reflexes are present but can't say any more at this stage'.

And then I took out my tablet and began emailing you.

I don't know what this has been. A way to bring you on the trip with me, I suppose. A way, perhaps, for you to feel one day that you did somehow come on the trip. There was something self-serving about it too though, I'm sure. I hadn't planned to do it. I thought I might keep a journal or something in which I'd write about the trip and maybe also about how I was dealing with the pain and guilt. But after I wrote that first email, before I'd even left, I began to find this more helpful, like it didn't take any effort or deliberation to do it. The words just flowed and filled up those empty hours where, for want of occupation and clarity, I would have otherwise just sat and ruminated. Or drunk too much. Or both.

It was probably because the exercise relied upon the fiction that you were still the same Paris that I've always known that I found it so absorbing. And that was probably a protection from my emotional reality. Or a way to make real and manifest my ever-diminishing hope that you will become that person again.

But it feels futile now. With Neevie – who was so good and supportive in those first few weeks after the accident – not being here, all my optimism has finally leaked away. Six weeks on, you're not really any better than you were: they've told me these last few weeks that your eyes open sometimes and that you make noises, grunt. But does any of this mean that your awareness is growing? That you have become conscious or are likely to become conscious any time soon? No. Not necessarily.

I see now in how cowardly and selfish a way I've dealt with things, but I'll make amends.

I'm coming home now anyway, and I have nothing to do when I get back, nowhere to live even, so I'll probably just come and sit by your bedside for as long as they'll let me each day.

Finally, one more apology: I'm sorry for what I said that night, about you being arrogant and entitled and self-righteous. I truly didn't mean it. Really I think you're brave and brilliant and principled and I just hope that you get to read this one day.

Goodbye, Paris, and I will see you soon.

Love Mark.

From: Paris Rosiello
To: Mark Rosiello
Jul 25; 23:17

Don't go home! Go back to the warehouse you idiot!

From: Mark Rosiello
To: Paris Rosiello
Jul 25; 23:24

Who is this??

From: D
To: Mark Rosiello
Jul 26; 07:42

Mark,

This is Danika, from my own email address this time! I owe you a sizeable apology for that email last night! I'm in Thessaloniki and I was logged into Paris's email account because I've been keeping an eye on it to let relevant people know what happened. Hope that doesn't seem too weird . . . turns out his email password is the same as his Spotify password, which he let me have (generous/trusting/careless man that he is).

I feel he'd be okay with me doing it, as he'd find the prospect of his unread emails just mounting up like in some kind of eerie digital purgatory quite bleak. Either that or he'd take a perverse delight in it. Anyway, I'm saving him a lot of admin for when he's fully recovered!

I'm actually slightly out of my depth now to be honest. It's pretty much become a part-time job in its own right. Your emails have been the highlight by a long way, amidst those from the local Labour Party group in Bristol he hasn't been to for seven years, six different political journals asking him to renew his subscription, and, worst of all, the low-key catch-up messages from friends around the world who haven't heard the news yet.

The 'weird glitch' email you received from Paris's account at the beginning of your trip . . . that was me. I'd just spent the night in the pub, after working all day and then sitting with Paris until visiting hours finished, basically without having left the office or hospital for two weeks before that. When I read your account of seeing Paris at the fundraiser, my wired, slightly drunken kneejerk reaction was to reply to tell you you'd got it wrong. I wanted to tell you Paris wasn't fobbing you off, he wanted to go travelling with you. I know because he told me that night – he was just being his usual holier-than-thou self about the Urb job. He did genuinely want you guys to do some travelling together this summer. When I told him that I'd suggested you come out and volunteer with us, he was really excited.

As soon as I'd started the message though, I realised it would be deeply unsettling for you to receive an email like that so I went to click delete but, pissed as a dog, I of course clicked 'Send' instead, and lo and behold Paris hadn't enabled the 'Undo Send' function on his email, which tells you a lot about the sort of guy he is, I think.

I worried that it would creep you out for me to suddenly reveal myself like that, so, when you seemed not to be that suspicious about it, I kept schtum, realising that you'd said yourself in your email to Paris that even though you thought he'd been dismissive, you didn't resent him for it and that you were feeling better about things. I remembered what you said to me the day I bumped into you at the hospital, that you thought taking yourself away for a while was the right thing to do and I got the sense that writing the emails was just part of that and it was really helping you in a lot of ways.

In fact, these emails have been pretty helpful for me too these last few weeks. I probably should have told you straight away that I was receiving them but by the time I'd found and finished the first one you'd already sent the next and I was kind of absorbed and didn't want you to stop sending them. I guess you were, in your own way, expressing a lot of what I was feeling about Paris and how to deal with what happened.

So I decided that I should tell you that (along with a bunch of other stuff I've been wanting to these last few weeks) but that I should do it properly, i.e. in person, so my plan was to meet you here in Thessaloniki. I'd been meaning to come out for a while anyway, to visit our Larissa base where we've just taken on a load of new vols and I had a week of holiday which I was due to take back in June, but after Paris's accident I didn't think I could leave London. Also, my boyfriend's been telling me all summer that I should get away – think he's a bit fed up of me not sleeping and thinks I need to take my mind off things. He's just freaked, I think, cos we're supposed to be moving in together soon and the idea of living with an insomniac is not appealing to him.

Anyway, I was pretty gutted when I saw your email late last night. Needless to say, I was once again sozzled after spending the evening at my mate's bar (it's been a pretty testing week here!) and again replied without thinking. I probably should have followed up straight away or got hold of your number or some-thing but I fell asleep almost immediately.

I spoke to Ilana this morning by the way and she told me Tom had been a wanker and she tried to call you back. I messaged Tom about it too and he was really apologetic. I think he feels awful, especially after he found out you're Paris's cousin.

I've told him not to feel bad – they are stretched and empathy is at a premium there, which has the really shitty effect that it can be very tough for volunteers whether it's their first day or

500th. And by the way, it's really not unusual for people to have the kind of reaction you had.

Also, I've been to the warehouse many times myself and I know how annoying those buses are. Enough to send anybody home early regardless of all the other stressful shit you've had going on.

Hope that's all helpful to hear in some way, and in case I now don't get to see you, here are the things I most wanted to say:

The main thing, and the one I feel worst about not telling you sooner, is that you weren't the last person to talk to Paris that night, I was. I'd seen you guys arguing so went out to talk to him after I saw you leave and that he was about to cycle off. I don't doubt he was condescending to you when you asked him about the trip; we know he can be like that and it's fucking annoying. And I can't pretend he wasn't hurt by what you said but, he told me, he was more annoyed with himself for being dismissive and not emphasising that he really did want to go for a drink with you to discuss it some more. He said he loved you and that he'd call you in the morning. When he got on his bike again, he was calm. So you shouldn't feel any responsibility for making him angry. He definitely wasn't angry by the time he was cycling home and, in any case, how he might or might not have been feeling as he did so had no bearing whatsoever on what happened.

I think you know this, but it was in no way Paris's fault, we can be almost certain. The media reports are suggesting the driver fell asleep at the wheel for god's sake. We just have to be patient in waiting for the police investigation to be completed but it shouldn't be too much longer before we know more.

I wanted to say as well that you shouldn't feel that you have abandoned Paris or the family by going away. You were there more than anyone else during those first couple of weeks remember. They're just worried about you more than anything, there's no resentment at you being away there at all. I actually saw your mum and dad a few weeks ago – they gave me some good allotment tips, which I hope to make good use of in about seventeen years when I finally get to the top of my local waiting list for a patch – and they seem to really understand that this is what you need to be doing at the moment. I mean, the main point is that you're working!! And even if you weren't, getting away for a bit would be a valid thing to be doing and everyone gets that.

I actually lost my dad a few years ago (cancer; we got eight months) – and after he died, I just couldn't stand to be at home anymore. That's when I went away to volunteer for the first time, in Calais. I was away for months and I lost myself in it a bit because what you're doing and what you're seeing is so all-consuming, but I had this gnawing sense that I had abandoned my mum and my sister. I felt like they'd both been so brave and dealt with it so admirably and 'properly', being at home with my dad the whole time and then being there for each other, whereas, while he was ill, I'd been working and going out and trying to escape into other things. And when I finally came home I went round to my mum's and just broke down and was more or less sobbing in her arms like a baby and saying how sorry I was and she was like 'you silly girl, you had to do this. This was the only way you could get through the pain, you had to keep moving. Everyone's different how they get through it. I'm always here for you whenever you need me'. Think she regrets saying that a bit now because I'm round hers the whole time eating everything in the fridge as she only lives down the road.

Anyway, I can empathise very directly with that need to be away, is what I'm getting at.

And try to remember what the doctors have said as well: that Paris has a good chance of further recovery, a chance of full recovery in time. We just have to stay patient and hopeful. I know how hard that is though.

So yeah, those are the main things I wanted to say. I'm here now anyway. Are you still here or are you now not here? If you're not not here, you should definitely come back to the warehouse today if you at all fancy it. Totally understand if not.

Dx

P.S. how's your cat scratch?

From: Mark Rosiello
To: D
Jul 26; 08:11

Really sorry to hear about your dad. I'm not not here. I'll come back to the warehouse now?
    P.S. cat scratch is healing well.

From: D
To: Mark Rosiello
Jul 26; 08:13

Yes! Come back now! See you soon (good luck with the bus).
    Dx

From: Mark Rosiello
To: D
Aug 03; 11:31

Hey,
    How are you?? How were the five coaches? I've thought of you a lot over the last couple of days, in most cases internally exclaiming 'fucking hell, she'll still be on the coach!' I applaud your commitment to 'futile consumerist stunts towards carbon reduction'. Considering you paid your one euro 'eco charge', I'd say your conscience over not forking out for the train instead is as clear as the pre-Anthropocene air. Anyway, you should be home by now. I hope you're on the sofa eating something nice and not feeling too tired ahead of going back to work.
    Really enjoyed hanging out with you and enjoyed getting to know you a bit more. Just wanted to say thank you, for a litany of things:
    Firstly, for encouraging me back to the warehouse and being

so cool and patient with me. I felt I did okay second time around, and I'm now pretty confident I know the difference between flour and sugar. In fact, I don't know if you heard, but just before we left on that last day, Tom told me I'd done a 'pretty good job' and that Paris 'would be proud'. Not fully convinced on that last score myself – he would have been decidedly unimpressed by the, for want of a better word, 'stew' I made for lunch on the second day – but it was a nice sentiment, I thought.

I'm really glad I did it, and I feel, dare I say it . . . rewarded. When I was packing all the children's clothes into the cases I had this weird epiphany, I think, stemming from the fact that what I was doing was, technically at least, pretty easy and yet, *and yet*, it made me feel better and more alive than almost anything else I've ever done, and that includes most of the times I've got high or had sex (primarily because I didn't feel guilty about this afterwards).

Probably very telling that I would make the experience about *me* and how *I* felt, and how *I've* discovered new insight for *myself* but it's about as *complete* as I've felt in a long time. Just felt I had to share that with you.

I hope I can make it back out there before too long. I want to see how the completed mural looks – hopefully Tom managed to amend my botched effort at sticking down the tiles. Never was very good at crafts, despite all those years of CDT at school!

Secondly, thank you for coming back to Athens with me. For *making* me go back, in fact. Have to admit, I thought it was a daft idea when you first suggested it, even accounting for how drunk we were, to spend my last two days off going back to a place I had just left. But leaving the city for a second time having negated those regretful feelings – to have walked through Exarcheia and not felt such a loner, and had such a great dinner with you there (who'd have thought Greek salad and chips could seem such a feast!) and to have the benefit of your insight into the situation and the people and the organisations there; to have revisited the Acropolis with someone to talk to about it all; to have actually made it up Mount Lycabettus at sunrise (I'm sorry if I became slightly . . . over-poetical there) . . . it was all . . . quite wonderful!

Thirdly, thank you for your reassurances about Paris. I am feeling a lot better about things as a result, I think. The conversation we had helped a lot. It was tremendously helpful to learn just how similar your experience has been to my own, and I'm beginning to accept that I shouldn't feel responsible and shouldn't feel guilty either for going away. I know there's nothing that I could really do right now. Spoke to my dad on the phone yesterday as well and he said they're doing okay and that Alan and Rosalind had been asking about my trip and Uncle Alan had been going on about his own travels in Europe in the '70s, which everybody'd already heard about a hundred times of course. So that was comforting to hear.

You're right that after the police investigation is done, we'll have a more substantial sense of what happened and what will happen next. And, in general, I'm even managing to feel more hopeful. Yes, it's important to focus on the positive aspects of what the doctors have said – that Paris is still young and fit; that patients are more likely to recover from head injury than other causes of damage to the brain; that the level of neurological damage stands him in good stead of recovery; that, relatively speaking, he wasn't in a coma for long and is now showing increasing motor responses. It's hard to keep all that in mind and not get caught in a spiral of thinking the worst and being affected by what you read on the internet about general outcomes and stuff. But I'm trying and I'm doing better, I think.

Fourthly, perhaps most importantly, thank you for encouraging me to send that email to Bethan Decker. I think if you hadn't, I would have just gone awol and then tried to go back into the office as normal in September.

Do you know the story about Larry David supposedly quitting his writing job on *Saturday Night Live* in angry and ignominious fashion, only to show up again two days later as if nothing had happened? Perhaps I'd do the same thing, I thought – just show up to the Monday Morning Hustle on September 2nd, with zero ceremony and never talk of Europe again.

But no, I sent the email as you suggested just as I was getting on the train back to Thess, telling her everything and asking if I could essentially be 'signed off' after Corfu and then I turned my phone off and slept the whole journey. When I got there, she'd replied.

Mark, I've tried to call you a couple of times and I've sent a couple of emails. I just wanted to say how sorry I am about your cousin. I wish you'd told me. Just before I heard from you, I'd actually been on the phone to Sarah Neevie (I hope you don't mind, it was just that I hadn't heard from you about Corfu logistics and I knew you guys were close when she worked here). She explained about Paris and I was just going to call you when I got your email. I really just wanted to check that you're okay and I'm sorry if . . . I've been . . . well look if I'd known I wouldn't have . . . well anyway, the main thing is that you're fine. And don't worry about the job. We'll get Florence from reception to go to Corfu and do the rest of the trip. I think she'll love it and, you know, it's actually doubly authentic because she's not even a copywriter! So that's all cool.

And look, I haven't said anything to anyone about what happened, only that you were unable to do the remaining dates because of other commitments and that's totally fine. But, uh, I do think you should perhaps let people know what's happened. In your own time. I think you'll be very much able to go back into your old role when you're back. That's what everyone's expecting anyway. Look, give me a call back if you want to, any time. Okay, all the best. It's Bethan, by the way. Ciao!'

I sent her an email back saying thanks for her message and sorry that I hadn't been in touch sooner because I was 'emotionally ravaged', which may have been a bit melodramatic in hindsight.

But the point is: it worked! As well as you said it would. Better even. So now I'm free. Don't even have to make that mad journey to Corfu, which is a relief. Shame as I'm sure it would have been lovely. Though not necessarily my scene. So now I'm off, on my own adventure until the money runs out. About to board the coach to Macedonia, in fact. Thank you for the idea – it's feeling like absolutely the right thing to be doing.

Anyway, hope you've made it back safely and hope everything's okay with Tristram! As you counselled me: so many of our worries on this stuff come from things we think might happen rather than just looking at what's going on in the present and it's fine for that to be a bit uncertain or ambiguous. (Was that what it was?? That's what I took from it anyway and it's helping!)

Speak soon. Missing you already.

Mark

From: D
To: Mark Rosiello
Aug 04; 19:52

Mark! I'm assuming you've heard the news from the hospital but in case you haven't: Paris might be showing initial signs of consciousness! Rosalind said that yesterday they brought in a new speaker to play music to him and were listening to *Kind of Blue* and when it got to Miles Davis's second solo on 'Flamenco Sketches' Paris opened his eyes and looked at the speaker for a few seconds (*so* Paris to be neurally stimulated by modal jazz!). She said she hadn't seen him actually *look* at anything before, so she ran and got the doctor but by the time they got back his eyes were closed again. *Buuuuuuuut* (to quote Bethan Decker) they said it's quite possible this was an indicator of awareness and that we should keep watching him closely and this morning Rosalind says his eyes keep flicking towards the speaker. So now they're going to assess him closely and do more tests and stuff because the doctors need to see 'sustained' evidence of conscious activity.

Fuck, I can't believe it. It's amazing. The next thing might be that they decide he's advanced to a 'minimally conscious state', which doesn't guarantee anything in terms of ultimate outcomes, but it's really fucking good news at this stage. I'm going to see him tomorrow. I'll let you know how he is.

I'm really buzzing but trying not to get carried away too!! Oh man, it's so hard.

I'll concentrate on answering your questions to calm myself down: the journey was somewhat ridiculous. The third coach had no toilet, or rather it did but somebody had tried to flush, according to the driver's announcement, 'something wrongful' down it. I genuinely thought I was going to die around Aachen. At Leuven, I discovered new reserves of strength. By Brussels, I'd almost transcended this earthly plain to a higher realm of bladderless Zen freedom.

In Ghent we stopped at a services and I finally got to have a massive piss. I've never felt happier. Sure, standing atop Lycabettus with you, watching Helios rise from hydrospheric depths, and sipping fresh coffee under the morning's glorious aureole was pretty good but those 30 seconds in a grimy motorway cubicle in North-west Belgium were the most beautiful of my entire life.

But yes, I am home. When I got in I watched eight episodes of *Seinfeld* and ate my bodyweight in Spinach Bites . . . I've become almost satirically vegan after eating an awful cheese sandwich in Ghent (there was no other option! Also I was basically high as a kite after the wee and had lost all self-control).

You're of course totally welcome for the coaxing back to the warehouse! It was a slightly selfish thing to do anyway because I wanted you there. Your white powder-differentiating abilities are truly second to none! And I'm pleased to hear that you're keen to go back.

Not claiming that I know you well enough to make assessments like this, but it seems very on-brand for you to put time and effort into doing something helpful and then feel bad about feeling good for it! I think it's totally fine and necessary that you get a selfish kick from volunteering. Isn't that, in the end, basically the only thing that drives us to do anything? The altruistic buzz? The ego satisfaction? (See *Friends* episode S05E04 'The One Where Phoebe Hates PBS'.)

I want to say my own thanks to you, generally for being such good company over the last week. Been feeling a bit knackered and disillusioned recently and having you around being so curious and keen to learn about everything has really buoyed me. You're a buoying boy.

I know I've harped onto you about how much I've got from reading your emails and that you find the whole thing slightly embarrassing, but I want to say it just one last time. After Paris's accident I, like you, was completely thrown. It's a weird thing because on the one hand, you're just forcing yourself to stay hopeful, not to give in to despair over the fact that everything might be about to change, that he might not recover or at least might not ever again be like the person we all know. On the other hand, you kind of have to begin to prepare for the worst. It's like grieving – and it obviously goes without saying that I'm so, so glad Paris wasn't killed – but the lack of certainty about how things will end up makes it all incredibly difficult, just in terms of processing it on a day-to-day basis. Having something to look forward to reading every couple of days, something to escape into, was just what I needed.

Obviously I waffled on about the relationship stuff to you the other night – thanks for being a good listener – so I won't say much more about it now. I think your distillation of what I was trying to get at seems right. I am definitely ready for him to move in – it was my idea after all! It's just that as the prospect gets realer, it gets a bit daunting. But it'll be all good.

Have you spoken to Neevie much?

I'm so excited for your onward journey. I'm glad Bethan has been understanding. Good to know the job's still there if you need it, I guess (though I'm betting you won't need it and by Christmas you'll be living on a canal boat in Bristol brewing craft beer from nettles or something!).

How's Macedonia??

Okay, right, back to pacing up and down with a sense of ambivalent, but ultimately *hopeful,* nervous energy.

Dx

From: Mark Rosiello
To: D
Aug 04; 20:14

Hey!

Yes I've just heard from my dad! So great!

He wasn't really very clear about what it means? What sense do you get? Have they changed the prognosis? It's not like he's communicating yet, is it? Guessing things don't progress that quickly but it's still great. Is he making eye contact then or is it just the speaker?

Sorry, so many questions. It's just so great. Wondering if I should fly home? What do you think?

Macedonia is cool. Just arrived in Skopje and now waiting for my Urb Host to get home. Yes, I bottled it and opted for an Urb rather than a hostel; sorry, feel I've let you down there, after your encouragement to embrace the relative merits of hostels. Just got slightly overwhelmed by the idea of being in Macedonia and took the easy option.

It's weird because on the one hand this is like one of the least familiar, most excitingly different places I've ever been in my cloistered little life. On the other hand, Man Utd are playing Real Madrid here tomorrow so there are loads of pissed, sunburned Mancunians wandering around looking lost in a sort of low-key angry way. Quite an uncanny situation all round. Anyway, feeling glad to be freer now.

Things with Neevie are . . . yep, ambiguous. We've spoken a bit, after that text I showed you in Athens in which I told her not to worry and that I hadn't expected her to definitely come. Which, as you said, was not very convincing at all. But she got in touch after Bethan Decker contacted her – she said she hoped I was okay with her explaining my situation etc. and that I was still having a good time – to which I replied that I was grateful to her for looking out for me.

So, I don't really know what to think. Time will tell, I guess. I'm more just overwhelmed with relief about Paris right now, I think. I've been ambivalently pacing too. I know it doesn't guarantee anything, but it's just the best we could have hoped for at this stage. Let me know how he is.

Mark

From: D
To: Mark Rosiello
Aug 05; 12:09

Hello,

So I went in early this morning before work and he wasn't 'awake' but I spoke to one of the nurses and she said the doctors have been in a few times to assess him and they were waiting for the senior neurologist to come and see him, which should happen early tomorrow. The nurse said they thought maybe there had been increasing signs of awareness but she couldn't say very much and we've just got to wait and see. But yes, his mum said he was showing eye contact yesterday and was actually blinking, which I haven't seen him do at all yet.

Don't fly home just yet, I'd say. Unless you want to, but if you're still enjoying being away then don't feel obliged. I don't know how quickly things will move here – apparently making the distinction between vegetative and minimally conscious states is something they want to be very precise about.

In the meantime, tell me about Skopje! Where do you think you'll go next? I hear Belgrade's a cool city (if that's not the very sort of sugary tourist platitude you're trying to eschew now).

Oh and I know you've said the email writing has served its use for you now but if you did feel like sharing accounts of your remaining travels I'd love to read.

Godspeed, champion!

Dx

From: Mark Rosiello
To: D
Aug 08; 16:34

Hello,

Thanks for the update, really appreciate it. Keeping everything crossed that we hear more good news soon. Sorry for the slow reply by the way – have been moving about a lot.

If you're absolutely certain you want more meandering, woozy reportage then here's my potted account of my passage north through the Balkans, somewhere I have greatly enjoyed exploring a small part of.

First, Macedonia . . . As I wandered through Skopje's melancholic bus and train station, which, in its cool-tiled, empty largesse, still seemed to bear ineradicable traces of its communist-era origins, I wondered smugly to myself, How many English people come here?

The answer, it turned out, according to my taxi driver, was 'thousands'.

'There are thousands of English people just arrive today,' he said as he pulled away from the station into the afternoon heat, as unrelenting still as it had been in Greece, adding, 'You must be here for the match.'

'What match?' I asked.

'Manchester United against Real Madrid in the European Super Cup! It is being played tomorrow night, here in Skopje!' he replied, aghast at my ignorance.

He told me excitedly that he had tickets for the game and that Manchester United was his favourite non-Macedonian team. I replied that it was mine too, nominally. Except, I left out 'nominally' for ease of comprehension. I asked who his favourite Macedonian team was.

'FK Vardar,' he answered, 'but they are not good. Macedonian football is not good. We are a small country. In UK they spend millions and millions on football. Here they spend 2,000.'

'2,000,' I found to be, in its blunt specificity, a very funny number to under-exaggerate with.

I asked if he'd heard of Hull City but, shockingly, he hadn't.

I hadn't planned on taking a taxi and had in fact planned to spend the afternoon walking around the city until my Host Mira returned from a week 'in the mountains', feeling that this would be the most apt way to begin to this free-spirited, drifting leg of my trip.

I hadn't anticipated, though, that I would still be laden with my big bag after finding the station luggage store 'full'. Added to this, and the heat, which made even the briefest departure from the shade more or less impossible, was the fact that I had no idea how to get to the city centre, where I planned to visit the Museum of the Macedonian Struggle, the foremost museum in the city according to Google Reviews, where it scores a respectable 4.2 stars. No choice therefore but to cough up the 200 denars (roughly £3) for a cab.

I asked if he'd ever visited the UK and he said it was too expensive to get a visa but that he would like to one day.

'We don't need visa to travel rest of Europe though,' he said cheerfully.

We drove past the parliament building, to which he pointed and remarked, 'That is where the Mafia lives!'

'Really?' I asked.

'No,' he laughed. 'It is a joke. Not Mafia.'

'But is the government corrupt?' I asked.

'Yes,' he said, turning serious. 'Very corrupt.'

Inside the neoclassical museum, upwards of 30 men and women in matching yellow polo shirts were cleaning the lavish atrium, some sweeping, mopping, polishing, dusting and wiping; others just kind of looking around for even the smallest speck of dirt to expunge. Otherwise this grand and preposterously clean space, with ice-white tiles, palatial staircase, and stained-glass dome ceiling held no staff presence. Maybe this is a fake museum, I thought, though quite what that would mean I had little time to ponder before a small, blonde woman came purposefully down the stairs, towards me.

'Hello! The museum is 300 denars,' she said, landing at ground level. 'It is by guided tour only. The next tour starts in 10 minutes. You can leave your bag in here.' She pointed to a fairly small cupboard along a side wall.

'Does it lock?' I asked.

'No,' she said. 'But it is watched always by a camera.'

Better able now to quell my paranoid instincts, I questioned no further the wisdom of leaving more or less all my worldly goods in an unlocked public cupboard, and just knuckled down to spending a good minute kicking and then shouldering the large bag into it. In the end, it was so comprehensively wedged in that I wondered whether I'd ever get it out again myself, let alone a potential thief.

This done, I sat down in a comfortable armchair and began flicking through an English-language tourist guide, while continuing to try and make sense of the cleaners. A moment later another guy walked into the museum and gave the same quintuple take that I had at the sight of the sanitary activity. Out of my earshot, he then had a conversation with the small, assertive woman (which I assumed to be the same one I just had with her, minus the bag part) and then sat down in an armchair opposite me. He was a guy in his mid-thirties, in shorts and T-shirt, with tousled brown hair and a face that, though friendly, bore the quality of having . . . seen some shit, you know. He looks like a quintessential Balkans-man, I thought. Then, in a strong Glaswegian accent, he asked me whether I was here for the museum tour too.

While we waited, we related our respective travelling experiences heretofore. I remained pretty vague on my own journey, telling him I'd 'come up through the Mediterranean' which he seemed to accept as a normal enough thing to say. He told me he'd flown into Zadar in Croatia. Deciding to take a few weeks off work (he was a social worker in Glasgow), he'd wanted to go somewhere inexpensive and as different as possible from Western Europe, 'somewhere where the alphabet's different,' he explained. Now a few weeks into his trip he'd been around Croatia and Serbia (and possibly Kosovo; I don't remember) and now he was weighing up his next move.

'I wanna do like a three seas tour,' he said. 'I've seen the Adriatic. And I might go to the Aegean and then the Black Sea.'

This struck me as the right way to travel somehow. A way that Paris would approve of.

For some reason I asked how he'd been 'doing his accommodation' and he told me he'd mainly just been turning up in places and walking around until he found a hotel or hostel he liked the look of or just going to a café and booking one online if he was tired.

I asked if he'd been using Urb at all. 'No,' he said. 'It looks complicated. Have you?'

'Couple of times,' I replied.

'Is it good?'

'It's fine,' I said.

At this point the diminutive dynamo returned and told us it was almost time to start the tour. I asked her whether there were always so many cleaners in the museum.

'No,' she laughed. 'They are here because tomorrow evening Manchester United will play against Real Madrid in Skopje and before the match the UEFA officials will attend a special dinner in this museum.'

Whether this was why visits were tour guide-only she did not say, but if, for example, you'd wanted to enter the museum as a visitor, hide overnight behind a mannequin of e.g. Kole Čašule, founder and former president of the Macedonian Writers' Association, and then, when the dignitaries arrived the following day, jump out and run towards UEFA president, Ángel María Villar, in order to ask him whether he's considered that the new changes to the Championships League qualification procedure might harm domestic football in smaller nations, you probably wouldn't have been able to.

The tour was interesting and increased my knowledge of Macedonia, a country whose strange, eventful history belies its minor size and status, by about 50,000%, which says as much about my near-total ignorance as much as the tour's thoroughness.

This encounter of the Macedonian Struggle (and my own to

get the bag back out of the cupboard) complete, my Scottish friend and I wandered around a bit. My initial impressions of Skopje as being, I suppose, socio-geographically 'basic' were made ridiculous by the city centre's many shops and cafés and rooftop bars, and by the city's Old Bazaar, one of the oldest and largest marketplaces in the Balkans. We sat outside a restaurant and he ate steak while I had a beer, still full from the cheese and spinach pie I'd eaten at the station (now pretty much a daily ritual for me), before progressing to a rooftop bar where my, by now, best friend from the whole trip – you excluded, of course – had a coffee and I an orange juice.

After a brief walk taking in the city's improbable number of bronze statues and more drunken Man Utd fans as well, followed by an unsuccessful visit to the Memorial House of Mother Teresa (closed for the day), I persuaded my Caledonian companion to have a final drink with me, effectuating a good, wide-ranging chat in which he indulged me with his superior knowledge of Balkan history and I described Glasgow as a 'beautiful city, amazing city' several times, before the swapping of emails and – only then – names (his is Jamie, mine remains Mark), after which I headed to my Urb. Quite fun just having a mate for one afternoon. Like being a child on holiday.

The Urb was nice – simple and modern – but I left it feeling pretty bad. It turned out that Mira, my host, had cut her holiday short to come back and let me in. She was clearly knackered, and I had to stand by uselessly while she made up my bed. I then couldn't get onto the wifi and accidentally woke her up to help me – turned out I just needed to turn my tablet off and on again. And then – I am so embarrassed about this I can hardly believe I'm telling you – I was very, very hungry, and, according to Maps, there was nowhere within a mile radius open to buy food. So I looked in the fridge and found, amongst the jars and spreads and old vegetables, a tupperware box of pasta with tomato sauce. And so I ATE THE PASTA, which, as was revealed following a loud knock on my door the next morning, had been intended as Mira's lunch for that day. Please don't judge me too harshly (I already judge myself). In short, I felt like the time had come to leave the Urbs behind.

In Belgrade (thanks for the recommendation!) therefore, I decided to heed Paris's (and latterly your) instruction at last and stay in a hostel. Not quite having pluck enough to emulate Jamie's approach of just turning up in the city and walking around until finding somewhere (which I was at least 53% sure would end up with me sleeping in the park, an outcome of which Paris would no doubt approve), I had booked 'Good Stay Hostel', which absolutely lived up to its name, as well as its 8.2/10 rating on the booking website and accompanying pull quotes: 'friendly staff', 'over four cereals!', 'the showers work'. Within half an hour of checking in and putting my bag down on my neatly made bed with neatly folded towel in my bright and airy four-person dorm, which was empty on arrival, and locking my valuables in a little safe on the wall (before unlocking them again almost immediately in case I needed them when I was out), all my fears about hostel life were allayed.

I suppose I feared chaos and noise and unavoidable human interaction, but Good Stay was a calm and quiet place, perhaps without the easy privacy of some of the Urbs I've stayed in, but also without all the fuss and guilty anxiety of some of the others.

In fact, lying in my clean single bed in the empty, sunlit dorm with the reassuring sounds of human presence from farther rooms, I felt great.

After a rest, I was ready to walk to the Museum of Yugoslav History. At first sight, Belgrade seemed more developed/prosperous/modern/concordant with my weird Western European prejudices than Skopje initially had. Just when I was about to decide the city's troubled past to be entirely undetectable, however, I came upon a massive militaristic billboard and then a stretch of buildings with entire façades missing, roughly exposing their abandoned interiors. A quick Google search led me to a website called darktourism.com, an improbably in-depth encyclopaedia of 'dark sights' throughout the world, which gives Belgrade **** on the 'Darkometer', for its 'bombing scars

. . . stunning sights on a scale not otherwise seen anywhere else in Europe'. This particular sight, the site claimed, represented 'the most dramatic bombed ex-government buildings' in the city.

After visiting the Museum of Yugoslavia, I finally felt I had a good, digested sense of the region's history, and how complex and brutal that story is. And now, as I made my way back to the hostel, it suddenly seemed that behind the burrito counters and the cocktail bars and the boutique cinemas, many ghosts were moving.

So yeah, anyway, if we ever get into conversation about the Balkan Wars or the former Yugoslavia again, I might actually have something to contribute rather than just saying 'I sort of remember that from the news' over and over again. In fact, in Belgrade, I also visited the House of Flowers, where Tito and his wife, Jovanka Broz, are interred, and saw a very interesting interview of an economist (whose name I failed to note down despite transcribing a large amount of what he said. . .) The point he made was that whilst Yugoslavia's economic stability came with censorship, free speech violations and demographic oppression, neoliberalism has led to accelerated inequality resulting in tensions which have fuelled the rise of nationalism across the region. But, comfortingly, he did also talk about a 'new social system' which will have to allow prosperity and development and yet maintain equality and liberty, the name of which, he said, would 'come by itself'. Brought me some vague hope anyway – hope it does for you too as you're sitting at your desk.

Next it was on to Zagreb. Just as I arrived, and was boarding a tram outside the central station, the sky suddenly turned night-time dark, even though it was still two hours from sunset. Everything went strange with lightning, then thunder and then rain – the first I'd seen since Paris.

Again, I'd booked the hostel in advance of my arrival, but whereas in Belgrade this had proven a savvy decision, here it didn't so much, as I learned first-hand the internet's incapacity to properly convey vibe. The Time Hostel *looked* more or less as it did in its photos, but it somehow just felt a bit . . . miserable. Perhaps I should have been more attentive to the review comments, where, buried deep, deep amidst an avalanche of foreign language assessments and lukewarm English appraisals such as 'good hostel', 'free juice!', were descriptors like: 'I think there were spectres in my room' and 'It was like purgatory but good location'. Having such a good, interesting time in general though, I didn't care much about the eerie vibe, certainly not enough to leave a comment. Bad millennial citizenship? Maybe.

High amongst the internet's 'Things To Do in Zagreb' lists was the Museum of Broken Relationships, which was not, as I expected, an evocatively named monument to Croatia's fraught historical relationship with its former Yugoslavian neighbours but actually a museum about actual breakups, taking the form of an exhibition of individual items symbolising failed relationships (almost exclusively of a romantic stripe), donated by members of the public. These were displayed on mounts or in cabinets with as much gravitas as was bestowed upon any item I've seen in any museum all summer. Alongside the objects – items of clothing including many bras, CDs, books, drawings, love letters, a large axe – were accompanying statements from their donors, ranging from the blunt and gnomic ('I bought her this. She didn't want it.') to the expansive and almost novelistic (which made me feel slightly less weird about my own sudden logorrhoea in the wake of Paris's accident).

There was a lot to stir the emotions – from the heart-rending to the bathetic and sometimes both at once – but the single item that absorbed and anguished me most was a copy of the computer game Football Manager 2006, a game that I played a great deal and, years earlier in its franchise, played with Paris too.

The game had been submitted by a woman in 'Pariz, Francuska' who described a relationship built on 'Love at first sight. Unmistakable'. It lasted, she wrote, for two years, 'and that's how long it took [. . .] to break up'. The video game symbolised for her 'all the things which were unbearable' about the relationship.

By donating it to the museum, 'separating from this very symbolic object', she hoped it would 'break the spell'.

After the catharsis of the museum, I strolled around the night-time streets and lost my mind a bit at the view of the city from the elevation of the Old Town, swooned at the buildings, ate an over-priced tuna steak and walked around some more.

More rain in the morning precluded a visit to Dolac market, the largest farmer's market in the city, which every Zagreb guide-book completely creams itself over. Instead went to the Museum of Arts and Crafts, a veritable dream-factory of bourgeois interiors. This is the only time in my life I can remember being deeply moved by furniture.

Next came Ljubljana, capital of Slovenia, population 280,000, with the swag of a city three times larger and the placidity of one three times smaller. Its beauty was fore-ordained by the scenery viewed on the train journey from Zagreb, an easy 140km course, running like an especially attractive contour on the face of Europe.

It basically went like this: *glistening wind-rippled lake – open field with storybook medieval castle – small town – glistening wind-rippled lake – open field with cylinder-towered church – small town – glist—(and on and on)*.

The mental serenity this scenery engendered was interrupted only by the embarkment of armed border guards checking passports. This happened at all international crossings in the Balkans, and then later again on the Slovenia-Austria border – even though Croatia and Slovenia are both EU member states – but not at any other borders as far as I can remember, even coming off the Italian ferry in Greece. This won't come as a surprise to you, I'm sure; I realise now this is likely because of what you told me about the EU's efforts to close off the 'Balkans Route' for refugees travelling through Greece towards Northern Europe.

After the eerie sterility of the Time Hostel, I wanted to be sure to find a hostel in Ljubljana with character and communal feeling, though as I approached the Slovenian capital I began to fear I might have opted for an establishment with an excess of said traits. I'd booked two nights at the Hostel Celica, a converted prison in the Metelkova Art Centre complex, formerly headquarters of the Yugoslav National Army. It almost felt like a parody of the kind of place Paris would choose to stay while travelling.

I'd been attracted by certain descriptive details from its website, details which were now, as arrival grew imminent, giving me pause – 'artistic cells'; the 'fun' of 'spending the night behind bars'; 'beer pong Sundays'; 'happy people'; 'sooooo much to do'; 'everything and more'. These details, coupled with the discovery that the Metelkova complex was more than simply an 'art centre' but more importantly a 'self-organised autonomous' zone (effectively a large squat) occasioned me to worry, as I got off the train in the late afternoon, that I wasn't quite as ready for an 'alternative' hostel experience as I'd thought.

But stepping through Metelkova's graffitied gate posts, to my glad surprise, I found nothing overtly offensive, or challenging or alienating. There was nothing that remarkable about any of it, in fact: it was just a large, expansive ex-industrial-looking site with visible demolition and dereliction but also bars and cafés and workspaces, most of which appeared to be closed as I arrived. There was graffiti everywhere but of a friendly, artsy ilk, not likely to scare a passing bourgeois. It was like Shoreditch – here I go again! – but not yet totally lost to commerce.

The guy at the desk who seemed to be, if not 'the owner' (it being unlikely a place like this could be owned somehow) but the 'person currently in charge', was a slightly ragged man of about 40 with the energy and air of someone a good seven years younger, with centre-parted neck-length hair and a goatee. His name, he told me, was Thomas. Rather than a traditional straight-armed handshake, his default technique was of a crooked armed/elongated high-five variety, which you'd think should be quite unbecoming for an older white man, but he managed to carry it off okay, despite the fact that I shaped up for the trad shake on the three or four occasions he felt it necessary for us to manually engage during my stay.

Later I took a walk towards the river, in search of food, and, just around the corner from Metelkova, came upon a vegetarian establishment, of a kind now cheeringly familiar: a slightly confused English name such as 'VegeNice'; a pleasingly naff illustrated logo, such as a smiling leaf or a carrot shaking hands with a bean; a bright and simple aesthetic; IKEA-ish furnishings; many posters advertising festivals and local charities; and a chalkboard menu listing dishes cheaper, healthier, more ethically derived, and not necessarily even a lot less nice than those served at rival carnist outlets. Here I ate a good burger and felt no need to do anything else, not read or scroll through Twitter or listen to a podcast. I just sat on my own on a stool and ate a reasonably decent veggie burger. I washed this down (not enough opportunities to *wash things down* in this life, I don't think) with a three-euro beer in a tremendous bar round the corner. Maybe I'll move here, I thought. It seemed a perfect city in which to just wash things down and live a chilled life. I then walked a few blocks and discovered a seething, scowling, selfie-stick-brandishing mass of tourists. Ljubljana is brilliant, but it turns out I wasn't the first to discover it.

Thomas had told me that 'everyone in Ljubljana' goes to Metelkova after the riverside bars have closed at about 1am, so I wandered back and found maybe a hundred or so people spread out over the concrete yard outside the hostel, watching a theatrical performance. A woman and two men were taking items of junk from a shopping trolley – a kettle, a computer keyboard, a mannequin's arm – and then, holding them in front of their faces, creeping, to a rumbling electro soundtrack, towards the encircling audience, most of whom were sitting and smiling respectfully. They placed the items one by one on the ground, before gathering them up again and putting them all back into the trolley save for one soft toy polar bear. This was placed ceremoniously on the ground and the contents of the trolley were tipped onto it. Then the music abruptly stopped, and a donation bucket was passed around.

I enjoyed this a great deal, though couldn't tell you why. You would have either, I reckon, loved it *or* hated it.

I wandered around and found the only bar in the complex which was open, a kind of shack full of grunge and metal memorabilia, projecting footage of a Soundgarden concert onto a large screen. N.B. I knew this from a caption; I'm not cool enough to be able to identify Soundgarden, though I do remember Paris having a poster of them in his teenage bedroom.

I bought a can of something and took it outside, where a load more people were sitting around in what was effectively a playground. Some appeared to be destitute types shouting at each other, some were teenagers, generally non-destitute, the rest were just your common-or-garden pre-middle-aged hipster tourists. Most were speaking in English.

Now, as a freewheeling, roadgoing, vagabonding raconteur, I expected I'd fit right in here, and make new friends in an instant. But as I sat down to join a small group of grungy young things at what seemed to be a non-moving merry-go-round, it quickly transpired they were probably the only people not speaking English in the whole outside area. They carried on chatting away in what I think was Russian, paying me no regard and eventually getting up and leaving a few minutes later. I stayed put, expecting others to replace them, but nobody did. I looked around: all the people nearby were locked in happy conversation and there came that feeling again, that everyone seemed to know each other and had no need of interruption from me. About halfway through my beer, I had begun thinking about bed when a man and woman about my age approached.

'Is anyone sitting here?' the woman said, Australianly.

'Erm, not at the moment,' I replied, trying not to give away the extent of my solitary plight.

'Mind if we join ya?' the man, also Australian, said.

I told them I did not. It turned out they were staying in the hostel too and soon we were neck-deep in conversation, ranging from the very banterous to the very sincere. They, Rosie and Nick, bought me many beers because I had no cash on me, and of course you can't use debit cards in an anarchist-squat-turned-weird-bars complex. I found them very agreeable: they lived in

Melbourne and liked art and theatre, when they could afford it, but 'to be honest' preferred comedy and cinema. They both worked jobs they didn't love – Rosie, similarly to me, doing marketing for a travel company, Nick as a planner for a biscuit brand. Neither knew exactly what they'd rather be doing. That was a big reason, they said, for why they'd come on their three-week trip to Southern Europe, to try and work out what they both wanted to do with their lives, although neither of them had got very far yet.

At about 2am we headed back to the hostel, where we found the lounge area empty, lit by a solitary lamp casting a welcoming glow over the beanbags and battered chairs. We all agreed that we didn't feel like going to bed. It was a nice feeling, as if we were enjoying each other's company too much to part ways just yet.

Rosie had a bottle of wine upstairs, so she went and fetched it and with the warm white wine my inhibitions dissolved and, almost against my will, I told them in great detail about Paris, everything that had happened. By the end of my monologue, Nick and Rosie were staring at me now and looking pretty galled in the candlelight.

It wasn't exactly what they'd signed up for, I guess, in electing to stay up and drink the wine with me, not exactly how they'd expected the evening to end: go out to a bar, fun, fun, fun, chats, chats, chats . . . decide to stay up and have another drink . . . and then a man you've just met talks for 20 minutes about his cousin's traumatic brain injury.

I told them I was sorry. This had all become a million times more serious than I'd intended it to.

'Don't apologise!' said Rosie. 'It sounds so fucking horrible.'

I emphasised that Paris is getting better, albeit slowly and that I'm okay. I told them about you, how helpful you've been.

'Danika sounds smart!' Rosie said.

'Definitely smart,' Nick averred, 'you wanna keep onto her, mate.'

Haha. Dunno why I'm telling you all this. Just thought that was a funny phrase. 'Keep onto her.' Not sure what he meant by it. Don't think he did really – it was nearly 3am now and we were all hammered.

On the stairs where we parted ways, we hugged and exchanged emails and half arranged to eat breakfast together but by the time I woke, they'd left the hostel, for – if memory serves – somewhere on the Croatian coast. I sent them an email to say sorry I missed them and that I hoped we'd meet again in London or Melbourne. Rosie replied straight away to say they hoped so too.

I hope I do see them again. I probably won't though, and that's fine too. Relationships are no less meaningful for being fleeting, and other such sentiments that prove to you my growth and wisdom . . .

That said, I do kinda want to 'keep onto you', whatever that means. What I don't want is to treat you like a therapist. I hope this hasn't been completely exhausting to read. I just wanted to share because it felt kinda necessary and cathartic and also because it was about you.

But yes, I know you wanted these emails to break up your daily toil and stresses, so to that end, here's something nice I did on my final Slovenian morning . . .

After breakfast I'd planned to do once again what I do best: go to a museum, have some lunch, go to another museum, have some dinner, have a drink, go to bed. But hearing about Rosie and Nick's peripatetic plans the previous evening, staying in the city for a day or two before barrelling off to some other exciting-sounding place I've already forgotten the name of, made me want to spread my wings a bit. So I took a coach to a place called Lake Bled, which sounds like where a satirical vampire might live but is in fact just a beautiful lake, apt for swimming in and walking around.

Well, I hope that was what you were after. Won't be at all offended if you're too busy to read. Know how much you've got on. Hope you're feeling okay, all the prep for the move is going all right and you're not feeling too overwhelmed by everything.

All best,

Mark.

From: D
To: Mark Rosiello
Aug 11; 11:37

Mark!,

Assuming your parents have told you the news!

I can't really believe it. Obviously we were hoping they were going to make that diagnosis, but part of me was preparing for the worst, or at least I thought it would take much longer. I was there this morning when the senior neurologist came in and said that she was content that he's now showing minimal conscious-ness, with his eye movement and blinking and even making small movements with his hands when they ask him to now as well! Also he now has a demonstrable sleep-wake cycle (though I keep having to go to work before he wakes up!), which is another really positive sign.

She said they can't give a renewed prognosis but said we should be pleased and that it might be time for him to be moved to a rehabilitation facility (it's fucking lucky his parents are rich, I tell you that much).

So no miracle moment of him waking up and high-fiving us all but definitely a meaningful advancement nonetheless.

As for coming home, I'd say stick to your non-flying pledge and don't rush. He's stable and improving and who knows, by the time you get back he might have made some really significant progress!

As for the situation at home, I have really not thought about anything except Paris and work for at least a week. Currently sitting amidst all Tristram's boxes, which he brought over last night before going off to Estonia to make a film about nation-alism. I said I'd make a start on unpacking them but now I'm just staring at them and truly cannot be arsed. Might just feign back injury and let him do them when he gets home.

That museum sounds amazing. Now I'm sitting here wondering what single object from all these boxes I could send to the museum if Tristram and I broke up. It's mostly broken camera equipment, I think, which'd probably serve as a metaphor for something, though I'm too tired to think what.

I wish I were still travelling with you. The prison hostel sounds really fun and it totally seems like you're embracing the adventure and throwing yourself into stuff. Whatever happened to that lonely man trying to look at Twitter on the party boat in Paris?

Glad you found Nick and Rosie too. You're very welcome to hold onto me haha. I'm not going anywhere.

Right, I better go. These boxes won't stare uselessly at themselves!

Give me another update – need something to read over lunch. Where even are you now??

Lots of love

Danika xxxx

From: Mark Rosiello
To: D
Aug 14; 20:06

Hello,

Yep, my mum called me as soon as she heard. I literally screamed 'YES!' in the street, and the attendant of a nearby tulip stand came and asked me to move away because it was 'bad for the flowers to have loud energy near them'.

Anyway, time to start making my way home then, I think. Haven't felt so happy in months.

Right now, I'm in Holland. I'd carried an idea with me for the last couple of weeks of going to Amsterdam, mainly because I was supposed be there anyway about this time, if I'd still been doing the Urb job. On Sunday though, I was in a bit of a sorry state after a few days in Berlin, which were so intense and exhausting that I'll have to save it to tell you about in person, I think, but essentially I tried and failed several times to get into the 'cool' clubs and ended up going to quite a weird one called Suicide Circus for 12 hours.

After that, the prospect of returning to a city I'd already visited about four times on football trips and stag dos and miscellaneous lads' weekends didn't hold much appeal. Also, a while back, I came across this article about how tourism has blighted Amsterdam and what contributions Urb has made to that. Predictably, this was confirmed by a bit of further googling, which revealed a mounting backlash against tourism in the city. I knew that I didn't need Amsterdam just now, and it seemed that Amsterdam didn't need me either. So I went to Rotterdam instead.

I wanted Rotterdam to be just a smaller Amsterdam, which it isn't really, though it is an appealing city in its own right. Even looking from the coach window at Eindhoven I felt calmed. Something about Holland, flat and green and true, promises that everything will be alright. And never have things felt more like they'll be alright than they did in Rotterdam.

Miles and miles of functioning docks. Skyscrapers. Trams. Canals. Bike paths. Small parks. Trees. (I appreciate I'm now just listing nouns; guess I'm just generally overexcited.)

I had a bed in a four-person hostel room but only one of the other beds was taken, by a man who was asleep by 10pm and out by 6am. Next door was a bathroom which looked out onto some trees. I took a soak and listened to an Audio Long Read about banter.

Later I walked into town, heading for a specific 'coffeeshop' I'd read about online, only to get there and find it was closed. A shame as it looked fun, with a nautical theme and small submarine-like pods, which I suppose allow you to get stoned while sitting inside a metaphor for your own drug-induced solipsism.

Now hell-bent on smoking a doob, I searched for another café. Turns out there aren't that many in Rotterdam. Or at least not as many as in Amsterdam. Rotterdam probably has a density of coffeeshops similar to London's density of pancake houses – there are a few around but you'd be lucky to find one just by wandering the streets.

20 minutes later I found one but it was takeaway only – a heavily secured booth selling bags over the counter. The woman

there directed me around the corner to another place and here, again past a bouncer and through a security turnstile, I entered a disarmingly over-lit shop floor where I bought a pre-rolled hash joint, as I reasoned that if I bought tobacco to roll with I'd just start smoking again, which is the last thing I want. A friendly sign suggested I buy a drink with my spliff before going upstairs so I bought an ice tea from a vending machine.

Upstairs was the barest room you could ever see. It had maybe 10 tables, most of them occupied, but otherwise it was completely undecorated. No attempt had been made at a theme or even the merest scintilla of aesthetic effort. The crowd were all men, a range of ages. Mostly quite scruffy but none seemed threatening. A man and woman, apparently a couple, entered and sat at the table next to me for a nice romantic spliff.

I'd intended to sit here a while and read about Dutch history on the tablet while smoking, as I'd done most evenings this summer (albeit with a beer rather than a spliff, and not Dutch history but history pertinent to whatever country I was in at the time) but I felt too restless: not quite edgy but certainly not able to sit and relax and concentrate. So, as soon as the spliff was done, I stepped out again onto the canalside.

In smoking specifically hash, I was trying to call back to an old high: being 15 and absolutely enamoured with everything, on the permanent brink of tripping. It was Paris who offered me my first experience of being stoned, when I was 14 or so, down a farm track near his house one evening in early summer. I must have managed one toke at most, but I remember walking back to the house as in a reverie, the York countryside rendered more Arcadian than usual. I remember Paris laughing as I climbed into my dad's car and told him I'd had a 'halcyon day' about six times. Not sure if he was oblivious or simply chose to seem so.

As I drifted along the canals of Rotterdam I felt a very mild version of that adolescent buzz but it wasn't quite the same. I wandered down Witte-de-Withstraat, renowned as the city's 'nightlife street', before spending absolutely ages trying to take a photo of a neon sign which read 'WITTY' hanging above the cobbles and which I decided would make a fantastic Instagram photo. In the end, the phone camera proved incapable of picking out the luminescent letters against the dark sky and I just had a load of photos of an iridescent blur. For the best really, as once I was less stoned I realised 'WITTY' would have made for a terrible Instagram photo – no great loss as I don't even have Instagram.

It was semi-balmy and the bar and restaurant terraces of WITTY were full. But I was not yet back on an even enough psychic keel to sit amidst the cheerful crowds, so I kept on walking and walking until most of the restaurants were closed. At around 11pm, all I could find to eat was chips but luckily, with chips being the national dish, it still felt special.

After the special chips, I was steadier in the mind, steady enough to drink a small beer and continue reading the Wikipedia entry for 'Holland' (great read, highly recommend) by a canal, before retiring to my quiet dorm.

The next day I walked and walked and walked some more. Took in the docks. Considered a boat ride. Decided against it. Considered the maritime museum. Decided against it. Walked some more. Hung out in the massive, modern public library building for a while, studying a map of Holland.

Next went into an architectural bookshop and found a fascinating little book about Rotterdam, which took the form of a kind of meandering poetic photo-essay. Particularly intrigued by a section on the strange hotels of Graaf Florisstraat, which offer rooms for 40 euros a day, not, apparently, for carnal activity but for drug mules, 'middle-aged men from all corners of the globe', carrying drugs within their digestive systems, who decamp in Rotterdam before exorcising said goods.

And that about brings you up to speed, I think. Better go and find something (chips) to eat and get an early one – need to be in good shape for my ferry crossing tomorrow.

How are you doing? Hope the boxes remain unobtrusive.

Mark

From: D
To: Mark Rosiello
Aug 14; 22:09

Hey,

Sounds like you've been having an amazing time! Looking forward to hearing about your Berlin exploits. Hope Suicide Circus made up for your aborted visit to Fabric. I'll come with you next year if you still want to go.

Rotterdam sounds great. I keep hearing amazing stuff about community projects there, a lot of which sprang from one initiative where residents turned an old Turkish bath house into a reading room and it inspired other people to do similar things elsewhere. Sorry about your disappointing spliff. Probably good that you feel you've outgrown it though maybe.

So you're getting the ferry back to England? Where do you sail into? So great that you'll get to see Paris soon. Your auntie says he's actually making eye contact now, as in actually holding her gaze for a few seconds at a time. Yet to see one of his conscious moments myself but am gonna be with him most of the weekend as your auntie and uncle are going to look at rehabilitation facilities near York for him to move to. Think it'll be a lot easier for them to be back at home and not living in an Urb!

Anyway, have a good crossing. You bloody love a ferry. I do too, although my affection for boats was slightly diminished a couple of years ago when I volunteered on a rescue boat off Malta for a few days and just felt deeply ashamed of myself the whole time for feeling seasick in front of people who had almost just drowned and/or had no idea what was about to happen to them.

In fact I think I was sick, on Paris when we took the ferry to Dublin as students. Although that might have also been down to the combined effect of the Guinness and the five or so goes I had on a motorbike game in the arcade, which I was playing to get rid of my euro change (and because I was really brilliant at it and kept beating Paris).

In the spirit of nostalgia for a misspent youth, I started looking at my old diary the other day around that time and then found what I'd written the day after your infamous trip to Bristol! I have zero memory of writing this or any of the details here really:

18th May 2006

Went to hustings for new SU officers. So asinine was crying blood by end. Got sense only about 10% had anything about them (i.e. not enough to fill positions) and rest were doing it either because dangerous careerists/latent crypto-fascists or thought it'd be a laugh. Latter detail not just a projection: at least nine actually said they were seeking election for 'a laugh'. Despair for our politics.

Got back to halls to find Paris in kitchen with young cousin from Hull who was in a k-hole. Paris had given him ket despite him (the cousin) never having had it and now was feeling v bad about it, though not so bad that he was prepared to let it ruin his own night. He (Paris) wanted to go back out to Mandrake and asked if I was staying in. Said I was and he asked if I could keep an eye on Mark (cousin) (who was basically asleep with head on table by this point), because 'I'd be in anyway'. Said I didn't really feel comfortable looking after someone overdosing on drugs and Paris said he had given Mark 'the smallest scintilla' over two hours ago and it was 'safe stuff' and so was probably overexcitement that had caused him to freak out and now he just needed water and sleep. Obviously sounds v similar to what had happened to me during fresher's, right down to the way he was splayed out at kitchen table in exact same chair.

Said I'd do it and Paris hugged me for ~40 seconds and told me he'd buy me 'the biggest breakfast I'd ever had'. Would do anything for that boy and don't know why.

He said he'd carry Mark to his room and leave door open so I could go in and check on him every so often but, being lazy, I just told him to plonk him on sleeping mat in my room, so I didn't have to move.

Pointless anyway as Mark didn't wake up for several hours. Actually quite pleasant having him there, sleeping on floor while I worked. Relaxing, kinda like in the way having a sleeping dog near you is relaxing.

When he eventually did wake up, he was v confused and sat up and looked at me and said, 'Are you Paris?'

Told him what had happened and he was ridiculously apologetic, saying last thing he remembered was everything feeling 'like a cartoon', and 'believing his own name was a lie'. Felt lucky was able to say had almost exactly the same experience myself and that I'd come through it with no lasting damage (that am aware of).

Made pasta for us both and he asked me about degree stuff, which I didn't really have energy for and then he started talking about his A-Level English Language Coursework about Ted Hughes, which I didn't have the energy for either, so tried to steer the conversation onto other stuff. He said he was going to Sussex next year and asked me what uni life was like. I told him it was mostly work and Amnesty volunteering as I'd tired of going out after about week three. Then talked about football for about half an hour, which I think was what he needed, as did I tbh.

Took him to Paris's room and he climbed straight into bed, still in his clothes. Overall a funny and welcome distraction and he seemed nice in a kind of 'Pigeon Detectives' way.

Hope you didn't mind me sharing that and that it brought you as much cringing amusement as it brought me, so much so, I was happy to write it out. I'm deeply sorry also for comparing you to both a dog and a Pigeon Detective. Neither is really a favourable, or fair, comparison.

And to be fair to Paris, I think he did buy me that breakfast, though I seem to remember he ended up eating a lot of it himself.

In terms of what's going on here, just so you know, things are a bit difficult with Trist and me at the moment. Won't bore you too much with the details but basically I think him moving in has put a bit of pressure and scrutiny on the relationship and I've suddenly freaked out because I'm just sitting here with these boxes while he's hopping around all over the place and it's like 'fucking hell is this just gonna be your London storage unit??'. Which is obviously unfair cos it won't always be like this and it'll feel less weird once he's unpacked and settled in and his work calms down a bit but I sort of got a bit pranged about it the other night and raised it with him over Skype (tip: never have a serious relationship conversation with Skype if you can avoid it; hard when your partner's on average 500 miles away from you) and he was thrown by it and like 'why didn't you say this before I moved in?' and I was like 'because I didn't know how I felt until you moved in, and also you haven't even moved in yet, you've just put some boxes in my spare room!' and he got quite annoyed, saying that I was the one who suggested he move in, which is basically true because he was renting this flat on his own and it just seemed to make sense, especially after Paris was no longer here and his parents came to get his stuff and suddenly the flat felt fucking empty (not to mention significantly more expensive rent-wise), but now it just feels empty but also has loads of boxes in it. Which obviously won't be the case soon but it's just feeling shit right now.

Anyway, too much information. Just wanted to bring you up to speed with the boxes etc. and now I've got all that off my chest I'll shut up.

Looking forward to seeing you once you're settled back in London. Where are you gonna be staying?

Danika.

From: Mark Rosiello
To: D
Aug 15; 20:37

Hello,

Writing to you from the 'Irish Bar' on the *Pride of Rotterdam*, which is ostensibly the same as all the other bars but has a big plastic shamrock over the entranceway. I did initially park myself in the Sunset Show Lounge before a vigorous trio took to the stage, looking something like a band from an arcade dance-mat game, and began belting out with mind-smothering exuberance a succession of pop hits from circa 2013. By the time they'd reached the first chorus of 'Moves Like Jagger', I'd made retreat to my current nestling place where my thoughts only have to compete with a gentle man called Fergal who's playing his guitar acoustically because the amp stopped working and whose repeated, vague calls for a 'technician' have gone unanswered.

I'm sipping a Guinness in honour of your nauseous maritime adventures though sadly I didn't find a motorbike game in the Megadrome Games Arena (a small room with some fruit machines in it).

Mercifully the sea is calm and, through the slightly greasy and satisfyingly porthole-like window, the sun seems a rosy arc on the horizon. The perfect situation, then, to reflect upon our first meeting and the general ridiculousness of my conduct, to come away from which being compared only to a dog and a Pigeon Detective feels pretty merciful. I remember that 'leather' jacket actually, which I got from Topman with my birthday money, bought specifically for the purpose of coming to Bristol, I think.

I'm glad to hear it wasn't a total chore to you to look after me and you were even glad of the distraction, though I'm sorry you weren't too enthused to hear about my Ted Hughes coursework. If unending over-analysis of militaristic similes about birds isn't your cup of tea then that's your loss, imho.

I have to admit I don't remember the experience in all that

much detail, though I do remember the general impression I took away of you as being very kind and patient or, more specifically, as I described to Paris in a text a few days later 'a life-saving angel'. Gendered hyperbole of the description aside, it's a sentiment I stand by, and one confirmed by your general friendliness to me at all our subsequent meetings and especially over the last few weeks. Genuinely couldn't have done it without you (I appreciate that by 'it' I mean had a really nice, fun extended holiday without having to do any work or anything at all onerous but still . . .).

Anyway, I'm actually sailing into Hull, where I'm going to see my mum and dad and then, I'm actually going to go to Edinburgh. Basically, I told Neevie I was coming home, and she said it would be good to see me and that I should come up and 'do a weekend' at the Fringe if I felt like it. And I thought, why not? Really no idea what the vibe's gonna be. Just can't tell how she feels or whether there's a 'thing' there really but it's a positive sign that she invited me up there. Hopefully I'll at least get some sort of clarity from it either way.

So I've booked myself a hostel bed, in a shipping container, two miles out of town. I'm trying now not to prang out too severely with regret over the decision. The hostel describes itself as a 'party hostel'. There will be vomit. And that's cool!

And then back . . . to London, which I'm weirdly looking forward to. Didn't think I would be. I'm obviously looking forward to seeing Paris again, and you, and just getting back to 'normality' a bit, even though I don't really know what that's going to entail. I guess I'll go in for the meeting at Urb, not that I have any raging desire to work there any more. But maybe it'll be good for a few months while I work out what I actually want to be doing.

Dyson is away filming a music video in Romania for a few weeks and he said I can take his flat in Shoreditch, which will mean a great fall from grace when he gets back and I have to find another damp room in Zone 3 and make my own gentrifying contribution to yet another neighbourhood. Nice of Dyson anyway. Had quite a funny email from him actually the other day saying the above and also that he had been reflecting on Florence and felt that he behaved like a dick and that he's decided to change his ways. He's realised, he said, that he really likes Chiara and they're now 'going steady' (whenever they actually manage to be in the same country at the same time – not easy with their work commitments!). They even fastened a padlock to a bridge in Paris a few weeks ago. I'm pleased for him. A steadier life will be good for him, I think.

As for me . . . it'll all work out, as Tom Petty says, and I shall return now to my pelagic reverie, as my summer's lease nears its date and the *Pride of Rotterdam* issues exhaust emissions to the unknowing air.

Sorry, ridiculous sentence. Should probably apologise for the rather aureate strainings of these emails in general. I suppose I just haven't been able to break the habit established in my very first missives to Paris. Being frank, I always feel a tremendous pressure to impress him in speech and writing, as eloquence seemed to always come so easily to him as I'm sure it will again in time.

Our first email exchanges would have come when he went off to Bristol. I remember his dad proudly telling us at some family dinner or other that Paris had 'his very own email account now' and my parents' murmuring scepticism in the car on the way home. 'It'll never catch on, this email business' my mother said. But of course, it did catch on and I shortly thereafter set up my own Hotmail account, initially for the exclusive purpose of emailing Paris, remarking upon his thrilling reports of clubbing in Bristol and late night, machine coffee- and tobacco-fuelled debates outside the library. In my responses, mostly about Ted Hughes and the tedium of Sixth Form life, I'd make frequent recourse to my thesaurus (a battered *Roget*'s from the family bookcase; I had no conception of equivalent digital resources at that time). And, on those occasions when I encountered Paris, in his new scholar-hedonist guise, in real life, I'd make recourse to pausing, frequently and lengthily, to find a word or phrase that would impress him.

I guess that compulsion didn't diminish after his accident, and if anything increased, as this thread will attest. I just hope he gets to read it one day. Also, really after a while I was doing it – i.e. throwing linguistic caution to the wind – for my own entertainment, and I've obviously failed to rein myself back in for your benefit, for which I'm sorry.

On this particular occasion I blame the Guinness and the music.

Before I sign off and give my full attention to Fergal, who's being increasingly drowned out by the drunken and uninterested patrons of the Irish Bar, I just want to say I hope things are okay with Tristram. It sounds incredibly stressful, but I think I can speak from experience now when I say that these moments of strife and uncertainty often precede moments of great renewal and happiness so I'm sure things will feel better soon. Thoughts are with you, hope you're doing okay. Right, better go, Fergal has just struck up, I want to say, 'Bridge Over Troubled Water' but it's genuinely too quiet to be certain.

Lots of love,

Mark

From: D
To: Mark Rosiello
Aug 16; 14:02

Hey,

I'm envious of your sea legs. Hope the rest of the voyage passed so tranquilly and the only troubled water you encountered was purely poetical!

And no need to apologise for the poeticism! I enjoy the words, as I've told you.

Oh my god yes, I've known Paris for 14 years and I've never properly got over that impulse to impress him. To be honest though, the very first time I met him I hated him. It was exactly what you say – a debate outside the library at night. I was outside smoking and losing my mind over some essay on 'Liberty and the State' or something and feeling like I was completely out of my depth and as if I was gonna have to admit that I was not cut out for the degree. Like, genuinely considering phoning my mum that next morning to pick me up. And there was this group of guys – and I think it was exclusively guys – all sitting around on benches smoking with this big curly-haired man standing in the middle, like some debate club Worzel Gummidge. Pontificating about Hobbes and god knows what other nonsense I had no real awareness of or interest in. And it just compounded this feeling that I was surrounded by white public-school boys affecting edginess.

I must have gone out to smoke three or four more times that night (it was a gruelling essay) and he was still there every time, with his little encircling band of guffawing sycophants. At one point I went over and asked one of them for a lighter and he said something to me, something that suggested a greater talent for self-deprecation than I'd given him credit for, based on first impressions, about how I might be able to give him and his friends – whom he referred to collectively as 'us procrastinating pseuds' – some help, as I was clearly getting on far better with the essay than they were. This, along with the admission that he knew we were on the same course because he had seen me in lectures and admired the thoroughness of my approach to note-making struck me as, if not absolutely creepy then at least a bit forward and ostentatious.

And it took me a while, in fact, to accept that such overblown addresses – made loudly outside the library or in the canteen or the union bar or across a hushing lecture hall – were not really done out of ostentatiousness or any intention to unsettle or undermine but just out of some overbrimming enthusiasm to connect with people. Once I was sure he wasn't trying to get off with me, he became one of my best friends.

He is obviously a ridiculous man, a towering straw-haired berserker of interrogations and monologues, and, no, I never overcame the compulsion to impress him either.

These aureate emails are a fitting tribute to him, I think. And yes, I'm sure he will get to read them one day.

I think you should try and keep the job option open if you can. Bethan sounds pretty understanding really. Why don't you just go back for a few months while you work out what you want to be doing? You should come and check out the charity's office in London btw. There're a lot of volunteering opportunities available and I'm sure there'll be a copywriting or comms role or something that you're perfect for that comes up either for us or someone else in the sector before too long.

Okay, so some quite big news but Tristram and I have decided to take a break. As I said, I think this move stuff has put extra pressure on the relationship, ironic cos we've actually seen less of each other since the move than at any point in the last three years, I think. But yeah, I guess it's made both of us question some stuff and whether it's actually what we want and whether it's actually right for us and the relationship, or whether it was just a bit of a reflex reaction on my part to suggest it in the wake of Paris's accident and for him just something he felt he was supposed to say yes to. He flew back from Estonia last night and we stayed up all night talking before he flew back this morning, so I'm working from home today but haven't been very productive and I'm going to the hospital in a minute, though I feel worse for him as he had to go and film in a NATO barracks for 12 hours today. Considering that and the fact I've kinda messed him around a bit, he was pretty decent about it all really. It's a complete headfuck but feels like the right thing for now. He's basically going to be away for like another month, so we'll have some time to think, but the break just feels like a definitive step after quite a long period of weirdness and ambiguity.

Anyway, just offloading again, but also one upshot is that the boxes that have been in the spare room all this time will now be gone. Tristram's hired someone to move them all out and into storage next week so the spare room will be free, in case you're still looking for somewhere to live . . . it would appease my ongoing guilt about it being a potentially habitable room just going to waste and I thought it could potentially work if you were just looking for somewhere for a few weeks when you leave

Dyson's place, while you decide what to do about work and find somewhere more permanent.

If you're theoretically interested maybe you could come over one night to have a look at the room and decide whether you can see yourself getting your Harry Potter on in there. Stay for dinner maybe. I could do us Greek salad and chips and I'll eat round the feta again. Maybe Wednesday night?

Also give us a shout if you want to coordinate visiting Paris once you're back. Hope your return to home soil is proving all you hope it to be. How's Edinburgh?

Danika.

From: Mark Rosiello
To: D
Aug 18; 15:07

Hello,

I'm sorry to hear about Tristram. Genuinely.

I know it's been a source of angst for a while now so I'm glad the break is letting you feel an easing up of that, but these things are always shit.

I'm on the train to London feeling completely exhausted but . . . in a good way. More importantly, at a grander, non-bodily level I'm feeling . . . a deep contentment but one underwritten by a kind of sadness borne out of recent experience. I look forward with a nervy optimism and I look back with a glad regret. I'm a mess basically, owing mostly to lack of sleep, plus being on a train on a Sunday afternoon, which always has the potential to completely confound me emotionally at the best of times.

To be fair to me, it's been an eventful few days.

Arrived in Hull on Friday morning under clouds so comprehensive and yet so translucent that it was as if the whole dockland was being viewed through the sepia filter of an early camera phone, which is exactly how I wanted it really.

As the *Pride of Rotterdam* neared her terminus, the Humber

swelled wide and grey, with marine inspiration; the chemical plant fumed slyly against the gauzy sky; cranes stood askant, as if stooping to make sense of the daedalean dock shapes. A few boats moved on the water, cars went like slow toys in the distant city.

It was strange to see it all still there, pretty much as I've always known it to be. I don't know what I was expecting really. That it would all have been flattened or something, turned to wasteland, or, not much more agreeably, to 'luxury development' that nobody from this area could realistically afford. But it hadn't; it wasn't.

Whence this feeling of contingency, this surprise at the persistence of the familiar but half-forgotten? Was it austerity or Brexit that made it, for a moment, shocking to see Hull *still there*? Or was it simply an amplified version of that age-old home-from-holiday feeling, which renders it a shock to see your house again and smell the hallway, and run up to your bedroom and find your things crouching just as you left them and see the dust particles dance in the shaft of sunlight which has landed in the middle of your bed, as it always has done at this time of day and always will.

That mid-latitude frigidity of autumn, first sensed in Holland, was now fully manifest. In the car park outside the ferry terminus I felt cold with no jacket on. The low-key familiarity of everything hit me like a blow to the head with a rolled-up local newspaper: the furrowed brow of the bus driver as he flicked out his cigarette at the sight of the newly landed luggage-wielding crowd; his Humber drawl as he explained five times over that he couldn't take cards or large notes; the feel of greasy sterling coins in the hand; the journey into town and the cemetery and the prison and the ASDA. It all seemed a world away from the creeping neon and helvetica, iZettle and ginger shot realm I had come to know. Still, things go on. And suddenly you're in the train station, under the arches, and it could be 1994 again and, giddy at having just watched the *Lion King*, you're running through the crowds to your mother's tired half-shouted condemnations;

or 2001 and you're holding Philippa Gill's hand and praying she doesn't judge you for how sweaty yours is, as you walk with her to the bus station and watch her get on the bus to Hessle and walk back towards the trains almost crying because you might not see her again for four days; or 2006, it's the Christmas holidays and you're stooping under a big backpack and feeling any fear that you might have changed irrevocably or that home might have changed irrevocably dissipate at the sight of a cancer hospice charity choir and drunken men dressed as elves stumbling about.

And then suddenly it's the present day and you're walking into the bar of the Royal Hotel and your mum and dad are there, really quite dressed up, if a fleece with a Matalan checked shirt counts as dressed up, which, in your dad's case it definitely does. And your auntie and your uncle are there too.

They were all smiling, and they all said 'hello' with almost harmonious prosody, and though it felt like a very deliberate moment – not one they had collaboratively contrived necessarily but at least one they'd instinctively cohered towards – it was a welcome one. One that said: we are all glad to see you, without qualification.

That notwithstanding, I felt conscious of just how little direct interaction I'd had with them these last few weeks and that feeling of slightly indefinable guilt began creeping back in.

'So nice to see you guys,' I told them. I don't think I'd ever called them 'guys' before.

'Ah well, we're up here this weekend anyway,' my auntie said.

'And when they said you'd be passing through today, we thought that's good enough for us then,' my uncle said, advancing on my auntie's explanation in a way that made the whole moment feel like a slightly prepared set piece.

My mother chipped in: 'Your dad wanted to go to the London Way next door for a fry up!'

'Aye but your mother said it wouldn't be posh enough for Auntie Rosalind in there!' my dad said, and we all laughed, even though it wasn't really a joke.

'This is more your sort of scene, isn't it, Rosalind?' my mother said.

'Oh definitely!' my auntie replied.

And we all laughed again.

Indeed, the setting did prove salubrious and the vibe conducive to the kind of interaction we all probably needed to have. I felt cheerful at the sight of all the people in the bar with their gins and wines and sparkling waters and pots of tea and curate stands of sandwiches and scones and whatnot, each laughing away affectionately under the chandelier shades and the frieze of jumping fish.

Alan and Rosalind told me about the rehabilitation places they'd be visiting over the weekend. There was one just a few miles from theirs that they were hoping would prove a good fit. I'd have to come up to see Paris there and stay with them a few days, my auntie said. I'd like that, I told them. Maybe you and I could both go up at the same time?

I asked if they'd heard much more about the police investigation and they said nothing too substantial. The police family liaison officer had told them that they expected the report to be completed by the end of the year – it's complicated because there's a lot of evidence to consider to do with working culture at the haulage firm. My uncle said he'd been talking to a journalist who's interested in that too, and the suggestion that the company's drivers are encouraged to (or at least not discouraged from) working illegally long hours. That could well have been a factor in why he fell asleep at the wheel.

'We shouldn't get ahead of ourselves, though,' my auntie said. 'We won't know anything, really, until the investigation's done.'

We all agreed, and then Uncle Alan asked me a lot of questions about my trip, I think keen to let me know that he had been to all the same places and probably knew more about them than I did, even though I'd been more recently, but he seemed interested enough in my reflections and everyone else did too, though to be honest having been away for six weeks I could come home and read out the Euro Currency Index and my parents would be on tenterhooks.

Perhaps it was that the trip came with such a ready discursive structure that it felt so welcome as conversational matter, and I went on for the best part of the hour, leaving out certain juicy details, naturally. Though they still each found something to enjoy. For my mother it was the sardine miracle of Madrid; for my father the (slightly airbrushed) account of my visit to our ancestral village; for Auntie Rosalind the Wellness retreat in Foix; and for Uncle Alan it was my Stendhal syndrome in Paris, which he himself had experienced many times, of course.

I'd just got about halfway through listing the onboard facilities of the *Pride of Rotterdam* when I realised that I was at risk of running late for my onward train and had to curtail my travelogue.

On the platform my uncle gave me a handshake and then a squeeze on the shoulder and then another handshake and told me that it had been excellent to see me and that he looked forward to comparing my experience in Edinburgh to his own 'trove of Fringe memories'; and my auntie hugged me for about eight seconds and called me 'love' several times – 'take care, love', 'lovely to see you, love', 'lots of love, love' etc. – which she'd never done before.

After I'd gone through the goodbye rituals with my parents and promised them I'd come 'home' again soon, I was away, first to Doncaster where I changed trains and then on to Edinburgh, where I arrived about 8pm, to see the sun, ringed with blue clouds, low over the castle. I hadn't expected to walk up the ramp of Waverley station and, as soon as stepping foot on the pavement, to see the sunset, especially sunset over a castle.

I hadn't expected, upon immediate exit of the train station, to see a castle at all, especially not a castle on a huge rock. I hadn't expected, either, to turn around and see the sea, away on the horizon and framed tightly, on one side by a hill with about five different monuments on top of it, including a mock-Parthenon, and on the other by another hill that seemed to aspire to be a mountain. In fact, I hadn't expected to be able to turn in just about any direction and have my head more or less blown clean

off, not only by the quality of each single element of the architecture and natural surroundings – a towering baroque hotel here
– a gothic monument, set amidst acres of greenery there – but
more by the notion that all of this could be contained within one
landscape. In short, I hadn't expected to experience the most
mesmerising moment of arrival I'd had anywhere all summer.

And I hadn't expected, either, to suddenly have my view
obscured by a map flapping in front of my face and to hear, just
over my shoulder, a familiar voice say:

'Hey, old pal.'

I turned and there was Sarah Neevie, looking simultaneously
exhausted and completely glowing, in one of those fluffy 'teddy'
coats that definitely shouldn't be fashionable but somehow are.
This, the first coat I'd seen in months, I think, was replete with
loads of little badges like Paris used to wear, except his were
always for political things, while Neevie's appeared to be promotional pieces for Fringe shows. Her hair was wet and she had an
redolent, melony, quite-recently-out-of-the-shower smell.

I'd texted her at Newcastle with my ETA and when she hadn't
replied I'd assumed it was just owing to her creative brain but
actually she'd wanted to surprise me. 'Do you want to do it or
shall I?' she asked.

'Hello! Do what?' I said.

'The map,' she replied, producing a sharpie from her pocket
and ripping the top off with her teeth.

'Oh,' I said, going giddy and gormless and unable to speak,
as I always do when I first see her.

'Turn around,' she said and so I did. Then she told me to take
my bag off, before resting the map on my back and digging into
it with the pen.

'There,' she said as I turned around again and she held up the
flapping sheet which I now garnered to be a fold-up map of
Europe, the kind you might keep in the car if you were driving
through France for a few weeks in the '90s. It was absolutely
massive, bigger than Neevie's arm span. She continued to hold
it aloft and I saw that she had drawn, in pens of various colours,

the route I'd taken, including, now, Hull to Edinburgh (except for a few sections between Greece and Holland left uncharted).

'You'll have to tell me the places I'm missing,' she said.

'I will,' I told her.

Then, smiling widely, she said, 'He-ey,' and hugged me.

She folded the map up with enviable adroitness and then we just stood for a few minutes and I told her how good I thought the view was and she explained what a few of the things were – that the castle's rock was in fact a 'volcanic plug'; that the hill with all the monuments was Calton Hill; that the big hill was 'Arthur's Seat' – and then she asked where my hostel was. I showed her on my phone and she said, 'Fucking hell, you're basically in Glasgow!' She was joking, she said, but that it was a long way anyway and did I really want to be sleeping in a ship-ping container with a load of drunk teenagers and wouldn't I rather just stay at hers?

I told her I would. And just as I felt a pang of uncertainty and confusion come on about actually whether this was the right thing to be doing, she said:

'You can have my bed and I'll have the sofa.'

The girl she was sharing a room with, she said, the company's social media manager, had 'had enough' and gone back to London, so I'd have a bed to myself. That she was so repeatedly emphatic about the prospect of my having a bed to myself I felt was, deliberately or not, a tacit indication of what the status of things was in Neevie's mind. And that I found the offer (of staying in a flat but not the same bed with someone I until very recently believed might have been my life partner) agreeable enough to accept was probably an indication of what I was feeling too.

And so it was that, after we'd dropped my bag off and chatted to her housemates – the cast of a musical about the friendship of Elton John and Eminem – who were all drinking vodka & Lemsips, in celebration of the fact that their show would be transferring to the West End, I sat with Neevie drinking whiskeys in a small pub, which sort of felt like the pub in *Trainspotting* but gentrified. It didn't come as a great shock to hear her explain how she was feeling about 'us'.

It was, I suppose, more or less what I'd anticipated: she always felt very glad of my presence at work; came to realise she enjoyed spending more and more time with me; she began to suspect she fancied me; she had a 'really fun time dating' me (it was at this point I knew for sure it was over); she felt we bonded a great deal after Paris's accident and hoped she'd been able to offer some support. I assured her she had.

She was so great in those first few weeks after the accident where I just needed someone to confide in, someone who wasn't directly affected by what happened. And she was amazing at going with however I was feeling at the time – being compassionate and patient when I was upset and needed to talk about it, and just so relaxed and funny when I need to escape from it all a bit.

But I guess maybe that's all it was: a relationship (if you can even call it that) suited to a particular set of circumstances: initially, two people feeling out of place in the same office; latterly, me being a bit of a mess emotionally and her being a bit of a legend about it, possibly to a slightly charitable degree.

And then maybe, as the weeks passed, she found it difficult to be there for me in the same way, especially given the distance now involved, and for my part, well, I had the emails and then, talking to you has been just . . . inordinately helpful.

As the pub emptied out and droplets of candle wax hardened on the table between us, Neevie concluded this account of her feelings. She said that although her ultimate reason for not coming to Athens was the job, it was around that time that she began thinking about things and she realised that in the time we'd had apart she'd missed me a lot more as a friend than as a romantic partner; she'd considered telling me sooner but hadn't wanted to ruin my holiday, which I guess it might have a bit, and she was glad she'd been able to talk to me about it properly, in person.

It all made sense. And that was how we found ourselves at midnight chinking glasses to toast a newly defined friendship, followed, finally, by welcome, peaty sleep.

Next morning (after insisting on taking the sofa and finding it comfortable enough), I left Neevie in the café doing her work, and took myself up Arthur's Seat, the mountain-like hill seen from the train station the previous evening. From here another sensational, mixed-up panorama: to the south rugged green hills; to the west the castle on its lithic base, the city and its motley palette of styles, Calton Hill and its follies; to the north the Hibs ground with floodlights as high as nearby tower blocks, housing estates, long Georgian terraces giving way to the sea, the Forth bridge and misty northern sky. Truly the Athens of the north.

The wind whipped my face. It was the end of August and everything felt suddenly *together* – Paris, the job, Neevie, Europe, the 30 pages of *Don Quixote* I'd read, every beer and every cathedral and every day-changing street scene, every Home and Experience, all contained neatly now within one summer – packed up and ready to be loaded onto the baggage conveyor of my memory.

Later, back at sea level, I watched some shows: an interesting play about the threat of monocropping as, I *think,* a metaphor for individualism, and an enjoyably ideology-free juggling show in a room above a pub.

Then I met up with Neevie and a couple of her mates, who'd just been to a show together by a young male comic and were arguing about whether it was a savagely satirical critique of bourgeois malaise under capitalism or just a man who didn't really know how to do stand-up properly hitting himself on the head with a microphone in a box for an hour. Neevie thought it was just 'an all-right comedy show, bit long'.

In the morning, just before I left, I showed her the missing routes on the map between Greece and Holland. She coloured them in with a red pen and when she was done, I asked her if I could keep the map, 'as a memento'. She took a photo of it, folded it up and handed it to me. I thanked her and packed it within my tablet cover. As I walked back to the station, having thanked Neevie for having me and telling her I'd see her at her birthday do, I decided I will donate it to the Museum of Broken Relationships (along with a very positive, very short caption).

So there we are. That was Edinburgh and now I'm on the train, on a Sunday afternoon and actually feeling not too bad, all things considered (and written about).

And just in case you thought I was ignoring your offer of the room, I'm not – just wanted to get the past tense all done and dusted, before saying that sounds a potentially perfect short-term thing. Dinner Wednesday sounds great too, and you can leave out the feta. I'll bring the Mythoses.

Mark.

Acknowledgements

Emma Herdman, Lily Cooper, Veronique Norton, Will Speed, Dom Gribben and Ellie Wheeldon at Hodder, and Vince McIndoe for the jacket.

Marigold Atkey for early encouragement.

Veronique Baxter at David Higham Associates.

Kitty Drake for companionship at an important time.

Daniella Isaacs for all sorts and Alex Woolf for reading tips.

Emily James for Wellness insights.

Kitty Laing & Isaac Storm at United Agents.

Joe Nunnery for patience and accommodation.

Simon Pearce and the Invisible Dot for Stories.

David Roper at Heavy Entertainment for accent tips.

Dave Story for advice, technical and artistic.

James Varley and Dean Burnett for invaluable neurological expertise.

And Ruby Riley whose cameo has been greater than words can convey.